Tales of the Country

BRIAN VINER

POCKET
BOOKS

LONDON • SYDNEY • NEW YORK • TORONTO

First published in Great Britain by Simon & Schuster UK Ltd, 2005
This edition published by Pocket Books, 2006
An imprint of Simon & Schuster UK Ltd
A CBS COMPANY

5 7 9 10 8 6 4

Simon & Schuster UK Ltd
Africa House
64–78 Kingsway
London WC2B 6AH

www.simonsays.co.uk

Simon & Schuster Australia
Sydney

A CIP catalogue record for this book is available from the British Library.

ISBN-10: 0-7434-9572-1
ISBN-13: 978-0-7434-9572-1

Typeset by M Rules
Printed and bound in Great Britain by
Cox & Wyman Ltd, Reading, Berks

For Jane, the wind beneath my wings,
the compost beneath my beans

Contents

Tales of the Country

1

Leaving the Toilet Handle Behind

Leominster, pronounced Lemster, isn't the town it was. It is said to have peaked in 1380. Still, apart from the occasional outbreak of cholera, a steep economic decline in the wake of the Industrial Revolution, and its modern status as the venue for the annual congress of the Test Card Circle, a group of people who gather to celebrate great television test card transmissions of our time, the subsequent 625 or so years have not treated it too badly.

And let me right away take back that slur on the Test Card Circle. The 2003 highlights – I quote from the official pro-gramme – included sessions called 'Saturday Night Almost Live, featuring something for everyone, with BBC and ITA music from the days of Test Card C right through to the Ceefax era' and 'Back To School – relive your childhood with those ITV Schools Intervals'. There was also a spontaneous debate about the celebrated incident, on Sunday, 9 October 1969, when the BBC2 tape was accidentally played on BBC1. The stalwarts of the Test Card Circle are the kind of people who make Britain such a wonderful country. I mean that sincerely.

But it's not just people who make Britain a wonderful place to live; it's places too. Places like Leominster. It is an unremarkable little town in many ways, yet it has some timbered buildings dating from 1450, which were shops then and are shops now. We Brits go on holiday to places like Greece and Turkey and ooh and aah when we hear that a building has been in continuous use as a retail outlet for over 500 years, yet here they are in north Herefordshire, containing skeletons of women who were forced to wait a bit too long while the original shopkeeper carried on a cheerful conversation with the person he was serving. Leominster's still like that.

It is also the town closest to where I live. Our house is in Docklow, about five miles east of Leominster, just off the Bromyard road. It is surrounded by open farmland, and we enjoy a marvellous view, on a clear day, of Lord Hereford's Knob.

To learn more about Lord Hereford's Knob, plough on. This book is the story of how a family – my family – adapted to living in the heart of the English countryside after moving from Crouch End, a fashionable area of north London. There are no funny Frenchmen or stubborn Spaniards in this story, but we still had a different culture to grapple with and a new language to learn. In Herefordshire, if you tell someone something that they find surprising, they might very well tell you to 'get up the brook, Leonard'. It means 'get away' or 'you don't say', but it seems to me a far more interesting exclamation. Which brook, and who Leonard is or was, nobody seems to know.

I was forty when, to the surprise of our friends in London, we moved up the brook, Leonard. This was a growing phenomenon in England. Between 1981 and 2002, the rural population had grown much faster than the urban one, by around 81,000 people a year compared with roughly 48,000. By 2002, just over 14 million people, or 28.5 per cent of the population, lived in districts officially considered rural. So we weren't exactly bucking a trend. But within our own social circle we were. And within a few months of arriving in Docklow, our lives had changed comprehensively.

For example, until I was forty I had considered the chicken, if I considered it at all, a creature to be eaten, preferably with roast potatoes, carrots, peas and gravy. I did not consider it a creature to be fed, watered and housed, let alone to be addressed as 'darling'.

These thoughts meandered through my mind one morning while visiting the henhouse to check for eggs. I opened the door to the nesting box to find Ruby, one of our Buff Rock bantams, in earnest mid-lay. 'Sorry, darling,' I said instinctively, and closed the door.

It took me a moment or two to realise that I had just called a chicken 'darling', an endearment previously reserved for my wife and three children. Was this what living in the country was all about, muttering sweet nothings to poultry? And if so, was it such a bad thing?

A couple of days later I was driving along the A44 to Leominster. It was a crisp spring morning. I was feeling Mr Toadishly pleased with myself for moving out of a crowded metropolis to such a glorious part of England, and altogether

3

bullish about life. I don't know if you can be toadish and bullish at the same time, but if it is possible anywhere, then Herefordshire's the place for it. And as I admired the pleasing silhouette of the Black Mountains, filling the horizon thirty-odd miles away across the Welsh border, I was suddenly overcome with the need to make a noise.

I inserted a CD, a Beach Boys compilation. Coincidentally, just as they, and I, started exultantly singing 'I Get Around', I spotted a hitchhiker slumped on the verge of the road, one grubby thumb unenthusiastically raised. I drew up, and turned the music off. 'I get around' was almost certainly not this guy's anthem: he looked as though he'd been there for a month.

He clambered gratefully aboard. It turned out that he was twenty-five, and decidedly down on his luck. His girlfriend had just left him and taken the car; he had no job and no prospects. But at least he wasn't on heroin, unlike 80 per cent, so he said, of the people he'd been at school with in Leominster. 'Get up the brook, Leonard,' I said. 'You what?' he said.

His company was depressing, but enlightening. It is hardly a secret that some country folk feel resentful towards 'incomers', especially those from London, and some of that resentment has to do with the former city-dwellers' almost wilful ignorance of the grievous social and economic problems with which many parts of Britain are afflicted. I didn't want to be one of those ex-townies who feel they know the countryside once they have worked out how to make toast on an Aga. It was strongly in my interests, I thought, as I listened to his tale of woe, to understand this dimension of country life.

All his old schoolmates had £50 a week habits, minimum, he told me, and he couldn't understand where they found the money; he was struggling to find £50 a week just to pay the rent. How unutterably miserable, I thought, to find yourself envious of friends addicted to heroin. But how miserable, too, to eke out 50 quid's worth of the stuff over an entire week. I had encountered people in London with £200-a-morning hard drugs habits, minimum.

I'd never felt much sympathy for them, just as it's hard to feel for a guy who prangs his brand-new Lamborghini. But how could you not feel desperately sorry for young people in a small market town with little money and less hope, squandering what money and hope they could muster on the contents of a syringe?

Anyway, just as my hitchhiker friend was puncturing the happiness with which I had started the journey, he cheered me up no end by sniffing the air inside my Volvo and saying, 'Are you a chicken-farmer then?'

I glanced at him in astonishment. Where, I asked, had he got that idea?

'I can smell chicken feed,' he said. 'I reckon you must be a chicken-farmer.'

I thought about this for a moment. We had lived in the country for only a few months. In that time I had done a lot of walking through the fields surrounding our house, golden retriever at my heels, waxed jacket rippling in the westerly wind, but I'd been told that I still looked quite a lot like a townie, maybe because even with my wellies on I still walked around rather than through the cowpats.

But to be assured by a lad born and bred in Herefordshire that I carried the whiff of a chicken-farmer, that seemed like acceptance indeed, almost a rite of passage. Laughing loudly, in fact trying to suppress a note of hysteria, I told him that I wasn't a chicken-farmer, but that we had bought three Buff Rock bantams and a Gold Sebright, which I'd just been feeding.

'Oh,' he said gloomily. 'If you had been a chicken-farmer, I was going to ask you for some labouring work.'

I felt suddenly depressed again. This A44, I thought, it's an emotional bloody roller coaster.

Eighteen months earlier, I had never even heard of the A44, let alone roller-coasted along it. We lived in a four-bedroomed, terraced Edwardian house in Park Avenue South, Crouch End, part of the London Borough of Haringey.

Crouch End, like huge swathes of London, sprang up between about 1890 and 1910 in an entrepreneurial flurry of house-building, intended to accommodate a new bourgeoisie of white-collar workers and their families. It lies to the east of affluent Highgate and the north of shabby Finsbury Park, and contains characteristics of both. There is a note of affluence in the shabbiness of Crouch End, and shabbiness in its affluence.

We celebrated the turn of the new millennium in Crouch End and had no plans to leave. Several neighbours had become dear friends and although they, like us, came from the provinces, we all considered ourselves Crouch Enders in much the same way as regulars at the Queen Vic consider themselves East Enders. It seemed like part of our being. We had even come to terms with the indecorous name Crouch End, with its faint redolence of lavatories and bodily functions. When an American I met on holiday started giggling, on being told where in London we lived, I went on the offensive. His name was Tray, which seemed to me far more embarrassing than living somewhere called Crouch End. I spent most of that evening trying to exact revenge by getting Tray to say 'the drinks are on me'. He never did, alas.

We bought our house in Park Avenue South in 1994, mortgaging ourselves to the hilt and slightly beyond. Until 1994 we could not have come close to making the repayments, but in January that year I began a fairly well-paid new job, for the *Mail on Sunday* newspaper. For five years before that I had banked an ordinary local newspaperman's salary – i.e. not much – even though I worked for no ordinary local newspaper: the *Hampstead & Highgate Express*, universally known as the *Ham & High*. Universally known as such in Hampstead and Highgate, anyway, which pretty much counts as universal on those rarefied slopes of north London.

I started there as a humble news reporter and loved it. There was a daily grind but it was not the daily grind endured by reporters on other local papers, of church fetes and school hockey results. Even the mundane stories had a unique north London tang. Typical was a phone call I received in the newsroom one day from a woman with a cut-glass accent. 'I'm from PHAFF,' she snapped. 'I beg your pardon?' I said. 'PHAFF,' she repeated, irritably. 'Primrose Hill Against Flash Floods.' It is still my all-time favourite acronym, and I sometimes wonder if they couldn't have kept it even once they'd sorted out the flash flooding, by finding another object for their ire. Perhaps they could have reformed as Primrose Hill Against Fast Food, or Primrose Hill Against Frederick Forsyth.

The editor of the *Ham & High* was a human terrier called Gerald Isaaman, who had been editor since around the time of the early Plantagenets. He used to boast that the *Ham & High* was the only local paper with a foreign policy; it was certainly the only local paper with book reviews contributed by, among others, Michael Foot, Melvyn Bragg, John Le Carré, Salman Rushdie, Tariq Ali, Fay Weldon and Margaret Drabble, all of whom, like all self-respecting liberal intellectuals, lived in the *H&H* circulation area.

We even had a full-time art critic, an unusual woman called Linda, who used to float through the office in voluminous kaftans, and rarely spoke to anybody. Linda expressed herself mainly through her writing, which was unfortunate, as none of us could make head or tail of it. Her greatest hour came when she delivered an obituary of a local ceramicist. 'The highlight of Alison Corrigan's career,' she wrote, in a rare burst of comprehensible prose, 'was the week she displayed her jugs in St Martin-in-the-Fields.'

It was hard leaving the *Ham & High*, but joining a national newspaper was the fulfilment of a long-nurtured ambition, as big a career highlight for me as it had been for the late Alison Corrigan to show her doubtless impressive jugs in St Martin-in-the-Fields. I became the *Mail on Sunday*'s television critic. My wife, Jane, whom I'd met at the *Ham & High* (where, as deputy news editor, she'd been my boss), was by now a producer on Radio 4's *Woman's Hour*. With our combined income we could just about afford to move to Crouch End, London N8.

We took with us our baby daughter, Eleanor. The following spring, in April 1995, our second child, Joseph, was born in the Whittington Hospital, Highgate.

North London seemed to us like a wonderful place to bring up children. There were playgroups and music groups and dance groups, many of them run by vegetarian women in smocks. We watched Crouch End, and neighbouring Muswell Hill, becoming more middle-class by the day.

It had not always been so. Muswell Hill was the home of Ronnie Barker's character, Norman Stanley Fletcher, in the incomparable sitcom *Porridge*. When Dick Clement and Ian La

Frenais created *Porridge*, in 1973, they must have reckoned that Muswell Hill was exactly the sort of dreary, down-at-heel area of London where someone like Fletcher might have lived. They could equally have chosen Crouch End, down the hill. Yet in 1997 the television writers Maurice Gran and Laurence Marks wrote a romantic comedy called *Unfinished Business* and set it in Crouch End. It starred Henry Goodman as an architect and Harriet Walter as an optometrist, very possibly the first optometrist in the entire history of romantic comedy. I wasn't sure of their reasons for giving a fictional character a career in optics, but they were bang on the nail to recognise Crouch End as having become the sort of place where architects and optometrists fall in love.

And then have children. In a playground one afternoon, 2-year-old Joseph dithered at the top of a slide, to the increasing exasperation of the little boy behind him. I stood at the bottom, encouraging him down. 'Come on, sausage,' I called. Eventually the little boy issued a formal complaint to his father, who wore trendy blue-rimmed spectacles and looked very much like an architect, probably married to an optometrist. 'Daddy,' he shouted crossly. 'Sausage won't go down the slide!'

It never occurred to the child that Sausage might not be our son's name. Nor, probably, to his father. Ironically, the rude American Tray would have felt perfectly at home in the playgrounds of London N8 and N10, which were full of men and women calling out wacky names. The sausage mix-up was understandable, because frequently they were names of things you could eat.

'Jambalaya, it's time to go home!'

'Saffron, stop being horrid to Roquefort!'

'Chowder, darling, you'll be late for Marmalade's party!'

9

In August 1998 we had another son, whom we rather unimaginatively named Jacob. We would clearly have to pretend, when he reached the swings, slides and roundabouts age, that he had been named after the cream cracker.

Jacob was born at home. We already felt umbilically attached to Park Avenue South, but almost literally so when Jacob slithered to the (plastic-sheeted) floor in our en-suite bathroom. The midwife who delivered him was a huge West Indian woman of blessed temperament and fabulous fruity vowels. Her name was Margaret Hill and she was the mother of Mel, who featured in the first series of Channel 4's *Big Brother* and enjoyed fifteen minutes of fame as dazzling as they were fleeting. When Jane phoned Margaret to report her first contraction, it was Mel who took the call.

This was another enjoyable dimension to living in that part of north London – the casual and often improbable encounters with celebrity. To Jane it seemed perfectly normal that Mel from *Big Brother*'s mum should be gynaecologically acquainted with her, although she did wonder, at the height of *Big Brother*-mania, whether she should sell her story to the *Sun* – 'Mel's Mum Saw My Bum'.

Meanwhile, most people we knew locally had at some point, in Marks & Spencer on Muswell Hill Broadway, reached for the same Gruyère and Parsnip Bake as Victoria Wood. Or if not Victoria Wood, Alison Steadman. But with due respect to those two admirable women, Crouch End had even hipper celebrities than Muswell Hill. The actor Neil Morrissey lived there. So did the DJ Andy Kershaw. The *X-Files* actress Gillian Anderson had been a schoolgirl there. It was repeatedly rumoured that Bob Dylan, of all people, had been seen house-hunting in N8.

Now, it is obligatory for anyone with a journalistic training to follow all references to Bob Dylan with the observation that the times they are a-changin'. It is something they teach you in media studies. But a-changin' the times they certainly were. As Crouch End became trendier, property values soared. And, despite our growing affection for the area, we found ourselves entering a phase of mild emotional instability, dubbed, by some Wildean wit or other, the 'metropause'. The metropause can apparently be defined as the midlife urge to leave the city, to swap a tiny garden for several acres, to exchange the sound of hooting traffic for that of hooting owls. Moreover, as I was increasingly working from home and Jane had quit the BBC, a move out of London seemed timely.

It was a weekend in Bath that turned us metropausal. I bet lots of people from London experience the onset of the metropause during weekends in Bath. We spent twenty-four hours with our noses flattened against estate agents' windows, detaching ourselves occasionally to eat, sleep and look after the children. But to our rather patronising surprise, houses in Bath, even the less Jane Austeny parts, were no cheaper than in Crouch End.

So our interest started radiating outwards from Bath, and we were particularly enticed by details of a late Georgian house in Frome, Somerset. We made an appointment to see it, and liked what we saw. In stark contrast with our fifteen foot square of back garden in Park Avenue South, it had an orchard and even an outdoor swimming pool. Inside, it seemed in good repair, a thoroughly comfortable family home. Amazingly, it fell within our budget.

We excitedly confirmed our interest to the estate agent, and resolved to check out the local schools before making a formal offer. On the long drive back to London, we stopped off at the home of a colleague of mine, who lived in Bradford-on-Avon and had invited us for lunch. 'Frome?' he said, when we told him about the house we'd seen. 'You do know that it's the incest capital of Europe?'

I have since heard this calumny directed at many places, both in Britain and abroad. Folk who live in Lockjaw, Alabama, will tell you that Hare Lip, six miles west, is the incest capital of America. But talk to the good people of Hare Lip and they will assure you that it is nearby Lockjaw where you are likely to see a brother and sister walking a pram containing a baby with its head on backwards. Someone I know recently defamed Much Wenlock in Shropshire in a similar manner. 'It is widely known,' said my informant conspiratorially, 'as Much Bedlock.'

It seems to be the fate of every other rural town to be known as the incest capital of Europe, if only by people in the neighbouring rural town, and even though nobody can ever supply any firm evidence, either in the form of hard statistics or misshapen townsfolk. Perhaps in Frome they insist that the dubious distinction belongs to Bradford-on-Avon. Whatever, I'm ashamed to say that I took my friend at his word. We joked that the town should have a sign saying 'Welcome to Frome – Twinned with Itself'. And I knew then that the hunt for a suitable house would have to resume.

What we considered suitable was this: a sizeable family house with a large garden, in a small market town or on the picturesque outskirts of an attractive city, with a decent primary school nearby. We didn't want to live in the sticks. We compiled endless lists of the pros and cons of moving out of London, and the pros and cons of staying put. Less pollution v. less culture; fewer muggings v. fewer restaurants; Arsenal, as our local football team, v. Middle Wallop Rangers.

Not least of the criteria we set ourselves was that the house had to be within walking-distance of a café with a cappuccino machine. In Crouch End I could set out from home in any direction and within fifteen minutes a gurgling cappuccino machine would be serenading me. When you work at home, on your own, such trivialities assume great importance.

Not that I was always at home. My editors at the *Mail on Sunday* kept coming up with offbeat projects for me, one of which, in May 1997, was to find out more about those curiously old-fashioned advertisements, which since 1961 had been appearing prominently in national newspapers headlined 'Does Your Memory Fail You?' or 'IQ of 145 And Can't Remember?'.

With the kind of tenacious journalistic initiative that enabled Woodward and Bernstein to rumble the Watergate cover-up, I discovered that the ads were placed by a company called R. & W. Heap, based in Marple, near Stockport. R. & W. Heap offered correspondence courses in mnemonics, a system of remembering things based on acronyms (such as the indubitably memorable PHAFF), word association and imagery.

Anyway, I phoned Bob Heap, the managing director, who said that he would be delighted to reveal more. He suggested that I catch a train to Macclesfield, Cheshire, where he would collect me and drive me to his office in Marple. He also said that after seeing my face for the first time, he would never, ever forget my name, thanks to his foolproof technique of making absurdist visual connections in order never, ever, to forget names. To lock Brian Viner into his memory he would visualise vines tumbling out of my brain, and the sight of my face thereafter would always trigger that image in his mind. I told myself that I'd prefer it if he just forgot my name.

Funnily enough, if I walked past Bob Heap in the street now, I'd never remember him. A woman giving a little curtsy on top of a mound of compost might come into focus . . . but no, I would not be able to remember why. The journey in his car from Macclesfield to Marple, on the other hand, I recall vividly. I was enraptured. It was a glorious day in early summer and the countryside looked spectacular, especially considering its proximity to Manchester. We passed buttercup-strewn meadows, followed by steep, dramatic hills, and even a man repairing a dry-stone wall with a pipe clenched between his teeth. Which takes some doing, I can tell you. Anyway, I got home that evening and said to Jane: 'How about Cheshire?'

Thus it was that we made an offer on East Cottage, a rambling Victorian farmhouse in the village of Broken Cross just outside Macclesfield. It was owned by a frightfully posh couple who, in that frightfully posh way, had allowed it to get, in parts, ever so slightly derelict. But otherwise it seemed to fit the bill. It had a brick-built office outside where I could hole up cosily with my Apple Mac, and an appealingly scruffy garden of about an acre, with a charming old dovecote. (Note to anyone hoping to sell a house in the country to people fleeing the city: erect a dovecote . . . it will probably clinch the sale.)

We didn't spot any doves, but East Cottage did have several slaughtered pheasants hanging in the larder. We presumed the frightfully posh people would want to take the pheasants with them, but at least dead birds in the larder emphasised the semi-rural location. Best of all, there was a café round the corner with a brand-new cappuccino machine.

Amid great wailing and gnashing of teeth – slightly moist eyes, anyway – we put our home in Park Avenue South up for sale. Pretty soon we found buyers, a pleasant family whom I'll call the Roses even though that wasn't their name. The Roses loved our house, which we found faintly troubling because we were by no means sure that we wanted to leave it. But the move to Macclesfield appeared to make sense. We both had northern roots. Jane's parents lived just across the Pennines in South Yorkshire; I had grown up in Lancashire. We had friends in and around Manchester. And getting from Macclesfield to London, by train if not through the Seventh Circle of Hell that is the M6, was a fairly straightforward business.

At first we bubbled with enthusiasm for the move. We put the children's names down for the King's School in Macclesfield, and at a Royal Television Society dinner I lurched up to Macclesfield-raised, King's School-educated Michael Jackson – not the troubled pop star but the then-chief executive of Channel 4 – and boldly informed him that I was going to live in his home town.

He looked at me with the mixture of incredulity and pity that you might get if you told someone you intended to challenge the world record for sitting in a barrel on top of a pole (currently 67 days and 14 minutes, of course). 'Great,' he said, humouring me. I slunk away. Jane's former colleague from *Woman's Hour*, Jenni Murray, was more encouraging. She loved her home in the hills outside Macclesfield, she assured Jane. On the other hand, it seemed significant that between Monday and Friday she lived in a pied-à-terre in Camden Town.

Slowly, my enthusiasm for Macclesfield began to wane. But whenever possible, I went back to reassure myself that we were doing the right thing. On one such visit, in December 1997, I had dinner with an old schoolfriend, Pete Venables, who lived in Wilmslow. I desperately wanted Pete to do a sales job on Cheshire, but he casually mentioned that he'd been in London the week before and had spent two cheery hours wandering around a beguilingly Christmassy Sloane Square.

'Wait a minute,' I said. 'You're supposed to be reassuring me that Cheshire is the place to be.'

'Oh it is,' he cried. 'I would never live anywhere else. And there are some fantastic retail parks opening up.'

Retail parks. Not since 'Open Sesame!' had two words had such a magical effect. The scales fell from my eyes and into my steak and kidney pie. Pete was a great guy, but I didn't want to live somewhere where retail parks were objects of ardour.

I tried to remain positive because I thought Jane was still keen. Besides, we'd already had a survey carried out on East Cottage, as had the Roses on our house in Park Avenue South. With the solicitor's fees, we had shelled out £1200. A date had been set for the exchange of contracts. But a few nights after my dinner with Pete, in an Italian restaurant on Upper Street in Islington, an area of London even trendier than Crouch End, my apprehension came spilling out.

We had just been to a pub-theatre, the King's Head, to see an actress friend, Sue Kelvin, perform a terrific one-woman show written by her husband, Chris Burgess. The lively cosmopolitanism of that evening, as well as the fact that Sue and Chris were friends, seemed to encapsulate everything we would be leaving behind. It wasn't that I no longer wanted to live in Cheshire, although I didn't. It was more that I wanted, with all my heart, to stay in London. To hell with the pollution, the traffic, the litter, the graffiti, the crime, and queuing to get into and then out of Ikea on the North Circular Road . . . they were just the horrid cumulative product of lots and lots of people. And lots and lots of people also meant shops, restaurants, cinemas, theatres, concerts, museums. Fabulous, life-enhancing things.

As it turned out, Jane had been feeling exactly the same. She had suppressed her doubts because she thought I was intent on making the move. Relief washed over us. We finished our pizzas quattro formaggio and ordered a celebratory tiramisu to share. It was official. We were post-metropausal. East Cottage and the building work it required need bother us no more. When some friends joked that we might have wound up in Broken Cross both broke 'n' cross, we howled the maniacal laughter of condemned prisoners offered a last-minute reprieve.

There remained, however, the difficulty of telling the frightfully posh couple and, worse, the Roses, that we were pulling out of the deal and therefore committing a crime considered by most estate agents to be on a par with mass murder, if not marginally worse: wilfully breaking the purchasing chain. So we made the cowardly decision to fib. We said that my work commitments had changed, requiring us to stay in London. Through their disappointment, the Roses understood. And would have remained understanding, despite having spent over £1000 for a full structural survey, had I not done something insensitive and stupid.

I still wrote a monthly lifestyle column in the *Ham & High*, and a few weeks later decided to write about our volte-face – a very Hampstead expression, after all. Naively, I assumed that the Roses, who lived in another part of the city, would never see it. But I knew it would go down a storm in north London, where people like to read that north London is a better place to live than anywhere else on the planet, and absolutely lap up stories about people who pull back from the brink of moving to the country, in favour of staying near Hampstead Heath.

A week later I got an angry letter from Mrs Rose. Some friends had sent them my column. We had told them one thing yet I had written another, she complained, and they were considerably out of pocket as a result of our seemingly whimsical change of mind. It was a fair cop.

Had we been nobler of spirit, and deeper of pocket, we might have offered to recompense them. As it was, I apologised and that was that. Except that the Roses then bought a house in a neigh- bouring road and overnight we started seeing them everywhere. In the park, on the bus, in the butcher's, in the medical centre . . . always there was either Mr or Mrs Rose, gazing at us reproach- fully and then looking away as soon as our eyes met.

Whenever we stopped in the car at a zebra crossing, they were the ones crossing it. When we walked across a zebra crossing, they were the ones waiting in the car, probably suppressing the instinct to slam down the accelerator and wipe us out. Even in my own home I started opening the toilet door tentatively. If we had taken a cruise round the Galapagos Islands, and alighted on a remote beach, the dark shape in the distance would not have been a giant turtle, it would have been Mr Rose. In Marks & Spencer on Muswell Hill Broadway, it was never Victoria Wood or Alison Steadman reaching for the same Parsnip and Gruyère Bake as me. It was always a frowning Mrs Rose.

Still, apart from being haunted by the Roses, we were happy to have recommitted ourselves to Crouch End. We threw ourselves into school fund-raising activities with renewed vigour. I started visiting a different café every day for my mid-morning cappuc- cino, just because I could. One day, I even ordered a treble decaff skinny peanut-butter double-jointed latte, or something of the sort, not because I truly desired it, but for the sheer Crouch Endness of it.

A couple of happy years went by. But gradually it began to dawn on us that the urge to leave London, the urge we had thought dead and buried, was reawakening. All the old desires we had consigned to our shiny, green London Borough of Haringey recycling bin – more space for the kids, more space for us, more space for the car, less litter, less graffiti, less crime, less pressurised schools – bubbled back to the surface.

Moreover, in October 2001 I would be forty. Some people buy leather trousers when they approach forty, others get a body-part pierced. I wanted to experience life in a different region of England (and maybe get a body-part pierced as well). Also, our daughter Eleanor was approaching secondary school age, and by then we felt it would be unfair to remove her from an environment she knew so well. If we were ever going to leave London, it had to be soon.

We more or less randomly earmarked three counties – Suffolk, Wiltshire and Worcestershire – and began the tiresome process of registering with estate agents. Over the next few months I became a property details junkie, hardly able to get through the morning without ingesting yet more details of moulded cornicing, dado rails, decorative architraves, chimney recesses, Belfast sink units and inglenook fireplaces. And what merriment we got from those property details, with their odd phrasing and indiscriminate use of capital letters. These things really shouldn't be left to estate agents. One house in Suffolk boasted 'a Norman Spiral staircase'; either a spiral staircase dating back to the Normans, or a staircase designed by the renowned architect Norman Spiral. We couldn't quite be sure.

Another place, in Wiltshire, was 'wonderfully located for access to virtually all points of the compass'. It was the 'virtually' that intrigued me. What could it mean? Were north, south and east within easy reach, but west an absolute no-no?

I became a reluctant expert in estate agents' jargon, with its championing of the euphemism. 'This property offers an excellent degree of versatility' meant, in short, a wreck. After a while I began to enjoy their efforts to sex up some obscure literary or historical connection. My favourite was: 'Crown House has recently undergone an extensive and sympathetic restoration programme, having been occupied previously for 106 years by the niece of Logie Baird.'

This begged several urgent questions, none of which the agent could answer. Had the niece of John Logie Baird, inventor of the television set, really lived in the house for 106 years? If so, was it some kind of record? What had she done that made an extensive restoration programme so necessary? And did she watch much telly? We'll probably never know.

Eventually, in summer 2001, after many weekend excursions up the M11 and along the M4 to look at houses, we found the place we wanted. Not merely wanted, in fact, but craved. Channing House (not its real name, for reasons that will become clear) was an elegant Georgian town house, a former coaching inn with a charming cobbled courtyard, in the attractive market town of Pershore, Worcestershire.

Channing House stood on the town's main thoroughfare, which was a bit of a drawback, as there seemed to be juggernauts rumbling by every two minutes. But the twenty-first century drawbacks rubbed shoulders with some stunning eighteenth-century features, among them a wonderful Georgian staircase. What seduced us above all, however, was a long and extraordinarily lovely garden, stretching down to a peaceful stretch of the River Avon. That, more than the proximity of heavy-goods vehicles, might have been why the house was just about affordable: the prospect every few winters of the River Avon peacefully flowing through the kitchen.

But to own that garden would be worth the odd flood, we thought. There was statuary and topiary, formal bits and wild bits, water features and archways, a ramshackle but characterful old greenhouse, and even a wooden landing stage. We were enchanted.

We were also, in retrospect, bonkers. It was all we could do to keep on top of our small patch of garden in London, which required about twenty minutes of attention every other week. The Channing House garden needed at least two hours a day of hoeing, mowing, weeding and feeding. Admittedly there was a trusty old gardener with a flat tweed cap surgically attached, but we weren't at all sure that we could afford him. Even if we could, it was a house for Mr and Mrs Monty Don or Mr and Mrs Alan Titchmarsh or Mr and Mrs Bob Flowerdew, not for the likes of us.

So naturally we made an offer. The house was owned by an amiable family called Powell, who had made a lot of money in agricultural machinery and literally had their eyes on pastures new – mother and daughter were keen riders and they wanted a place where they could graze a few ponies.

They were asking marginally less for Channing House than the value of our Park Avenue South house, thanks to the unstoppable gentrification of Crouch End.

The Powells accepted our offer, as long we could quickly exchange contracts. We felt sure we could. Our estate agent, a short, doughy guy called Michael – the kind of man who would be supplied by Central Casting if you asked them to send you a spiv of extreme, over-the-top spivishness – told us that our house would definitely sell within forty-eight hours of our putting it up for sale. We put it up for sale. A week later he said: 'It's very odd that there's been no interest. There seems to have been a sudden downturn in the market.'

We kept calling the Powells to assure them that we were committed to the purchase, and returned several times to Channing

House to plan exciting things like whose bedroom would be whose, as well as to check out the nearest cappuccino outlet.

The only thing that seriously troubled me about Channing House was that the splendid Georgian staircase wound around a splendid Georgian stairwell, with a drop from top to bottom of at least fifty feet. Let us leave Worcestershire for a moment, and venture to southern Spain's lovely Costa de la Luz. Two years earlier, while on holiday there, little Jacob had fallen head first out of a restaurant window. We had been having a merry lunch with some friends when, unnoticed by any of us, Jacob somehow manoeuvred his chair over to the open window. By the time I looked over, less than a minute after I had last smiled at him chattering at the table, all I saw was a flash of blue sandals and yellow socks as he toppled out.

The window was forty feet high, overlooking a beach. But there was rock beneath it, not sand. I hope I never experience a more agonising thirty seconds than those it took me to dash down the steps, certain that he would at the very least be badly injured.

The sound of him crying was like a choir of angels; it meant he wasn't unconscious or worse. There was a crowd of aghast Spaniards around him, and a woman holding him. By some miracle he was unharmed, apart from nasty grazing. Apparently, if you're going to survive a fall out of a forty-foot-high window, it's best of all to be a cat, but otherwise to be very drunk or very young, because drunk people and small children don't stiffen in anticipation of impact. Even so, we kept hearing the Spanish word *milagro*, meaning miracle, and it did seem like a kind of miracle. When we returned to the same spot a few days later, we half-expected to find a shrine to the Virgin Mary.

But just as miraculous to us was that within fifteen minutes of the accident, there was an ambulance on the scene with a paediatrician on board. This was a tiny fishing village, an hour's drive from the port of Cádiz, which was the nearest settlement of any size. Had a similar accident befallen a Spanish toddler in a remote fishing village in England, it was hard to imagine an ambulance turning up inside quarter of an hour, let alone a paediatrician. On the other hand, in England the window would probably have been shut. We were asked if we wanted to take legal action against the restaurant, but we blamed only ourselves for being less vigilant than usual; a common phenomenon, I have since been told, on family holidays, especially family holidays in Spain, where you see two-year-olds on the backs of mopeds.

Jacob's accident had made me neurotic about the danger of small children falling from great heights. But in the case of Channing House I tackled this neurosis by mentally positioning a big squidgy sofa at the bottom of the stairwell. Not the prospect of flooding, nor the obvious perils to small children of a river at the bottom of the garden, nor even my own particular dread of heights, eroded my conviction that this was where I wanted to live. And Jane felt the same.

We registered the children with a nearby primary school. I even looked into the cost of a second-hand dinghy with an outboard motor, and daydreamed of chugging along the Avon with three happy kids, a wicker hamper and a dog very much like Timmy in the Famous Five books. All we needed, for the wind to start stirring our willows, was a buyer for Park Avenue South.

Meanwhile, the Powells' estate agent – a pukka, rather superior chap from Knight Frank, who hardly seemed to come from the same planet, let alone the same profession as Michael – or 'Sudden Downturn' as we now called him – casually told us that there was interest in Channing House from another party, who had offered more than us, but seemingly wanted the house only as a second home. The other party did not need a bank loan, he added. They were cash buyers, and by implication, considerably richer than us.

'But Mr and Mrs Powell would rather sell the property to you,' he assured us. Evidently, they wanted Channing House to be a full-time family home. It would effectively be ours as soon as we could fix a date for the exchange of contracts.

We would happily have fixed a date for the exchange of bodily fluids, never mind contracts. But no buyer materialised. On 10 September 2001, we talked to the bank about a bridging loan. On September 11, the Twin Towers of the World Trade Center were destroyed. If there's ever a good time to take out a bridging loan, and I'm not sure there is, it's plainly not in the aftermath of an apocalypse. A few weeks later the man from Knight Frank phoned to say that the Powells felt compelled to sell Channing House to the other interested party.

We were devastated. Obviously, September 11 lent some valuable perspective to those feelings of devastation – friends of friends had died – but Channing House had seemed so perfect. We could hardly bear to think of someone else moving in.

Bizarrely, that someone else turned out to be the former pop star Toyah Wilcox. A woman who had lent her voice to *Teletubbies*, as Toyah had, could lay claim to reserves of goodwill that in our house would never entirely evaporate. Nevertheless, she plunged in our estimation. If we had had any of her records, we would have ritually jumped on them. So when later she appeared in a six-page spread in *OK!* magazine, pictured in her beautiful Worcestershire garden alongside the glorious River Avon, she very quickly acquired a bushy moustache, silly glasses and horns. It was the least we could do.

In the meantime, sympathetic friends and relatives told us

that the loss of Channing House was clearly meant to be, that things would turn out for the best. We smiled wanly, like the newly bereaved being told that time is a great healer.

I know, it's preposterous to compare our emotions to feelings of bereavement. But anyone who has set their heart on owning a property, and then seen the deal fall through, will understand what I mean. There was once an episode of *Coronation Street* in which Hilda Ogden coped stoically with the death of her idle but beloved husband Stan, then broke down when she opened his spectacles case. For us, for a couple of weeks, the Channing House particulars were Stan Ogden's spectacles case.

And just to rub it in, those Toyah Wilcox interviews kept on coming. It seemed as if we could hardly open a magazine or newspaper lifestyle supplement without reading about her fabulous house and garden.

However, she did say that she had visited the house in her childhood when it was a tearoom, and that when she had again walked through the door 'I just burst into tears; I knew we had to live here.' Fair enough, I thought. Maybe she wanted it even more than we did. Besides, she had been able to fill the garden with sculptures, including (I read) a life-sized terracotta warrior on a horse given to her for Christmas by her husband Robert Fripp, of the rock group King Crimson. That was far more in keeping with such a magnificent garden than the small terracotta plant pot, not including a horse, that I might have given Jane as a Christmas present.

Once again we shelved our plans to leave London. My fortieth birthday came and went without me living in a small market town or even getting anything pierced. But we continued to receive property particulars, mainly because we couldn't be bothered to let the agents know we had stopped looking, and on a cold

January morning in 2002, unenthusiastically opened a buff envelope containing details of a house in Herefordshire called Docklow Grange.

We realised instantly that the desire to leave London, which we had again thought dead, was again only dormant. It surfaced once more when we read the details of Docklow Grange. Yet the house failed our criteria on several important counts. For one thing, it was in the middle of the sticks. Docklow was a dot on the road to the Welsh Marches between Bromyard and Leominster. A walk to get a cappuccino on a winter's day would require thermal long johns, a compass and probably an ice pick. Besides, we had never even vaguely considered Herefordshire. It seemed much too far from London. Much too far from everywhere.

For another thing, Docklow Grange was way more than we could afford. In 1999 I had moved from the *Mail on Sunday* to become a columnist and interviewer for the *Independent*. They paid me well, and I also had a reasonable freelance income, through interviewing famous people for the *Radio Times* and *Sainsbury's Magazine*. But the price of Docklow Grange was laughably higher than whatever we could muster by selling our house, our car, our life insurance policies, Jane's body and even my cherished collection of Shell 1970 World Cup coins. Unfortunately, we couldn't expel the place from our minds.

The photographs made it look immensely handsome, a large, ivy-clad, early Victorian house, almost certainly with a resident ghost. It also came with nearly five acres of grounds and three adjacent self-catering holiday cottages, which made us wonder whether we might be able to buy just the house and grounds, and leave the cottages out of the package, bringing the price almost within reach. We phoned the agent – Grays of Ludlow, in Shropshire. They confirmed that the owners, Mr and Mrs

Openshaw, could possibly be persuaded to sell the house on its own. We made an appointment.

On 17 February 2002, just after 3 p.m., we turned for the first time into the drive of Docklow Grange, the house that was to become our home.

It was a miserable day. The journey from London had taken over three hours, including the inevitable pause to let the Roses, the family who had almost bought our house in Crouch End four years earlier, troop across a zebra crossing. The windscreen wipers had been swishing to and fro the whole way, fighting a persistent drizzle. It was not a good day to view a property. On the other hand, there could hardly be a better day. If it appealed to us on a dreary February afternoon then what pleasures might it offer on a warm day in June?

Mr and Mrs Openshaw turned out to be a couple in their early sixties, who had lived in Docklow Grange for twenty-three years, raising two children there. They manifestly treasured the place and we could understand why. Inside it was huge, rambling and brimming with character, with enough original features to make an estate agent swoon. The particulars had promised 'magnificent' mouldings and the mouldings did not disappoint. The particulars also promised a butler's silver safe, and there it was, a nineteenth-century strongroom with a vast iron door. And parliament hinges – colossal hinges that enable heavy oak double-doors to open flat against the wall. Mr Openshaw showed me his parliament hinges in the same rhetorical what-do-you-think-of-that? manner with which some men show other men a new tattoo, or a trick involving the foreskin.

We stayed for over two hours, hugely engaged by the Openshaws, the house and the dim prospect of living there. The house had a faded grandeur, albeit faded, in some places, to the point of invisibility. There were cracks in the ceilings. There was woodworm. Mr Openshaw was a heavy smoker and the walls were stained with nicotine. It needed a new kitchen. It needed rewiring. It needed redecorating. Heaven knew what else it needed. And yet we were smitten, as much by the outside as the inside, even in the drizzle. Unusually if not uniquely in the world of estate agents' particulars, the photographs undersold the place.

The red sandstone house, built circa 1850, stood at the heart of a hamlet of eleven cottages, most of which were clustered around an ancient stone cider press. At the back of the house was a formal lawn with an old stone font in the middle of it, a croquet lawn and dense woodland. In the woodland were two enormous wellingtonia trees, particularly fine specimens according to Mr Openshaw, and marking the western boundary of the grounds there was a delightful ha-ha – which incidentally is defined in my *Reader's Digest Universal Dictionary* as 'a walled ditch . . . sunk in the ground to serve as a fence without impairing the view', its name, and this is the bit I really like, deriving from expressions of 'surprise at finding such an unexpected obstacle'. In other words, it could just as easily have been called a bugger-me.

Beyond the ha-ha there was a spellbinding view towards the Black Mountains, spellbinding even in the drizzle. In the foreground was open farmland, yet it looked more like rolling parkland. There were two plantations of birch, beech, ash, horse chestnut and sycamore trees, and the glint of a pond or a lake beyond them. Around the other side of the house there were a couple of peacocks strutting around, and an elderly Muscovy duck standing solemnly in the shadow of an old clocktower. There was also, yes, a dovecote. And a Gilbert Scott telephone box. It was utterly charming, almost a caricature of rural England in bygone times. Had David Jason as Pop Larkin come strolling round the corner, rubbing his hands and saying 'perfick', we would not have batted an eyelid between us.

We asked the Openshaws why they were selling up. They explained that their children had left home, and Mrs Openshaw had since been seriously unwell. The house had become way too big for them. So they had decided to convert the nearby barn (Mr Openshaw, rather fortuitously, was an architect specialising in barn conversions) and to sell the house and its three adjoining cottages.

They confirmed that they might sell the house on its own, but would much prefer to sell the cottages with it. They had originally owned all eleven cottages, running them as holiday lets. Four of these they had already sold, and four they wanted to retain, to fill with long-term tenants. That left the three actually attached to the grange: Woodlands Cottage, Yewtree Cottage and Manor Cottage.

The Openshaws showed us round the three cottages. They were all charming, in a basic kind of way. And they yielded an income, Mr Openshaw told us, of around £19,000 a year. I did some mental arithmetic, and worked out that if we could increase the cottage income, if the Openshaws would accept a lower offer, and if we again mortgaged ourselves to the hilt, we could possibly scrape together enough for the whole estate. Whatever, we realised that the Openshaws were right; the cottages had to be part of the package. Which in itself was an exciting prospect. Jane and I had long fantasised about running a small hotel or upmarket bed and breakfast: self-catering holiday cottages offered a perfect opportunity to get involved in the hospitality industry without having to make fried breakfasts for strangers.

The downside to my calculations was that I'd always been rubbish at mental arithmetic. We probably couldn't afford it at all. But it seemed irresistible, and the Openshaws made it plain that they wished to see the house filled with children again. They told us that, as yet, we were the only family interested. We were definitely in with a shout.

We drove back to London in a whirl of excitement and uncertainty, put our house up for sale – again – and swiftly made a formal offer to the Openshaws, quite a bit less than the asking price, which to our amazement they accepted. But obviously we had to sell before we could buy, the minor consideration which had clobbered the Channing House deal.

In the few months since it had last been on the market, our house in Park Avenue South had apparently leapt in value again. It was now worth almost exactly three times what we had paid for it in 1994. This time 'Sudden Downturn' got us an acceptable offer in the first week. And a couple of months later, after a full complement of those infuriating ups and downs obligatory in all property transactions in England, contracts were exchanged.

The buyers were a youngish couple with a baby, whose hearts were set on our house no less than ours were set on Docklow Grange. This gave us a kick. Some people can be coolly pragmatic about selling their homes, but we even had sentimental ties to the upstairs toilet-handle, which for some odd reason had been what Jane chose when the midwife, Margaret Hill, advised her to focus on something while she was squeezing Jacob out. Like the Openshaws, we wanted our cherished family home to become another family's cherished home.

On Friday, 12 July 2002, we moved, forcing ourselves to do the unsentimental thing, and leave the toilet-handle behind. We had lived in Crouch End for eight years, three months and four days, and all our children had taken their first steps there. It would be melodramatic to say that it was like being separated from a limb, but the pain *was* almost physical.

The evening before we left, we had a farewell party, using packing cases as tables and chairs. I looked round at the immediate neighbours who had become our closest friends. They were fine people, without exception interesting, caring, hospitable and fun.

I looked at Paul and Jacky from next-door-but-two. Their 7-year-old daughter Holly and our son Joseph had been born three days apart; they loved each other like brother and sister.

I looked at Ali and Chris from just a few houses further down. Their three kids, Lauren, Rosie and Jake, were the same ages as our three, and devoted friends. Ali had grown up in Sheffield, close to the South Yorkshire village where Jane grew up. They had so much in common, not least an endearing if sometimes disconcerting capacity to call a spade a bloody, blasted, chuffing spade.

I looked at Rebecca and Derek, who lived two doors from Ali and Chris, and whose two lively, engaging boys, Thomas and Benjamin, we had watched grow. Derek came from Blackpool, just across the Ribble estuary from my home town of Southport. He was a terrific guy, who'd been a fireman and now owned a shop in Islington selling contemporary rugs. There was probably no man in the world better able to advise on the flammability of certain floor coverings, or more equipped to heave a Turkish kilim over his shoulder.

We had shared with Derek the anxiety and the adventure involved in opening a shop of his own, and I thought again of the conversation he'd had with his Blackpudlian mother, when he told her that he'd decided to call the shop 'Tribe'. There was silence at the other end of the telephone line, followed by a weak 'That's nice, love.' It later emerged that she thought he intended to call his rug emporium 'Tripe'.

I had laughed at that story until the tears ran down my cheeks. These were people with whom we had shared so much fun and laughter, and although I knew that we would never lose contact, nor would we ever again enjoy their company on a daily or even monthly basis. They, and so many others like them in Crouch End, were our kindred spirits. Where were we going to find kindred spirits in Herefordshire? Were we mad to turn our backs, and our lives, on all this?

We couldn't quite shed the suspicion that we were. Earlier that day, Jane had bumped into an acquaintance who was going with her husband and kids to live in Malawi for three years.

'How scary,' said Jane.

'But what you're doing is much scarier,' the woman said. 'At least we're coming back.'

She was right. After all, once we had taken our foot off the London property ladder, it would fall with a resounding clatter. If we were desperate to move back to London after a year or two, we would never be able to afford a house as nice as the one we were about to leave. Besides, it wouldn't be fair to uproot the children again. No, this move, for better or worse, had to be permanent.

The following afternoon, after extended goodbyes of ferocious poignancy, I climbed into the car without – for the first time in eight years, three months and four days – a single rueful thought for the excellent parking-space I was about to leave behind. In Crouch End, as in so many parts of residential London, convenient parking-spaces are of incalculable value, like saffron to the ancient Phoenicians. There had been times when I was about to get into my car to drive somewhere, but decided to walk or take the bus, rather than give away a prime parking-space to someone who might not cherish it as much as I did.

Our friends stood on the pavement, waving. Tears were shed. At five past two we took our final leave of Park Avenue South. Jane cried all the way to the North Circular Road, and all the way to the Hanger Lane gyratory system. Which on a Friday afternoon in summer, in the horrendous motorised crush to get out of London, amounts to a very long cry indeed. It was a good job I was driving, since visibility for her was reduced to about a yard. On the other hand, a yard's visibility is all you need on the North Circular on a Friday afternoon. At least we'd never be making *that* journey again.

2

Lord Hereford's Knob

The 154-mile journey from Crouch End to Docklow that Friday afternoon took us four hours and twenty-five minutes, the last hour and a half of it behind an I Can't Believe It's Not Butter lorry.

'I can't believe it's not going any faster,' I said. Jane made a noise acknowledging the joke, but it was closer to a grunt than a chuckle. She had cheered up since the Hanger Lane gyratory system but not much. It seemed like a terribly prosaic start to our new life, being stuck behind an I Can't Believe It's Not Butter lorry. I resolved that in future I would eat only spreadable Lurpak. I also realised that the country-road dawdle behind a large and impassable vehicle might become every bit as familiar as the interminable tailback on the North Circular. Still, at least I would have hedgerows to look at, rather than Ikea and Leather World.

This last thought made my stomach lurch. I could scoff all I liked at Leather World, but for years it had been a landmark on my journeys home. What would my landmarks be now? In the *London A–Z* I had shared a page with Alexandra Palace, hallowed site of the very first BBC television broadcast. It seemed like a distinguished page to live on, a page of real cultural significance. In the *Collins Road Atlas of Great Britain*, on the other hand, I now shared a page with somewhere called Bagwyllydiart, which as far as I knew wasn't famous for anything except possibly an unusually high concentration of consonants, that might have stumped even Carol Vorderman.

As we turned off the M5, and passed signs for Worcester and Malvern, I was reminded of the A-Level General Studies paper I had sat at King George V School, Southport, in the summer of 1979. I am usually revisited by old exam papers only in my sleep; whenever I'm anxious about something I dream that I'm about to sit three hours of French Literature having done absolutely no revision, a trauma which is more than worthwhile for the sheer joy of waking up to realise that I will never, ever again be asked to translate chunks of *La Peste*, by Albert Camus.

I'm told that, in some shape or form, it's a common dream. But I am not usually given to thinking back while awake to exams from so long ago. The reason I did so now was that in that General Studies paper there had been a series of five questions all referring to an accompanying map of the Severn Valley, and an attached railway timetable. All the questions went something like this:

Assuming an average speed of 40 m.p.h., and a departure time of 8.25 a.m., but accounting for a ten-minute delay for road-works just outside Hartpury, would it be quicker to travel by car from Malvern Link to Gloucester, or by train on the 7.38, changing at Worcester Shrub Hill, taking into consideration a five-minute delay at a signal box just outside Tewkesbury?

Once you consulted the map and the train timetable, the answers were not difficult to work out. Afterwards, my friend Rob Waggett asked me what I had thought of the exam. 'Not too bad,' I said. Rob almost exploded with indignation. 'Not too bad? What about those questions about getting from Malvern Link to Gloucester? I've never been anywhere near Malvern fucking Link.' I said I thought that the map and timetable had been easy enough to follow. He looked at me, horror-struck. 'Map?' he shrieked. 'What map? What sodding timetable?'

I'd been cheerfully telling this story ever since, not least, through my student years, as a memo to myself to absorb every word of every question on an exam paper. And here I was, with Worcester Shrub Hill and signal-box delays just outside Tewkesbury about to become part of my everyday life. It wasn't an unpleasant thought, particularly, but it was definitely a thought.

There was one immediate benefit to celebrate, though. As we finally turned into our new drive I accelerated before braking, just to emphasise the noise of tyres on gravel. Our gravel. In London the midnight drive round the block in third gear, repeatedly cursing while looking for a parking-space, had become a Saturday night ritual. Now we could park a pair of pantechnicons outside our house if we wanted.

Which, happily, we did. Scarcely half an hour after us, our two vast removals vans arrived and I cruelly drew a measure of consolation from the thought that some poor sod had probably been sitting in his car for an hour and a half behind a GB Liners removals van. An I Can't Believe It's Not Butter rep, with any luck.

Eventually, four sturdy men began the process of unloading our worldly goods. It was a job that would take them the rest of that day and most of the next, yet our worldly goods did not fill much of Docklow Grange, to put it mildly. We felt like characters from *The Borrowers*. A dresser which had dominated our dining room in London now looked like doll's house furniture. We'd had a shed at Park Avenue South which had loomed large just outside the utility-room door. Every time we wanted to get from the kitchen into the back garden, we'd had to squeeze past the shed. Here, two strapping removals men placed the same structure against the far wall of the orchard, and some weeks later when I asked Eleanor to fetch some barbecue charcoal from the shed, it took her half an hour to find it.

I was reminded of Jane's Auntie Jose, a diminutive Yorkshirewoman of little formal education yet who could effortlessly produce imagery, even in postcards from Lanzarote, that was the equal of anything written by Virginia Woolf. She had come back from her last holiday complaining that the hotel swimming pool was too small, and the whitewashed walls around it too high. 'It were like postage stamp in t'middle of a squash court,' she observed. She'd have known just what to say about our shrunken dresser, and our invisible shed.

At least the Openshaws had left the three cottages furnished, if not entirely to our taste. It was just as well they had. The following day, our first in our new home, we had a week-long holiday let starting in Yewtree Cottage. The family, from Liverpool, had apparently stayed several times before. It was strange to think that they would feel at home before we did. In fact, the first thing they asked was: 'Where are the peacocks?' We hadn't even noticed that the peacocks were missing. It turned out that the Openshaws had abruptly sold them because one of the neighbours complained that they kept fouling his path, and apparently peacock poo has peculiarly adhesive properties. In truth we weren't sorry. We had enough to wrestle with without incontinent peacocks, not least the holiday cottage business.

We had all kinds of plans for the cottages, things that the Openshaws had never done. We wanted to offer home-cooked dinners, so that guests, especially those arriving on a Friday night after the kind of journey we'd just had, could have a meal waiting for them in the oven. And once we'd got that service established, we planned to offer dinner in the house itself. Jane would cook, I would be maître d', and the children would be bribed to stay upstairs. Then, once we'd done a few of those, we would advertise as a venue for small wedding receptions. If the business took off I might have to do less journalism and more wielding of smoked salmon canapés.

My other, rather grandiose scheme was to host literary, musical, theatrical and culinary weekends at Docklow. The idea was that people would stay in the cottages but come into the house for a lecture or recital or drama workshop or cookery demonstration, given by an expert. About a month before we moved, I had interviewed the actress Vanessa Redgrave for the *Independent*. As I left her ground-floor, mansion-block flat in Chiswick, west London, she asked me where I lived. 'Crouch End,' I said, 'but we're about to move to Herefordshire.'

'Oh reaaalllly,' she said, her pale blue eyes flashing an interest which seemed more than mere politeness. 'I was evacuated to Bromyard during the war. I haven't been there for years. I would love to see it again.'

So I told her about Docklow Grange, scarcely six miles from Bromyard, and my arty weekends idea. I cheekily asked if she'd be willing to come and do a workshop or give a reading and she said she would, although I didn't discount the possibility that she was trying to humour me in a desperate bid to get me out of her flat. Still, she gave me her e-mail address, and I walked away down Chiswick High Road with an irresistible vision of the formidable Vanessa Redgrave performing some Chekhovian monologue in our Docklow drawing room – uninterrupted, I hoped, by Jacob yelling from the downstairs loo for someone to come and wipe his bottom.

Whatever, all that was for the future. Our task right now was to keep the cottage business ticking while we established ourselves in our new home, and to divert the children's thoughts from the many friends they had left behind. The cost of that diversion was precisely £400, which is what we paid for Milo, a 7-week-old golden retriever puppy. The children, particularly Eleanor, had been begging for years to have a puppy. But a terraced house in London is no place for a big dog, and when anyone suggested a small one I very firmly put my foot down – always a risky manoeuvre, of course, when you're dealing with small dogs.

In a house like Docklow Grange, however, it seemed almost obligatory to have a big dog. The Openshaws, indeed, had once had a St Bernard, which by all accounts had been the size of a small elephant, and had once pinned Mrs Openshaw's elderly father to his bed for the best part of two days. Or maybe it was two minutes. I do remember it being a good story, anyway.

In a blatant act of calculated parenting, we arranged to collect Milo on our first full day in Docklow Grange. On the internet we had found a breeder of pedigree retrievers who lived in the

Golden Valley on the other side of Hereford, and a month before we moved we chugged up there with the kids to choose a pup from a litter of eight. They were all sweet little balls of pale fur, but the sweetest of them was Milo. We decided to call him Milo after one of the characters in the pre-school children's television series *The Tweenies*, although well-read adults would later assume that he was named after Lieutenant Milo Minderbinder in Joseph Heller's powerful anti-war novel *Catch-22*.

'Milo? Ah, you named him after Milo Minderbinder in *Catch-22*, of course?'

'Of course.'

The children's excitement at the prospect of taking delivery of Milo had been a useful tool in those last few weeks in London, which we used to chisel away at their unhappiness over leaving their friends. And Milo was a happy distraction, too, during our first few days in Docklow Grange – as tiresome as it can be, when you have dozens of cases to unpack, to have to attend to piddles on the carpet.

We all fell instantly in love with Milo, but I had never owned a dog before and it took me a while to adjust to a dog-owner's mindset. In Leominster one day I realised with a start that a poster featuring an accusing finger in the manner of Lord Kitchener's, above a caption screaming 'Have you wormed your pet?', was directed at me. Before, if I'd noticed the poster at all, I'd have relaxed knowing that the finger was pointing somewhere over my shoulder.

Of course, it wasn't just a dog-owner's mindset that I now had to acquire, but a country-dweller's mindset. And excited as we were to be rattling around in our rambling new house, meagre as the likelihood was of us ever tiring of hearing our children telling us that the dog had done a poo-poo in the ha-ha, there was no doubt that our new life would take some getting used to. After all, the population of Docklow was about ninety, significantly fewer people than had lived on our side of the road in London. Nor was there a single shop. For the last eight years a four-minute walk was all it had taken to buy a pint of milk and a loaf of bread; now, there and back, it was a twenty-minute drive.

Docklow could scarcely be called a village. There was no village hall, no village green, no village pond, and no twitching net curtains, if only because the houses were too widely scattered. There was, however, a delightful old church, St Bartholomew's, dating from the twelfth century. And a seventeenth-century pub, the King's Head, which had recently changed hands. The new owners were Roger and Jean, a couple in their fifties. Roger was a former merchant seaman, but Jean was altogether the saltier of the two, a waspishly witty Glaswegian with a décolletage that could have, and in her younger days probably had, stopped the traffic on Sauchiehall Street.

We warmed instantly to Roger and Jean, who seemed to me everything that the licensees of a country pub should be. They were warm, welcoming and willing to give me pints of bitter on tick. I was thrilled to have a local again. In Crouch End I had only gone to the pub to watch the odd big-screen football match. Here, I sometimes went three nights on the trot. I hadn't done that since I was a student. It seemed like merely a matter of time before I had my own tankard hanging behind the bar, and a look of withering contempt for anyone who dared to sit in 'my' chair playing with 'my' dominoes.

Roger and Jean had encouraging plans for the King's Head, too. They wanted to improve the quality of the cooking, to make it a destination for its food alone. As it was the only establishment we could walk to without wearing out a pair of stout boots, we were delighted. And when they told us that the King's Head had been short-listed in the 2002 Flavours of Herefordshire competition for the best use of local produce, I would have turned a celebratory cartwheel, or at any rate a hesitant forward roll, had I not just eaten a portion of Jean's delicious but killingly rich strawberry shortcake.

Several of our new neighbours, however, did not share our enthusiasm for the transformation of the King's Head. By making the pub more upmarket, in the process removing the dartboard and the pool table, Roger and Jean had alienated some of the regulars. Mostly farmers and farmworkers, they still came in to sup but looked around with palpable disapproval at the changes, including, it seemed to me, me. I might have been innocently tucking into the strawberry shortcake, but to them I was dancing on the grave of the lamented pool table.

I hoped that I would eventually be able to share a nice pint and a good story with these men. I knew they told good stories. I heard one of them telling his mates that a pal of his had been pulled up on the A44 by a young policeman, who in a rather patronising manner had lectured him on the dangers of exceeding the speed limit.

'I was only doing fifty-five miles an hour,' he protested.

'Yes,' said the copper, 'but what if Mr Fog had suddenly come down?'

The man sighed, and decided to meet condescension with condescension. 'Then I would have placed Mr Foot on Mr Brake and put on Mr and Mrs Headlight,' he said.

There was a short silence. 'Let me express myself more clearly,' said the policeman. 'What if mist or fog had suddenly come down?'

It may have been an urban or in this case a rural myth, but it was a funny one. They seemed, this group of guffawing, cider-drinking farmers, like a companionable bunch. It would be pleasing at least to get the odd smile from them. But clearly a smile was not my due by some kind of seigneurial right. It would have to be earned.

I knew all the tales, of course, about people moving to remote parts of England and not being truly accepted by the locals until they'd put thirty winters behind them. Bloody cold ones, ideally. It doesn't mean that in the meantime they are shunned or even treated coolly, just that for decades they are broadly considered, as the charming expression goes in Herefordshire, as 'buggers from off'.

In our case this possibility was compounded by three further factors: one, that we had moved into the locality's big house; two, that we had come from London; three, that I was a national newspaper columnist, and a columnist, moreover, who had started writing a weekly column called 'Tales of the Country'. It had never been my plan to chronicle our life in the country in weekly instalments, but one week I stood in for my colleague on the *Independent*, John Walsh, who wrote a column called 'Tales of the City'. When John returned from holiday I was asked to carry on.

I enjoyed writing about our new life but it was also hazardous. In trying to write positively about the countryside, I risked appearing smug about our decision to quit the city. Worse, in trying to give some sense of how we grappled with life away from the city, it might seem that I was poking fun at them country folk and their funny ways.

Inevitably, I offended some readers; it might be argued that any self-respecting columnist should. The rather worrying thing was that some of the people I unwittingly offended lived nearby.

I didn't really expect to find a severed cow's head on the doorstep one morning, but it was mildly troubling to think that I might stand innocently in front of someone at the bank who recognised me from my picture byline and harboured a dislike for me.

One day, I received the following letter from a man who lived in Kimbolton, three or four miles away.

Dear Mr Viner,
We, like you, are incomers, having moved here at the end of 1980. It is a pity you do not restrict your contributions to the *Independent* to your sporting interviews, as your Tales of the Country are exceedingly trite and patronising. The arrogance of Londoners is quite breathtaking. What a shame you don't use that column to address some real local issues such as the lack of a swimming pool in Leominster.

Hey ho, on a positive note I cannot believe the number of times you appear to have emptied your septic tank. Something is wrong. We have emptied ours twice in 22 years. If correctly sized (capacity about one-third daily total intake, ie say eight people @ 250gpd = 2000 gal/3 = 667 gal), in practice a 750 gal fibre glass bottle would be OK. However, the real key is the French Drain or nitrification tile or perforated plastic pipe which takes the septic tank's effluent. It must be of sufficient length (c +150ft) and surrounded by coarse/medium gravel.

Yours sincerely, Arthur J. Kirtley

This, it occurred to me, represented a new turn in the evolution of the poison-pen letter. Mr Kirtley hadn't sent me his shit, but considered technical advice on what to do with my shit. I was almost touched.

As for his suggestion that I should use my column in the *Independent* to address issues such as the lack of a swimming pool in Leominster, I wondered how fascinating that would have been to readers in Ruislip or Budleigh Salterton. He would doubtless raise the same point with regard to my musings about our apple trees, or indeed the troublesome septic tank, except that domestic hassles are, paradoxically, universal.

Whatever, it bewildered me that my 'trite' subject matter so enraged Mr Kirtley that he felt compelled to write. Had I been regularly coming down hard on the Palestinian Question I could expect a bit of abuse, but it seemed odd that someone should get so indignant on behalf of a misunderstood septic tank. Happily, there were many more nice letters than nasty ones. And lots of people very sweetly wrote with advice, recommending local sights and plant nurseries, or simply offering tips such as how we as novice poultry-keepers should deal with a broody hen.

A newspaper column about forsaking the city for the country was nothing new, as was wittily pointed out by my colleague Miles Kington. Miles e-mailed me to say that his friend Stephen Pile, of the *Daily Telegraph*, had chronicled his own move out of London in a series of articles with roughly the following themes: 'The Hell of Living in London!' 'Why I Must Get Out of London!' 'Why I Have Finally Made the Break!' 'Ah – the Country at Last!' 'Why I Still Miss London!' 'The Hell of Living in a Wood with Five Million Mosquitoes!' 'Move to the Country, and the World Comes to Stay!' 'Why I Have to Get Back to London!' 'Ah, London – How I Missed You!' 'The Hell of the Country!' 'Why I Sometimes Miss the Country'! 'Twickenham – It's Just Like the Country, Really!'

I chuckled nervously on reading Miles' e-mail. But I felt reasonably sure that my country chronicles would not follow the same pattern as Stephen Pile's. For one thing, our move out of London had not been fired by negative feelings towards the city. For another, the chances of us winding up in Twickenham were very slim indeed.

I took the point, though, that it was a fertile furrow I was ploughing. I knew, for example, that the great American humorist S. J. Perelman had written brilliantly in the *New Yorker* about his fifteen years in the backwoods of eastern Pennsylvania. In one dispatch he said:

> I wouldn't live in the city if you paid me a million dollars a year. Well, let's say 42 dollars a year. How people can exist side by side with utter disregard for each other, never prying into anybody's business, is beyond me. In the country, folks are more matey; there is always an extra stiletto for the newcomer and a friendly hand ready to tighten around his throat. The moving men have hardly kicked the rungs out of your Chippendale chairs before neighbours spring up like mushrooms, eager to point out any flaws you may have missed in your place and gloat over your predicament.

Perelman's dispatches might have related to a different country in a different era, America in the 1940s, but that made them no less relevant. Had I read them before rather than after we moved to the backwoods of northern Herefordshire, I might have hesitated a while longer before stepping into the unknown.

Another began:

Every now and then on a breathless August evening, I like to draw up my easy chair before a glowing fire, puff on a calabash and stare thoughtfully into the flames. The heat is unendurable and the calabash makes me nauseated, but like a bachelor remembering his summer sweethearts, it helps me recall the architects who have almost remodeled my quaint old stone farmhouse. For the money I have spent on blueprints alone, I could have razed the house, erected a replica of the Taj Mahal, and retired to Sun Valley. If I ever adopt a coat of arms, it will show a ravenous drafts-man . . . over a shield marked 'Soft Pickings'.

In other words, old houses in the country are a money pit. There is even a film called *The Money Pit*, which I still haven't been brave enough to watch, although I understand that it stars Tom Hanks as a successful lawyer whose wealth is quickly sucked dry by a house with a leaking roof, rotten floorboards and much else besides.

At least we knew that the roof on Docklow Grange was reasonably (although not entirely) watertight. And none of our new neighbours had turned up to point out any flaws in the house or gloat over our predicament. Only one person, a guy called Mark, told us that he wouldn't live in our house for all the cider in Herefordshire, largely on account of the antiquated plumbing system and the vast old tank in the attic filled with stagnant water. Mark was our plumber.

As for another S. J. Perelman crack about living in the country, that fifteen years of it taught him that 'a corner delicatessen at dusk is more exciting than any rainbow', I couldn't imagine ever feeling the same way. Which is not to say that I am unmoved by the sight of a corner delicatessen at dusk. Rare indeed is the corner delicatessen, at dusk or any other time, past which I am able to walk without shelling out £3.89 for a styrofoam tub of chilli peppers stuffed with feta cheese, or some other such essential.

But a vivid rainbow framing our own few acres of green and pleasant land, that was a spectacle almost worth the mortgage on its own. And the sunsets! Never mind all the cider in Herefordshire, not for all the chilli peppers stuffed with feta cheese in Muswell Hill would I swap our sunsets, now or ever. Ever since boyhood I had had a thing about sunsets. It was probably passed on to me by my parents, with whom I used to stand in our back garden in Southport, watching an orange sun dipping behind the sand dunes. 'Oooh,' my late father would say, as the last sliver of orange brushed the top of the dunes. 'Oooh,' my mother would add. 'Oooh,' I would chime in, as the sun finally disappeared from view. And then my mum always said the same thing: 'I wish I could paint.' It was a sacred family ritual, and no concessions were made if I had a friend to play. He would have to stand there too, oohing.

In all the places I had lived since I left Southport – Scotland, France, America, London – I had never seen comparable sunsets. But those in Docklow were even better. Above the Black Mountains the whole sky was suffused with pink and purple, night after night. Oooh.

Just as when I was a child, nothing and nobody was allowed to hinder my appreciation of a good sunset. One September day, distressingly soon after we had moved in, the septic tank overflowed. As I hadn't yet had the letter from Mr Kirtley informing me that the real key was the French Drain or nitrification tile or perforated plastic pipe, and that it must be of sufficient length (c +150ft) and surrounded by coarse/medium gravel, I phoned

Dyno-Rod. But just as the Dyno-Rod man was explaining what he had done to resolve the situation, I caught sight over his shoulder of a most wonderful sunset, an absolute belter, 7.5 on my personal Sunset Scale with 10 being the virtually unattainable maximum. 'Excuse me,' I said. 'Look at that! Oooh!'

The Dyno-Rod man, who had been talking enthusiastically about effluent, didn't seem to share my rapture. Which was a shame because sunsets, like all great natural phenomena, are even better shared. Jane and the children had become used to me herding them over to a window to gaze at a crimson sky. I had even done it in Crouch End. And they normally indulged me by making most of the right noises. At least I hadn't started saying, 'I wish I could paint.'

If the children were indulging me, I knew that I had a fellow sunset-phile in Tom, the gardener we'd inherited from the Openshaws. Tom would often join me as I stood looking west in a state of suspended bliss, gazing upon such a pinky-orangey-purply glow that you could almost believe there had been a diabolical terrorist attack on the SAS base in Hereford, eighteen miles away. One evening we stood together in silence for fully five minutes, bonding over a setting sun. I would have kissed him, if it hadn't been for the stubble on his chin.

Tom came in once a week and was as engaging a fellow as you could hope to meet. He was about twenty-three when we first met him but endearingly childlike; a little praise went a gratifyingly long way, and a lot of praise lifted his spirits for about a month. At the end of his stint Tom frequently solicited praise – 'Have I done well today?' – but the praise was never undeserved. He planted bulbs and weeded flowerbeds as though his life depended on it, and despite his childlike nature, could identify every tree and shrub and flower like a veteran horiculturalist.

'What's that tree with the lovely red leaves, Tom?' I asked one autumnal afternoon.

'It's known as weeping Jerusalem,' he said, looking at it lovingly.

Often he would add a charming bit of countryside lore. 'Some people round here think that if you rub a leaf from a weeping Jerusalem against your temple you will never get a headache.' That sort of thing. He reminded me a little of Chance the Gardener, the Peter Sellers character in the film *Being There*, whose aphorisms about the life cycle of a garden – 'you must plant new shrubs when the soil is warm' – are mistaken for profound insights into the American economy.

Anyway, as I was standing in the garden one day admiring the westerly view, Tom appeared at my elbow.

'Have you ever seen Lord Hereford's Knob?' he asked, excitedly.

Somewhat taken aback by the question, I considered my answer. At university I had played football with one or two members of the minor aristocracy, and showered alongside them afterwards, but none of them was called Lord Hereford. Besides, I knew that he was probably referring to an interesting topographical feature, as indeed he was. 'Unfortunately not,' I said. He pointed out a hill on the horizon. 'I think that is Lord Hereford's Knob,' he said.

After I had described this exchange in my newspaper column, I received an e-mail from a reader, Dr Norman Mills, who informed me that there is another hill, close to Lord Hereford's Knob, called Myarth. 'Perhaps you have no need to worry unless and until you can claim to see both at the same time,' he wrote. This information appealed greatly to that side of me, which may in fact be the whole of me, that appreciates saucy innuendo and terrible puns and thinks the Carry On canon of films to have been one of the twentieth century's great cultural landmarks. Was there ever a better line in any movie than the one uttered by Kenneth Williams as Julius Caesar in *Carry On Cleo*: 'Infamy, infamy – they've all got it in for me!'? I think not.

A few months later, incidentally, we befriended a splendid woman called Rosemary, the mother of Eleanor's classmate, Louisa. Rosemary, though she had lived in the Welsh Marches all her life, had been unaware of both Lord Hereford's Knob and Myarth, and was as amused as I had been to learn of their proximity.

In fact she and Jane – two full-grown and not unintelligent women – spent about an hour one morning quite literally howling with laughter over a conversation Rosemary had had at a party the night before, in which she asked an acquaintance, whom she knew to be a hiking enthusiast, whether he had ever made it to the top of Lord Hereford's Knob? He said that he had, many times. 'But you've never been up Myarth?' she added, in mock solemnity. 'No,' he said with a note of regret. 'I never have.'

The visibility of Lord Hereford's Knob on a clear day was not Docklow's only connection with the English aristocracy, however. There was a much more sinister one.

On Sunday, 13 September 1987, in Kempton, a hamlet a few miles north-west of Ludlow near Shropshire's beautiful Clun Valley, an elderly, myopic former guardsman called Simon Dale was found bludgeoned to death in his home, Heath House. A shocked neighbour, Mrs Spencer, told the police that Dale had given her the name and contact details of his ex-wife, the Baroness Susan de Stempel, in case there was ever an emergency. This was probably not the kind of emergency he'd had in mind.

Mrs Spencer added that she knew Dale and his ex-wife did not get on; something to do, she thought, with disputed ownership of Heath House.

Detective Sergeant Dave Clarke, from Ludlow police station, and Detective Inspector Derek Matthews, the duty officer in Leominster, duly set off to convey the terrible news to Baroness de Stempel, who lived in Forresters Hall, Docklow.

The definitive account of what happened next is contained in an engrossing book called *The Trials of the Baroness*, written in 1991 by Terry Kirby, who coincidentally would later become a colleague of mine at the *Independent*. We had lived in Docklow for all of a week before two people, quite independently of each other, lent me well-thumbed copies of Terry's book. Clearly, there was no point knowing where the nearest post office was, or what night to put the bins out, if you didn't also have a working knowledge of the Baroness de Stempel story, the most exciting thing to happen to Docklow in a millennium.

In a nutshell – although a large nutshell, because it's a complicated tale – DS Clarke and DI Matthews took a while finding the house that night, not least because they were looking for somewhere rather grand. In fact, Forresters Hall was, and is, two adjoining stone cottages opposite the church. It was 12.30 a.m. when finally they knocked on the door, and they found the Baroness curiously uncurious to find two policemen on the threshold. When Matthews broke the news of Dale's death, the Baroness and her grown-up children, who were also Dale's children, scarcely flinched. Which did not necessarily suggest complicity in his murder, merely that they were all card-carrying members of the English upper classes and had been intensively coached at public school in the finer points of emotional repression.

Baroness de Stempel was the great-great-granddaughter of one of Britain's most imposing moral crusaders, William Wilberforce. Best known for driving the abolition of the slave trade in the British West Indies through the House of Commons in 1807, he had also been one of the founders of the formidably named Proclamation Society for the Suppression of Vice. He was, in other words, a bit of a spoilsport. But obviously a man of fierce rectitude who would have been ashamed of his descendant. For as the investigation into Dale's death unfolded, it was discovered that Baroness de Stempel, with her second husband the Baron, and two of her children, had defrauded her elderly and wealthy aunt, Margaret, Baroness Illingworth of Denton, of all her money and possessions, forging her will and any number of documents authorising bank transfers, and sending valuable heirlooms off to be auctioned. So much for the venerable family tradition of suppressing vice.

All this embezzlement was initiated in Docklow, where Lady Illingworth lived with the de Stempels from February to December 1984. They then decided that they could no longer care for her, and in November 1986 she died in a nursing home, more or less destitute and apparently unloved.

For such a tiny, seemingly insignificant place, Docklow looms large and significant in Terry Kirby's book, and indeed became almost a euphemism for villainy at the 1989 fraud trial of the Baron, the Baroness, and her children Marcus and Sophia.

There had earlier been a murder trial, at Worcester Crown Court, at which Baroness de Stempel, Marcus and Sophia were cleared of killing Dale. The murder remains unsolved. But for defrauding Lady Illingworth the Baroness was sentenced to seven years in jail, and the Baron to four years. He was a 'congenital liar', a 'monumental snob' and a 'man without courage', said counsel, and that was counsel for his defence. Sophia got thirty months and Marcus eighteen months. The biggest show of emotion from the family was William Wilberforce turning in his grave.

When we arrived to live in Docklow we were unaware of any of this. I had a dim recollection that there had been a Baroness de Stempel and that she had been involved in some scandal in the 1980s, but that was all. It was not long, however, before people started mentioning the de Stempel affair: Mrs Openshaw told me that she used to see the Baroness furtively using the Docklow Grange telephone box. Nobody, though, had been on anything more than curt nodding terms with her. She evidently regarded everyone in the area as her social inferiors; exhibit A, a letter to Terry Kirby from Askham Grange women's prison in which she wrote that 'the one thing money can't buy is breeding, don't you agree?' Plainly, incarceration did nothing to diminish her extraordinary hauteur.

Unsurprisingly, Susan de Stempel did not return to Docklow when she was released from prison. What became of her or her family I have no idea. Forresters Hall is still there, occupied by people of rather less social distinction and rather more integrity. And Docklow's flirtation with notoriety is long gone.

Having said that, when we arrived here there was one person in the vicinity who had had fifteen minutes of notoriety; another person of whom old William Wilberforce would have mightily disapproved. This was a woman called Carla, who had once gloried in the exciting alias of Miss Whiplash. As you will recall if you're half as interested as I am in these matters, Miss Whiplash had rented a London flat from the then-Chancellor of the Exchequer, Norman Lamont, in which she dispensed her services as a 'sex therapist'. There was no evidence that Lamont ever availed himself of her particular brand of therapy, but a scandal broke when he tried to evict her using public money. Later, with the proceeds of selling her story to the tabloids, she moved from London to a house in Hampton Wafre, the adjoining parish to Docklow, where she lived in the company of about 200 ducks – less trouble, presumably, than politicians.

We found out about her presence in the locality when Tim, the local pig farmer, dropped round one morning soon after we had moved in. Tim was gathering signatures for a petition against a proposed telecommunications mast at Hampton Wafre, and top of his list of signatories was Carla. Indeed, Tim said she had asked him if he wanted her to make representations to a certain Cabinet minister.

'I know him,' she said, with what I can only hope was a twinkle, 'extremely well.'

It delighted me that the former Miss Whiplash, though now retired as a sex therapist, was still prepared to grapple with a controversial erection. I don't know whether she did make a call to her friend the Cabinet minister, but Tim's petition was unsuccessful – not least, perhaps, because you could get a signature from every living person round here and still barely fill one side of a sheet of A4 paper. It's sheep whose support you need if you're to get anywhere with petitions in these parts.

Anyway, up went the telecommunications mast, and in due course I heard that Carla had moved away. The only contact we had with her was indirect, through a delightful young woman called Livy not long out of Hereford Cathedral School, who had resourcefully advertised her own services – as a house-sitter rather than anything less wholesome – in the *Hereford Times*.

Every summer since 1997 we had spent ten days at a hotel just outside Padstow in Cornwall. It would have been more popular with our children to tell them that we were cancelling Christmas than our annual holiday in Cornwall, so in 2002 we went as usual, even though we had been living in Docklow for little more than a fortnight.

But we needed someone to look after the house and the holiday cottages, and Livy fitted the bill perfectly. Afterwards, we stayed in touch. And a few weeks later she told us that she had been asked to house-sit for a woman who lived near us with a battalion of ducks. It could only be Carla and indeed was. When we next saw Livy, my mother-in-law, Anne, was staying with us. 'What's she like?' asked Anne, meaning Carla.

'Well,' said Livy, gesturing to her knees, 'she's got tits down to here.'

Livy was not to know that my mother-in-law, while a marvellous woman and by no means a prude, is not someone who ever bandies around the word 'tits', nor ever really gets it bandied in her direction. Jane and I shrank back into the shadows, while Anne uttered a self-consciously robust 'really?', as if Livy had reported that Carla had a new Magnet kitchen.

I don't know where the stupendously well-endowed Carla went after leaving Hampton Wafre. Although I never met her I will always think of her fondly, largely because she helped to exorcise any lingering regret that I would no longer bump into Victoria Wood and Alison Steadman in M&S. It was so much more fun to have neighbours who preferred S&M.

3

The Kon-Tiki Expedition

The weather helped us to settle in. Since the day we arrived it had been remarkably fine, and although there were a couple of weeks in August when a massive low-pressure zone hung over the western side of Britain, those were, true to form, the two weeks we had chosen to take our holiday in Cornwall. So it piddled down on us there, while in Docklow there was virtually unbroken sunshine. We found rivers to swim in, and wonderful walks, and explored our nearest centres of population – Leominster, Ludlow, Bromyard and Hereford – when all were looking at their best.

And we simply hung out in the garden, where I developed a worrying obsession for blackberry-picking. I had never had a garden with fruit in it, had never known the pleasure of picking my own soft fruit, but the garden at Docklow Grange was full of blackberries. By the end of August I was unable to pass a bank of brambles without rushing back into the house for a basket, or even a ladder.

'But, daddy,' wailed Joseph, 'you said you'd play football with me.'

'And I will, darling,' I said, 'but I've just spotted a really fantastic clump of berries.'

Once I started I couldn't stop. It took nightfall, hunger or a desperate need to pee, whichever came first, to get me back into the house. And although my usual pain threshold was lower than a centipede's football studs, when it came to blackberry-picking I was fearless. Thorns and nettles held no fear in pursuit of the perfect blackberry, and when I did eventually wander back into the house, with a full basket, I looked as though I'd run into Zorro in a really bad mood.

Neither Jane nor I had ever lived in the country. As I've written, I was brought up in Southport, on what was the Lancashire coast until the 1974 boundary changes, when to much general harrumphing it became Merseyside.

Jane grew up in Hoyland, near Barnsley in South Yorkshire, not far from some lovely countryside but by no means in it. We were both small-town northerners with a thin veneer of London sophistication. And sometimes altogether the wrong veneer. When we were having our kitchen refitted in Park Avenue South, the cupboards that were installed had a gloss finish rather than the matt on which Jane had set her heart. She expressed her disappointment, in no uncertain terms, to the fitter, Trevor. He in turn grabbed his mobile phone and called head office, and in his agitation got her name slightly wrong.

'Mrs Veneer is doing her nut about the finish on these cup-boards,' he said.

Anyway, the point is that we were cheerfully clueless about life in the country. And like all city-dwellers who move to the sticks we anticipated problems that did not materialise, just as we failed to anticipate others that did. For some reason we thought that every trip to the supermarket would be like the Kon-Tiki expedition. We solemnly decided that we needed a long checklist, which we would have to take with us on the weekly supermarket trip, to remove the nightmarish prospect of getting all the way there, then all the way home, to find that we had forgotten to buy any baked beans. That would be disastrous, reminding us in the worst possible way of the shopping conveniences we had left behind.

As it turned out, Safeway on the western fringes of Leominster was a fifteen-minute drive. We could cover those seven miles far quicker than it had ever taken us to get from Crouch End to our favourite branch of Waitrose, in Ballards Lane, Finchley. And if we wanted some thrilling variety, there was a Sainsbury's in Hereford (twenty minutes), a Tesco in Ludlow (twenty-five minutes), and a Waitrose in Malvern (thirty minutes). Not to mention good old Somerfield in the heart of Leominster (ten minutes). Even in times of heavy snowfall, we would probably not go hungry.

Inside our first week in the country, indeed, many of my negative preconceptions were shot down like grouse.

For example, in London, as a man constitutionally incapable of coping with the slightest electronic malfunction, I had had a hotline to MR Systems, Apple Macintosh suppliers and repairers based just off the unsalubrious Holloway Road. Whenever I had a problem with my Mac, like figuring out exactly how to switch it on, I phoned MR Systems. *In extremis*, they would send round a service engineer for £70 an hour. What, I had wailed inwardly, would I do when my computer misbehaved in Herefordshire?

It happened on day one. My Mac had been disconnected by the removals men, and inevitably I couldn't work out which wires went where. With untypical resourcefulness I had drawn a little coloured map of the back of my Mac before we left London, but with characteristic hopelessness I couldn't interpret my own drawing. I found a battered business directory in our phone box – the one Baroness de Stempel used to frequent – and with a heavy heart looked under computer supplies. There was a shop in Leominster but, as I'd expected, they told me they didn't make house calls. I wondered what Errol from MR Systems would charge for a trip up the M5? Probably no less than £1000. Plus VAT, of course.

But the man in the computer supplies shop suggested I call Ross at In-vision, the telly shop. I did so, and Ross said he thought he would be able to reconnect me. I asked when he might be able to come out to Docklow? Errol at MR Systems usually needed three or four days' notice for a house call. He pondered the situation. 'I could probably be with you,' he said slowly, 'in about twenty-five minutes.'

Ross turned out to be a sunny young fellow with a relentless supply of gags and one-liners; he observed that finding certain Mac parts in Herefordshire was like 'finding Lord Lucan riding Shergar', which did nothing to ease my concern that we had left the media heartland that is Crouch End for the media wasteland that is north Herefordshire. Nevertheless, two hours, three mugs of tea and getting on for a thousand one-liners later, Ross not only had my computer up and running but had tuned the telly and connected the video-recorder as well. I would have hugged him, but didn't want word getting back to the King's Head.

I asked Ross what I owed him. He did a few sums and, after telling me why the chicken crossed the road and how I might hide an elephant in a cherry tree, arrived somewhat arbitrarily at the sum of £25. Just to recap: he had turned up within a half-hour of my phone call, wired a computer, tuned a telly, connected a VCR, and reminded me what the landlord says to the white horse who comes into his pub ('I've got a whisky named after you!' 'What, Eric?'). For £25, Errol of MR Systems wouldn't have put in his contact lenses.

It appeared that the cost of living in the country was going to be considerably less than the cost of living in the city, although that, as it turned out, was a premature calculation not taking into account the hundreds of pounds a month we would end up stuffing in our petrol tank, to say nothing of the way an old house in the country eats into a Barclays Bank deposit account like Desperate Dan eats into a cow pie.

Moreover, just as Ross embodied the positives we had not expected, so 800,000 flies embodied the negatives. Nobody had warned us that the countryside was full of flies, not to mention moths built like prop forwards, with big, leering faces. Looking back, it was astoundingly naive of us not to realise that we would share our house with myriad other living creatures, including a spirited band of mice of whom I gradually grew rather fond. After all, we were surrounded by fields and woods. The only living creature that we could have done with seeing more of, in those first few weeks, was the very one that was scarce: *Homo sapiens*.

At 177,800, the population of Herefordshire is about 40,000 less than the population of the London Borough of Haringey. Yet Haringey occupies just 2963 hectares; Herefordshire 164,306. Off the top of my head, this means that in Haringey, every person has 0.01368546975 hectares of personal space, whereas in Herefordshire it amounts to 0.92410573678. Quite a lot more, anyway. And even by the standards of a scantily populated county, we were living in a particularly unpopulous bit. In the most densely populated parts of the county, such as downtown Hereford, there were between 20 and 33 people per hectare. In our electoral ward, grandly called Hampton Court after a castle a few miles south of us which predated the more famous Hampton Court on the banks of the Thames, it was between 0.2 and 0.3 people.

Later, this would become a source of smug satisfaction to us: it can be oddly uplifting to walk for two hours on a Sunday morning in June through some of England's most glorious countryside and to see not a single person other than those directly related to you.

But from time to time in those first few weeks, the empty lanes of the Welsh Marches contrasted unfavourably with the clogged arteries of Crouch End and Muswell Hill. According to the 2001 census, there resided, in the combined parishes of Docklow, Hampton Wafre and Grendon Bishop, just 214 people. Of these, ten were aged below four years, five between five and seven, and five more who were either eight or nine. So the chances of our kids sauntering out into the fields and making lots of friends of their own ages were on the limited side. Jane and I had more chance; in the three parishes combined there was a whopping forty-seven people aged, like us, between thirty and forty-four.

Nevertheless, the question that had nagged at me as I surveyed the room on our last night in London seemed no nearer a resolution: where would we find kindred spirits?

It was not quite true to say that before we arrived we knew

nobody who lived in Herefordshire. I had discovered that Bill Anton, an old friend of mine from my time at St Andrews University, lived with his wife and kids about three miles away from Docklow, but I hadn't seen him for at least fifteen years and we had never met his wife, let alone his kids, so, socially speaking, all our eggs were in a pretty unfamiliar basket.

It transpired that the Antons could scarcely have been sweeter or more welcoming, and he hadn't changed except in two fundamental respects: I had to get used to the fact that the rotund bloke I had known as Bill was now (a) svelte and (b) Rupert, which I vaguely remembered had been his real name all along. In the 1980s he had reckoned, probably quite rightly, that as a student he would get along better as a Bill than as a Rupert. His parents, however, loathed the name Bill. And this led, I now recalled, to some considerable awkwardness whenever university friends phoned him at his family home during the holidays, and asked for Bill. 'There's nobody here by that name,' his father used to respond, tartly. Things later took a surreal turn, incidentally, when we found that Rupert was actually his middle name, and that his given first name, which he had discarded altogether, was James.

Anyway, we took immediately to Bill's/Rupert's wife, Louise, and they quickly became good mates. But they had their own busy lives to lead. We needed to make friends of our own.

It wasn't that I didn't look. Jane teased me that in the King's Head I was inclined to engage in conversation anyone who caught my eye for a split-second, in the hope of finding someone to talk to about Everton's prospects for the new football season. Clearly, I was turning into the sad nutter on the train, the one with whom it is always a mistake to make even the most fleeting eye contact. But so was Jane. She came home from the post office in Leominster one day to report that she had overheard a couple of cheerful, witty women of about her age chatting in the queue behind her, and had worked hard to overcome the impulse to turn round and say 'Please will you be my friends?'

I don't mean to suggest that we were starved of human contact; Herefordshire might have a low population density but it's not quite the Russian steppes. Yet Jane missed her pals even more than the children missed theirs. Every few weeks in London she had gone out for a night on the razzle with her mates Ali, Rebecca, Kirsten and Andrea, highly attractive women of great style who on nights out – and nights in for that matter – dressed only in black, with the occasional reckless foray into dark grey.

The dress code for urban trendies, now that I come to think about it, is no less rigorous than it is for those gentrified country-dwellers who feel naked if they're not wearing a Barbour jacket and buckled green wellies. And yet it was those same urban trendies who in our first few weeks in the country kept asking, by the people-carrier load, whether I yet had my green wellies and waxed jacket. If I was feeling pugnacious I liked to point out that they were pots calling the kettle black – with the occasional reckless foray into dark grey. But more often than not I laughed along, and when we were invited back to London for a party given by Kirsten and her similarly chic husband, Lawrence, I debated whether to pitch up wearing a flat cap and wellies.

'Don't,' advised Jane, wisely. 'It'll be funny for the first two minutes and then you'll spend the rest of the evening feeling an arse.'

'I should be so lucky,' I quipped lightly. All the same, I wore mostly black.

A week or so later Jane got an invitation that seemed to sum up the social realities of our new lifestyle. It was an invitation from the kind, companionable but inescapably sixtysomething Mrs

Openshaw to go with her to an Aga cookery class in nearby Ledbury, which as it happened coincided with a girls' night out in London to celebrate Andrea's birthday. The symbolism seemed cruel, and yet Jane returned, not as full of alcohol as she would have been after an evening at Pradera tapas bar on Hornsey High Street, but no less full of beans.

The Aga demonstration had been inspirational, she reported. The woman who gave it, a home economics teacher from Cirencester, even showed how you can fry an egg directly on the hotplate, eliciting a gasp from her audience when, with a dramatic flourish, she then closed the hotplate lid over the egg. Clearly, tapas and rioja were not essential to a cracking night out in Herefordshire; all you needed was an Aga and a home economics teacher. Jane, meanwhile, obviously feeling liberated from the girls'-night-out dress regimen, wore mostly red.

As for the question of kindred spirits, we knew that once the children started at their new school near Ludlow in September, we would start meeting like-minded people. We also knew that we were not helping ourselves by encouraging friends and relatives to visit us every weekend. We had moved into Docklow Grange on 12 July; not until mid-October did we experience a weekend on our own as a family, either at home or striking out to discover the infinite pleasures of the Welsh Marches. It was no wonder that we all felt vaguely unsettled. But we could also understand our friends wanting to see what we had moved to. Besides, we were excited about showing them.

This seems as good a point as any in this book to consider the pros and cons, when you have moved out of the city to live in the country, of being visited by urban friends. 'Move to the Country, and the World Comes to Stay,' as Miles Kington put it in his neat synopsis of Stephen Pile's city v. country chronicles. It is a topic frequently addressed in broadsheet newspaper 'lifestyle' articles, which not infrequently relate an amusing tale that the late Malcolm Muggeridge used to tell against himself and his wife, Kitty.

Apparently, the Muggeridges once stayed for a weekend with some friends in Somerset, and had what they considered to be a nice time. By early evening on the Sunday they reckoned it was about time to be motoring back to London, so thanked their friends and exchanged affectionate farewells, before climbing into the car and chugging off. No sooner had they reached the end of the lane, however, than Kitty realised she had left her hat in the back garden. Rather than ring the doorbell and go through another series of goodbyes, she walked around the side of the house intending to discreetly collect her hat, which was when she noticed the owners dancing a merry jig in the conservatory, singing 'They've gone, they've gone, they've gone!'

I can relate to that episode; Jane and I have danced that very jig. Not after waving goodbye to all our friends, or even most of them, I should quickly add, but certainly those few among them who expect us to cook for them and ply them with alcohol, which is fair enough, but also to wash up after them and make their beds, supply them with morning newspapers, entertain them with anecdotes and look after the needs of their children while they admire the westerly view.

Actually, the anecdotes are an optional extra, but everything else is considered their due. We have one friend, in particular, a bachelor, who no doubt fancies that we are pleased to hear him say, as he repeatedly does: 'I love coming to Docklow, it's always so restful.' And we think, if you'll pardon the vulgarity, 'No wonder it's so bloody restful, you've barely got off your arse for forty-eight hours. King Tutankhamun probably did more to help around the house.'

Moving from the city to the country means that all those city friends who used to come to your house for dinner occasionally now come for the entire weekend, and delighted as you always were to look at them over a glass of Chianti at midnight, you're not necessarily as enthused by the sight of them over a mug of tea at daybreak. Ditto their kids. The appealing little urchins who used to stay for a couple of hours playing wholesome dressing-up games before being picked up by their mums and told to say 'thank you for having me' are the same bruisers who now slope in for breakfast and slope out again looking pissed off when you tell them that, sorry, you're out of Coco Pops.

Coincidentally, another St Andrews friend, Kevin Pilley, tackled this very issue in a splendidly sardonic article he wrote for a magazine called the *Countryman*, in May 2003. Kevin is a freelance journalist now domiciled in rural South Wales. With his kind permission, and in return for a pint of cider or even two, I reproduce part of his article here.

One of the reasons you buy a house in the country is to show it off to people who live in the city. House guests therefore are very important. Their views as to how you might improve your home and make it more comfortable should be valued. To ensure that our hospitality keeps up with the ever-increasing standards of our friends and family, it is prudent to reassess the facilities and services on offer. Living in the country we have a lot of friends and family coming to stay with us. We always seek to anticipate and satisfy our guests' requirements. To ensure that everyone enjoys themselves, I have produced the following questionnaire which I leave on their bedside table for them to fill in at their leisure.

How did we serve you? Your opinions and insights are extremely valuable and we want to make every effort to ensure that you are completely satisfied. Thank you for staying with us. We hope to see you again soon.

OVERALL:

How would you rate your stay? Excellent/fabulous/average/fair/poor/atrocious.

Were you happy with the service you received from your old school-friends/distant cousins/old neighbours? Yes/No.

How much money have you saved on laundry, electricity, food and other household expenses? An enormous amount/quite a lot despite paying out £10 for a bouquet so we didn't arrive empty-handed and appear we were imposing/a fair bit/enough/not as much as we would have liked.

If you return to this area, what is the likelihood that you would choose to stay with us again? Definitely would/very likely/depends if you expect us to have a pub lunch/depends whether next time we can get away with buying drinks to accompany the pub lunch/not if you don't do something about that ruddy cockerel.

How was your reservation made? By direct invitation/totally out of the blue/pure cheek/recommendation of mutual friends and fellow freeloaders.

Would you say your stay was: Very relaxing/restful/ tense and unrelaxing/an imposition.

YOUR STAY:

When you arrived was your accommodation ready and what you expected? Yes/No. If no, please indicate what was not in order (room size/sheets/view/welcoming coffee and biscuits).

How would you rate the general road/rail/air network from your home? Very good/good/muddy/not good for the suspension/could be closer to cut down on travelling time.

Did you have to carry your luggage to your room yourself? Yes/No.

Did your pets enjoy their stay? Yes/No.

Cleanliness and maintenance of residence: Comfortable and quiet/no spiders or mice/poor.

Did you have to queue at any time for the bathroom or WC? Yes/No.

Did you find the house quiet enough when you slept in until 10.30 a.m.? Yes/No.

Were you disturbed by anyone coming in to your room with a cup of tea? Yes/No.

Was your room cleaned satisfactorily while you were in the sitting-room with your feet up reading the newspapers? Yes/No.

Were you happy with the overcoat you borrowed when you went for a walk? Yes/No.

Were your meals served promptly and well prepared? Yes/No.

Did you receive an early morning newspaper? Yes/No.

How would you rate your hosts for: Smiling and opening doors for you/passing you things/taking responsibility to answer questions and resolve problems/organising social and leisure activities/anticipating your needs?

Please let us know the names of any members of the host family who were especially helpful or rather grumpy at having you around for such a long time.

What was the primary purpose of your visit? Pleasure/short holiday/reunion/guilt.

Was the clean, fresh country air clean and fresh enough for you? Yes/No.

What could we have done, apart from vacating the premises, to make your stay more enjoyable?

What additional facilities would you welcome?

Thank you for your co-operation. We would be grateful for any other suggestions you may have which would make your next stay here even more enjoyable. After all, our only purpose in moving to the countryside was to provide a relaxing holiday for you and your family.

Please tick box if you would like to be informed of future special events.

And that's it. Kevin always was a master of pointed sarcasm, and his sarcasm has clearly got pointier in the years since we were at university together. It's a questionnaire that should raise a chortle from anyone who has moved from city to country, and from anyone who hasn't, perhaps a pained 'What's so funny about that?' But needless to say, I would hate our friends to take offence, especially those among them who were invaluable in helping us to settle in. Ali and Chris, for example, and Paul and Jacky, our muckers from Park Avenue South, worked like dervishes in helping us to clear the conservatory, which contained not only an improbable amount of flora and fauna, but very possibly the lost tribe of Machu Picchu. There was even a bloody great stagnant pond in the middle.

Undeniably, the Openshaws' conservatory had had a kind of jungly charm, but we were keen to reclaim it as a functional room. For the best part of two days we pulled out geraniums by the lorry-load, with a heavy heart (and a sharp saw) got rid of a rather beautiful amaryllis, and cut down a gnarled old tree that had twisted round the century-old girders like something out of a Harry Potter film. As for the pond, my father-in-law, Bob, came and filled it in. He had read something about stagnant ponds, even in Herefordshire, attracting mosquitoes.

Let me tell you about Bob. Bob is the father-in-law not from hell but from Homebase. He makes those skilled handymen in home improvement shows on television look like fumbling idiots. Docklow is to Bob's toolbox what Tombstone – or was it Dodge City? – was to Billy the Kid's six-gun. He is, in short, the father-in-law that men like me need. The most useful thing I can do with my hands is to let my fingers do the walking through the *Yellow Pages*.

Bob, by contrast, is never happier than when confronted by a challenging bit of DIY, whereas I'm one of those for whom DIY stands for don't-involve-yourself. But for all that, he and Jane's mum, Anne, like my own mother and stepfather, had been awash with anxiety when we first showed them Docklow Grange and declared our intention to move in. Where we saw period charm, they saw heating bills. Where we saw rooms on a wonderful scale for entertaining, they saw heating bills. Where we saw acres of characterful oak floorboards, they saw heating bills. To say nothing of the cost of decorating, repairs and maintenance, inside and out. They could see that the kids would have a ball in the garden and woods, but hell, Jane had grown up happily enough in a modest bungalow near a colliery; I, in a three-bedroomed semi backing on to the Southport–Liverpool railway line. It wasn't as though there was any family precedent for living in a Victorian grange with a croquet lawn and a ha-ha.

To their eternal credit, the older generation mostly kept their apprehension to themselves. We were so struck on Docklow Grange that nothing was going to put us off, short of discovering deathwatch beetle and a headless corpse in the cellar. And had it been deathwatch beetle without the headless corpse, or the headless corpse without the deathwatch beetle, we still would probably have bought the place.

impressively, and while poor Hannah howled, suggestions of remedies came flying in from all directions.

The remedies were definitely on the homoeopathic side. One woman told us to press half an onion against the sting, another to use a cold tea bag as a compress, while another advised Hannah to dance three times around a sycamore tree waving a spotted handkerchief. OK, she advised no such thing. But it wouldn't have surprised us if she had. Eventually an onion was produced and it did the trick, while a cold tea bag was held in reserve. It was good to be reminded that even with Safeway, Sainsbury's, Waitrose, Tesco and Somerfield within easy reach, certain situations called for old Herefordshire cures handed down from mother to daughter since medieval times.

'Is that an old Herefordshire cure handed down from mother to daughter since medieval times?' I asked the woman kindly pressing a half-onion against Hannah's arm.

'No,' she said, 'it's an old Australian bush remedy. I used to live in the Outback.' Ah well. That was nearly as good.

By the end of the children's summer holidays we felt as though the settling-in process was well underway, a notion only slightly undermined by Jacob, just turned four, who kept asking when we would be going home. 'This is home, darling,' we said. 'No,' he said, crossly. 'I mean our Park Avenue South home.'

School changed all that, as we had hoped it would. The children's education was one of the main reasons we had left Crouch End. Not that we were dissatisfied with St Mary's, their Church of England primary school in Haringey; indeed, we had been pretty desperate to get Eleanor, our firstborn, in. But the process of getting a 5-year-old into a decent state primary school in London was not without torment.

At that time St Mary's Infant School was run by a redoubtable head teacher called Mrs Morgan, who invited prospective parents to meet her but left them in no doubt that she was vetting them, rather than the other way round. Several friends with kids already at the school told us, with only slight hyperbole, that Mrs Morgan's interviews could reduce strong men to quivering wrecks, and on the day of our appointment I approached her office with trepidation, not least because it was the first time I had set foot in an infant school since I was an infant myself. I felt like a tot again, reasonably sure that I would burst into tears if anyone asked me why I hadn't brought my black pumps with me, or told me oversternly to put the beanbags away.

We were ushered in. 'Your daughter's name?' barked Mrs Morgan, in her best Peggy Mount manner. 'Eleanor,' said Jane. Mrs Morgan wrote down Eleanor's name. 'And parents' names?' she demanded, turning her steely gaze on me. In little more than a squeak I gave her the names of my mother and stepfather. It was Jane's turn to look at me askance. 'Actually, parents' names are Jane and Brian,' she said.

Despite my gaffe, Eleanor was accepted into St Mary's and in due course Joseph followed. By then the formidable Mrs Morgan had retired, to be replaced by her less scary deputy, Mrs Cumbers, a woman of whom I will always think fondly, if only because she once told the children that when she was growing up in Norfolk she attended a school called Beehive Lane, and that every schoolday morning for five years she unwittingly got the words of the Lord's Prayer wrong, solemnly intoning, 'Our Father, Who art in Heaven, Hello Beehive Lane, Thy Kingdom come, Thy Will be done . . . '

That's a story to gladden the heart of anyone who, like me, is ropey with lyrics themselves. It was only a couple of years ago that our friend Ali finally realised that John Denver was leaving on a jet plane; she always thought he was leaving on a freight train. And Mike, a dear old friend from school, remembers his mum's interpretation of a lyric in the Simon & Garfunkel song 'Cecilia'. In the song it is confidence being shaken daily but Mike's mum always used to think it was 'you're shaking my carpets daily' and was never quite sure how such a diligent approach to housework fitted into a song about being in love with a fickle woman.

In many ways St Mary's was a very good urban school, but we knew that as soon as our kids approached secondary-school age we would be sucked into the morass of angst which in London claims most middle-class parents of woolly liberal leanings. Neither Jane nor I had been to fee-paying schools and saw no reason why we should pay for our children's education if the state would provide. But even when it came to local comprehensives there was endless debate as to which was the best, and once you threw grant-maintained schools, voluntary-controlled schools, independent trust schools and God knows what other kind of schools into the mix, it became a nightmare.

Moreover, just when you thought you had heard of every decent school in north London, someone would upset your equilibrium by bringing up some establishment you'd never heard of before, casually mentioning that they had heard great things about Logarithm Grove School for Girls, or had you noticed that Our Lady of the Venn Diagram was shooting up the league tables? And off you would rush to phone yet another school secretary for yet another bloody prospectus.

One high-spirited evening, out with our good friends Kim and Will, we hatched a dastardly plan to invent a school entirely, then repeatedly drop it into conversation, and see just how long it took before this mythical school was chattered about by the chattering classes.

So it was that Dame Sally Allen's – founded 1891, fantastic crop of A-Level results, high percentage of Oxbridge candidates, handily located between Clissold Park and the Arsenal – rose out of our alcohol-enhanced imagination. We started casually mentioning it as another of our secondary-school options, inventing more and more 'facts', for example that the newsreader Julia Somerville was a former head girl and that the sixth-form lacrosse team had been south-of-England champions for the last five years. To our delight, about a week later, Jane was asked by a woman she scarcely knew whether we had considered entering Eleanor for the highly regarded Dame Sally Allen's, an excellent seat of learning between Clissold Park and the Arsenal? Somehow, Jane kept a straight face. 'Yes,' she said, 'we've got the prospectus.'

Jane and I were dismissive of the vogue for scrutinising school league tables; all I wanted to see from a league table was that Everton FC wasn't too close to the relegation zone. Still, it didn't hurt to read that 58.5 per cent of rural pupils were gaining five or more GCSEs at grade C or above, as opposed to 46.7 per cent of urban pupils. The chances were that our kids would get a better education in the country. And in Herefordshire, we knew, there would be altogether less angst about schooling, both primary and secondary, if only because there were altogether fewer schools and altogether fewer children. That in itself was a concern. In 2002 there were 31,500 children in Herefordshire, aged fourteen and below. In Crouch End, there were 31,500 children in the playground in Priory Park on a Sunday afternoon, if the weather was half-decent.

Rashly, and contrary to all the wise advice given to parents thinking of moving out of the city, we had set our hearts on buying Docklow Grange before checking out the local primary schools. However, the Openshaws pointed us towards the nearby village of Spindlebury, where their own kids, long since grown up, had gone to school. We made an appointment to be shown round.

Spindlebury Village School was charming, but so much smaller than St Mary's that we thought it would increase the children's feelings of dislocation. We had expected the grass to be greener on the other side of the fence, but not this green, and not with quite so many sheep grazing on it. The school had about sixty pupils, and the head teacher, understandably, could hardly contain her excitement that we might be about to add three more. At a stroke we would be increasing the pupil body by 5 per cent. But even if our children adapted quickly to such different sur-roundings, we weren't sure whether we would. At St Mary's, Jane had chaired the Parent Teacher Association, and played a big part in the organisation of an endless series of fund-raising quiz nights, bingo nights, summer fairs, winter fairs, autumn fairs, seventies discos, pantomimes, barbecues and jumble sales. Together, they constituted a sizeable chunk of our social life. It was hard to imagine Spindlebury filling the void.

Whichever school we chose, there would also be a striking ethnic contrast with St Mary's. At the time of the 2001 census, in our parish and the two adjoining parishes, the percentage of white people as an ethnic group was an unequivocal 100. In the entire county it was 99.1 per cent. Herefordshire had only 1576 people of 'ethnic groups other than white'. Again, as a useful point of comparison, in London I would say hello to 1576 people of ethnic groups other than white on my way to buy a morning paper. Our friendly neigbourhood baker thought that this was why we were selling up. When we told him that we were moving to the countryside, he nodded sagely and said, 'Good idea, get

81

out before we're bloody overrun. That's why the wife's sister and her husband moved to Gravesend.'

I didn't challenge him, or tell him that actually we were worried about leaving a multicultural environment behind. I wish I had. But I didn't particularly want to confront the unpalatable truth that our cheerful baker of the past eight years, who gave each of the children a complimentary gingerbread man whenever they walked into his shop, appeared to have racist views. It was cowardly, but I moved the conversation on to our usual topic, that it wasn't a bad morning although I understood there was a reasonable chance of showers later.

At St Mary's, our children shared classrooms with kids from African, Afro-Caribbean, Asian and Greek Cypriot families. One of Eleanor's friends, Esther, had moved from Sierra Leone and matter-of-factly told her classmates what it had been like living in the throes of civil war. This helped Eleanor to understand the hardships faced by others, and to count her own blessings, more valuable for any child than the principles of long division. We knew we would be unlikely to encounter any refugees from African war zones in the Welsh Marches.

However, we began to recognise an element of liberal posturing in our concerns about turning our backs on multiculturalism. It wasn't as though we spent our evenings at Bangladeshi social clubs; our friends in London could hardly have been a more homogeneous bunch of middle-class white people. In fact, I later provoked an angry letter to the *Independent* when I wrote in my column that, far from the countryside representing homogeneity and the city diversity, we had found almost exactly the reverse. After a few months in the country we had friends of all ages, rich and poor, gay and straight, whereas in London we knew hardly anyone who was not as white and heterosexual as we were, from the same income bracket and with similar educational qualifications.

The letter to the *Independent* was from a woman who lived in Crouch End. If all our friends had been like us then we clearly should have got out more, she thundered. Her Crouch End friends included (I paraphrase, but only slightly) mute Indonesian chieftains, bisexual Iranian acrobats and wheelchair-bound Inuit basket-weavers, aged between 7 and 104. Which was as maybe, but I couldn't write about anyone's life except my own.

As for our children growing up in the overwhelmingly mono-racial environment of north Herefordshire, we reached the conclusion that we would always be their parents, and they would therefore be unlikely to turn into raging Fascists. Moreover, millions of kids grow up in the English countryside without the misconception that England is for whites only.

While we looked for an appropriate school in Herefordshire, I thought back to 1987, when I first moved to London, and then to when Jane, Eleanor and I moved to Crouch End, in 1994, and considered how pressing concerns about one's new home reflect evolving priorities in life. In 1987 I moved into a small ground-floor flat in a rather shabby mansion block near Lord's Cricket Ground. My concern then was the proximity of a good pub and a decent squash court.

By 1994 we had a baby and wanted a house with a garden, although we dithered over Crouch End because it seemed too far from the centre of London and there was no underground station. I worked for Associated Newspapers in Derry Street, Kensington; Jane for the BBC in Portland Place. How the hell would we get to and from work? But one evening as we were driving to look at more properties in and around Crouch End, we realised that tens of thousands of people managed to get from there into central London every day, and so would we. This realisation came half-way down Cranley Gardens, which links Crouch End with Muswell Hill and is otherwise dubiously notable for the fact that it was once the address of the mass-murderer Dennis Nilsen. Whatever, St Paul had his road to Damascus; we had our Cranley Gardens.

We had a similar revelatory moment while fretting about leaving north London for north Herefordshire; we weren't the first to up sticks for the sticks, we wouldn't be the last, and if others could make it work, so could we. It had been madly impetuous of us to buy the house before finding a suitable school, but we were reasonably certain that one would turn up, and sure enough one did.

Like St Mary's it was a Church of England school, and although not as big as St Mary's, it was comfortingly bigger than tiny Spindlebury. It was in a lively village not far from Ludlow which I'll call Stamford Heath, about eleven miles from Docklow. Plainly, a twenty-two-mile round trip, twice or more a day, was less than ideal. Not so much a school run as a school marathon. But at least eleven miles hereabouts could be covered in twenty minutes or so. This was another statistic which begged comparison with the urban south-east. Our journeys from Crouch End to see Jane's sister Jackie and her family in Wimbledon had on one or two miserable occasions taken more than two hours. It hardly ever took less than an hour. Yet that was eleven miles, too.

The other difference between driving in Herefordshire and driving in London was road rage. Or rather, the lack of it. One morning, after dropping the kids at school, I decided to drop in at Safeway in Leominster. At a set of traffic lights, mine was the fourth car in a line of six, which in Leominster counts as an unusually nasty tailback. While I waited for green, I happened to glance at the newspaper lying next to me, and by the time I looked up, the three cars in front were long gone. In London, or probably any large city, you'd be lucky to escape from such a situation with anything less than a tar-and-feathering, yet from the two drivers behind me there came not a toot. I could probably have read the paper cover to cover without provoking so much as a brief, apologetic parp.

Contrast this with my favourite example of metropolitan road rage, starring my dear sister-in-law Jackie. She was once driving sedately along Roehampton Lane in south London, unaware of the welling anger in the man driving behind her. At a set of red lights he was finally able to pull alongside her, but he overshot slightly, so reversed until he was exactly level, from where he could snarl across and give her the finger. Jackie looked ahead as impassively as she could, trying to appear unruffled by the fact that, not two yards away, a fat man with a crewcut and very possibly LOVE and HATE tattooed on his knuckles was screaming abuse at her. He then started revving furiously, intent on roaring away from the lights first, but forgot that he was still in reverse gear. As soon as the lights went green he slammed his foot on the accelerator and screeched into the car behind him, sitcom-style, while Jackie moved off in leisurely fashion, clocking the carnage in her rear-view mirror.

There was none of that carry-on getting our children to school. Victoria Wood, my acquaintance from the Parsnip and Gruyère Bake aisle at Marks & Spencer in Muswell Hill, used to do a marvellous routine about the streets of north London getting clogged up every morning with enormous four-wheel drives fitted with bumpers strong enough to repel marauding rhino, manouevred by slim, manicured women with a single tiny child on the back seat waiting to be dropped off at the Fluffy Bunny Montessori School. In Herefordshire, too, there were women taking their kids to school in four-wheel drives, but then there was every chance that they might have to negotiate the odd mud slide.

Compared with north London, driving in Herefordshire was a pleasure. Which was just as well, because in the first term, with Jacob at a mornings-only nursery in the same village, the daily school run entailed three journeys there and back totalling sixty-six miles. Even when I could do one or more of the trips to lessen Jane's load, it was still costing a fortune in petrol. There were Boeing 747s with a more modest fuel consumption than our Volvo. And when she had to do all three trips, there was scarcely a time of day when she was not about to set off to or from Stamford Heath.

On the plus side, the children settled in at Stamford Heath immediately, which lifted a hundredweight of apprehension from our shoulders – don't ask me what that is in kilos, ask them. It was a wonderful school, run by a superb headmaster whose passion for West Bromwich Albion FC was, as far as I could tell, his only character flaw.

At the end of the children's first week at their new school, Jane and I were cock-a-hoop. We cracked open a bottle of champagne and I don't mind telling you that we went to bed that night and the earth moved.

It was the first time, and almost certainly the last, that an earthquake had ever had Brick Kiln Lane, Dudley, as its epicentre. It measured 4.8 on the Richter Scale and although nobody was hurt, twelve people walked into Dudley police station in their nightclothes to report it, which to my mind was worthy of front-page news around the world. The earthquake was close enough to us for Joseph to be juddered out of bed, much to the disgruntlement of his brother and sister, who had slept soundly through the whole thing. I woke up but assumed that the rumble was a low-flying RAF jet on night exercises. Other than earthquakes, low-flying jets were the only interruption to Docklow's tranquillity, very much to Joseph's delight. For a while, every picture he painted featured a pointy-winged jet with a bright orange flame shooting from its behind, and when my aunt asked him what he enjoyed most about living in the countryside – expecting him to rhapsodise about making dens in the woods or swimming in rivers – he said without hesitation: 'The really loud aeroplanes. They're so wicked.'

But the children *had* made dens in the woods, and swum in rivers, and had spent a blissful summer holiday in Docklow, visited every weekend by another batch of London friends. Now, as we moved into autumn, it was time to immerse ourselves in Herefordshire.

The children's happiness mattered more to us than our own, but then their happiness and ours were mutually dependent. A warm, Ready Brek-style glow enveloped me when I looked out of the window to see them, in their new school uniforms, gambolling in the fields with new playmates.

All the same, there were adjustments to be made. Not long into the autumn term, Eleanor was told that her all-white class was being taken on a 'cultural exchange' – to a school in Wolverhampton. 'I'm very much hoping that Miss Wood will come back enthused by bhangra dancing,' said the headmaster, whose excellent initiative it was. The curious thing from Eleanor's point of view was that the school in Wolverhampton was almost exactly like St Mary's.

We were making adjustments at home, too, slowly getting

used to living in a settlement scarcely big enough to be called a hamlet. I began to feel positively indignant on behalf of that much-maligned adjective 'parochial', which, although defined in that useful *Reader's Digest Universal Dictionary* of mine as 'of, supported by, or located in a parish', appears in recent years to have acquired an overwhelmingly pejorative meaning, becoming almost a euphemism for 'narrow-minded'.

Parochial is one of the many alarming words people in the city use to warn of the dangers of moving to the country, and in fairness, as a city-dweller myself I was frequently guilty of sniggering at the 'parochialism' of rural folk.

One year, we were invited to a New Year's Eve party at the home of our former next-door neighbours in Park Avenue South, Neil and Bridget, who had moved to Suffolk, and there fell into conversation with a couple who lived in a nearby village called Little Happening, or something very much like it. I asked where they were from originally. 'I've lived in Little Happening all my life,' said the woman, proudly. I asked her husband whether he, too, was a Little Happeningonian born and bred. He snorted with derision. 'You're joking,' he said. 'I come from Middle Happening.'

This exchange had seemed hilarious to me and back in London I got a great deal of mileage out of it. Yet here we were living in Docklow, which very probably made Little Happening look like downtown Las Vegas. We were becoming 'parochial' and proud of it.

In mid-October I took Eleanor to a harvest-festival service at Docklow church. There had been an annual celebration of the harvest at their school in London, with pupils lugging in produce to be donated to 'the poor', although it often struck me as I watched them gravely handing over their donations to the teacher that even Jamie Oliver, let alone the poor, would have struggled to create a satisfying meal out of a tin of pilchards, a packet of ginger nuts and a bunch of unripe bananas.

Here in Docklow, however, for the first time in all our lives, a successful harvest really was something to celebrate. The livelihoods of not a few of our neighbours depended on it.

Following the service, I took Eleanor home and then walked back across the fields to the King's Head, for an auction of harvest produce with not a single tin of pilchards to be seen. It was about as parochial as an evening could be – organised by and proceeds for the Parish Council, produce donated by a small posse of good people who had grown it, harvested it, carted it from their homes to the church, and then from the church to the pub, in some cases then to buy it back at auction and cart it home again.

The lots might have struggled to make it into a Sotheby's catalogue but one, a tatty box containing a swede, some carrots, a cabbage and an award-winning onion, did attract a high-spirited telephone bid of £3.50. Propping up the bar, feeling for the first time almost like a local, I had a wonderful evening. 'Next, one rather large radish,' said the auctioneer, pillar-of-the-community Eddie Crowley, holding up a vegetable the size of a cannonball. 'It's a bloody beetroot,' someone shouted. That this exchange seemed hilarious was very likely something to do with the five pints I had consumed of Butty Bach, an excellent local brew. But even in sobriety I would have enjoyed myself.

I took my leave of the King's Head at around midnight, and struggled in an undignified fashion over a stile, giggling stupidly as I went. With one hand I carried a hessian sack containing a cauliflower, about twenty apples and some crocus bulbs, with the other a torch to guide me around the ubiquitous cowpats. I felt as if I had just played a fairly significant supporting role in an episode of *The Vicar of Dibley*. I felt, more to the point, quite blissfully parochial. This living-in-the-country lark might just suit me, I decided, as I stepped around a cowpat only to trip over the carcass of a dead rabbit.

4

Rumpy-Pumpy in the Canadian Hot Tub

One October morning, Jane was cleaning Manor Cottage after one couple had departed and before another couple arrived. We had been living in Docklow for three months. For me, working life had continued much as before. Thanks to the internet revolution, I could file my newspaper columns as easily from north Herefordshire as from north London. But Jane had had to embrace what is impolitely known as skivvying. Her mum gaily told her about an exchange she'd had in Barnsley with the mother of one of Jane's old schoolfriends. 'Is your Jane still a high-flyer at the BBC?' this woman asked. Anne reported that she had replied, 'No, our Jane's a cleaner now.'

Jane took this in the light-hearted spirit in which it was

intended, but her mum, unwittingly of course, had taken a wire brush to a raw nerve. When Jane had been issuing instructions into Jim Naughtie's earpiece at Broadcasting House, she had little expected to be earning an income ten years later by cleaning up after holiday-makers in Herefordshire. On the other hand, Jim Naughtie was nothing like as interesting to work with as the Great British Public on holiday.

Take the couple who had just left that October morning. He was tall, bespectacled and bearded; she was short, bespectacled and had a slightly less full beard. I don't wish to offend academics, many of whom are a great deal trendier and better-looking than I am, but I felt reasonably sure that academia was where they came from. Maybe they were both lecturers, those over-earnest ones, who keep bits of breakfast in their whiskers in case they fancy a mid-morning snack, and look as if their idea of a good time in bed is some light banter about nuclear physics. On which lofty subject, I am reminded of the story a favourite comedian of mine, Arnold Brown, likes to tell about an encounter in the early 1950s between Albert Einstein and Marilyn Monroe.

The screen goddess was famously in awe of men with mighty brainpower, which is why she later fell for and married the playwright Arthur Miller. And apparently it is true that she and Einstein met. One might even speculate that the elderly physicist, then in his seventies, was as captivated by Monroe as she was by him. Anyway, the way Arnold tells it, they had dinner together in Los Angeles and then went back to his hotel for coffee.

'Albert,' she breathed, fluttering her eyelashes. 'Will you do something for me? It would make me a very happy girl.'

'I vill try, my dear. Vot is it?'

'Will you please explain to me your Theory of Relativity?'

Einstein gave her an avuncular pat on the knee. 'I'm sorry, my dear,' he said. 'I never go zat far on a first date.'

The couple in Manor Cottage looked as if they, too, would hesitate before discussing Einstein's Theory of Relativity on a first date, going only as far, perhaps, as his thoughts on Brownian Motion. They were decidedly frumpy, anyway, which is why Jane was so delighted to find a pair of dice under the four-poster bed, one bearing the names of six parts of the body – hands, feet, bottom, thigh, breast, stomach – while the other was stamped with six physical actions – kiss, stroke, lick, rub, suck and the rather intriguing 'wash'. It would be just my luck, I thought, to embark on a game of sexual frolics and end up getting my stomach washed, as if I was about to have my appendix taken out.

Whatever, this episode taught us never to judge a book by its cover, least of all a book on nuclear physics. I wondered whether to send the dice back to the two academics in a small Jiffy bag, but I decided there was an outside chance that, scrupulously as Jane swept and tidied, the dice might have been left by the people who'd stayed in Manor Cottage before them. Imagine that, them receiving in the post a pair of saucy dice with a Docklow Grange compliments slip, if in fact the dice hadn't been theirs to start with. Such are the dilemmas with which holiday cottage owners are faced. Still, whoever had brought the dice, it was gratifying to find that our guests were enjoying themselves, if ever so slightly galling also to find that they were enjoying themselves more than we were.

Clearly, some people could take care of their own leisure needs. Others, though, relied very much on us, wanting to know where the best walks were, the best pubs, what was market day in Leominster, Ludlow and Bromyard, where there was decent fishing to be found, what the opening hours were to see the Mappa

Mundi in Hereford Cathedral. And it was no good saying, 'Sorry, we're new to the area ourselves.' We needed to do a crash course in the Welsh Marches.

We also needed to make the cottages our own. The day we arrived to live in Docklow was a happy day for the man who owned the Cheap Skip Company in Bromyard. We filled six skiploads with furniture and knick-knacks from the cottages, and carted off a similar tonnage to charity shops and recycling centres, self-consciously aware all the while that the Openshaws, now resident in the nearby barn conversion, might catch sight of us turfing out the fruits of their hard work over the years. I kept half-expecting Mr Openshaw to scurry over and say indignantly, 'Well if you're going to throw out that print of a cockerel standing insouciantly beside a wagon wheel, we might as well have it back.' The house and the three cottages, and all their contents, were ours now. We could do what we liked. But that didn't stop us feeling awkward about the refurbishment operation.

Still, we pulled up our sleeves, mainly in order to write cheques to tradesmen, and got on with it. Manor Cottage and Yewtree Cottage were given new bathrooms; Yewtree Cottage and Woodlands Cottage got new carpets, supplied at cost by my old friend Bill/Rupert Anton, who very conveniently was the sales and marketing director for the Carpet Foundation, a commercial alliance of the nation's leading carpet manufacturers, and whose face to this day practically goes into nervous spasms, like Herbert Lom's in the Pink Panther films, if you whisper into his ear those sacrilegious words 'stripped floorboards'.

We spent a fortune on the cottages, far more than we had budgeted for, but gradually they began to acquire the look we had had in mind. We now needed to step up the marketing.

The Openshaws already had a website, but like much else, it

needed updating. I suppose that's the twenty-first century for you; websites need updating along with the plumbing and the wiring. My father died in 1976, when I was fourteen, and I sometimes wonder what I would tell him about first if he came back to life. I would certainly have a lot of explaining to do. Cashpoint machines, the fax, the mobile phone, the pound coin, Mr Bean, the Channel Tunnel, Viagra, the euro, Madonna, Channel 4, the demise of wooden tennis rackets, the Falklands War, spread-betting, the M25, Jordan's breasts, the Premier League, 9/11, breakfast television, the fall of Communism, Richard and Judy, Ant and Dec, Posh and Becks . . . where would I start? And just when he thought I'd got him up to speed, I'd say, 'Oh, and by the way, Dad, there's also this thing called the world wide web . . .'

The guy who had designed the Openshaws' website was called Adrian Pitt, and he'd done a pretty good job, so we saw no reason not to keep him on. Adrian advised us to develop a separate site to attract overseas custom, a dot.com rather than a dot.co.uk. This would be aimed principally at Americans, not that Americans, as a general rule, tend to cross the Atlantic when they perceive the global situation to be a bit on the volatile side.

As their leaders are usually the ones who have made it more volatile, this has always struck me as rather unfair, especially now that I am myself, in a very small way, in the tourism business. The reward for Britain supporting the United States every step of the way to Baghdad in 2003 should not have been an invitation to Tony Blair to address Congress, it should have been an undertaking on the part of every American of sufficient means (and with a Burberry raincoat, that essential accessory for all Americans of a certain age coming to England) to take a fortnight's vacation somewhere in the United Kingdom. Not necessarily Herefordshire, but not necessarily not.

Adrian asked us to supply twenty-five key words for both websites, so that when any of those words were entered into a search engine, up our cottages would pop. But there was no point using the same twenty-five words to appeal to Americans; to them, indeed, some words designed to attract British holiday-makers would be downright off-putting. One such was 'homely'. My friend Dana, who lived in Dallas and worked in the travel industry, advised me that in the USA 'homely' does not evoke warmth and cosiness, as it does here. There it means plain or unattractive.

As well as certain words meaning entirely different things in America – as you will know if, like me, you once subjected a friend from Illinois to a sleepless night by informing him that you would knock him up first thing the following morning – there is also the curious phenomenon of them using entirely different words. For example, they have a tendency to turn familiar nouns into unfamiliar verbs, which Jane and I encountered one autumn/fall when we were driving through New England and kept passing inns proudly advertised as 'fully fireplaced'.

Another American friend, Doree, once sought my advice regarding a weekend in the Cotswolds. She and her partner wished to go 'antiquing', she said. Could I recommend a hotel with great antiquing nearby. Accordingly, through gritted teeth, we made antiquing one of our key dot.com words, on the basis that Leominster is without doubt one of the antiquing centres of England. Or olde England, for our friends in the Burberry rain-coats.

Once we'd settled on our fifty key words, we also had to think of ways to elevate our Herefordshire cottages above the many others advertised on the internet. Although we had intended to wait until we were fully on top of the rental enterprise before offering home-cooked meals to our guests, we decided that we might as well go the whole spit-roasted hog and promote it from the start.

We set a price of £9.50 per head for two courses, which seemed pretty fair. It would be just as good as plenty of pub grub but cheaper, while at the same time giving us a modest profit, and the idea was that dinner would be waiting in a low oven when guests arrived in their cottage, filling the place with mouth-watering smells. Just the ticket after a long haul up or down the motorway.

The first customers to order a meal were the Warburtons, who came from Barnsley. And with them came the first indication that, while there are some hard-headed businesswomen in the cottage-rental business, as adept with spreadsheets as with the cotton and polyester sort, Jane was not yet one of them. 'How much is dinner?' Mrs Warburton had asked on the phone. Raised near Barnsley herself, Jane felt a wave of unprofessional solidarity, compounded by the suspicion that coming from South Yorkshire, the Warburtons might consider nearly a tenner a head a bit bloody steep. 'It's seven pounds fifty each,' she said. 'Right,' said Mrs Warburton, approvingly. 'That'll be fine.'

Jane's inaugural meal as a professional cook was chicken casserole followed by blackberry-and-apple crumble, the sort of thing she could normally do with her eyes shut, and in this instance perhaps should have done. It couldn't have made things worse.

Until that point culinary disasters had generally been my speciality. Which is not to say that I am inept in the kitchen, just that I always seemed to be the one doing the cooking when things went catastrophically wrong.

I once prepared beef-in-beer, a Delia Smith recipe, the day before a dinner party. I cooked it, tasted it, pronounced it quite staggeringly delicious, and left it in the oven overnight for warming up the following evening. When the time came to serve up, I had another taste, and this time nearly vomited. It had been delicious, and now it tasted almost literally like shit. At the time, we lived in that ground-floor mansion-block flat near Lord's Cricket Ground. And as Jane and I urgently debated what had gone wrong, all too aware of our guests sitting expectantly round the dining-table in the other room waiting to be served, we noticed that the kitchen window was ajar. So we reached the only possible conclusion: that someone had climbed in through the window, opened the oven, maliciously slipped a turd into the casserole dish, and climbed out again. Later, a chef friend offered an explanation that was arguably even more plausible, that in the process of cooling down and then being warmed up, the beer had fermented.

But if that was my disaster, this was definitely Jane's. There was no problem with her casserole, but the crumble was consigned to the top oven of the Aga, and Agas, while wonderful contraptions in many ways, do not release cooking smells. By the time she remembered it, with the Warburtons due to arrive at any moment expecting dinner, their blackberry-and-apple crumble looked as though it had passed through a blast furnace.

A word here about Agas. They inspire a strange kind of evangelism among those who own them, a bit like Morris Minors and Citroen 2CVs. If the Aga were roadworthy, there is no doubt that on certain Sundays every summer you would see long lines of them being driven from London to Brighton by hearty enthusiasts.

My friend Dominic has one, and when we, too, acquired one by moving to Docklow Grange, he could hardly contain his delight at being able to welcome us to the club. He talked us through the multifarious uses of an Aga, and solemnly pointed out that the lower oven was ideal should we ever need to thaw out a frozen robin. It remains a source of some disappointment that we have never had an opportunity to do this. Sometimes I wonder whether I should stick a robin in the freezer, just so that I can then thaw it out in the Aga. But getting hold of it in the first place could be tricky, and besides, I wouldn't want to have to explain to anyone what my intentions were.

By contrast with Dominic, people without Agas generally regard them with tremendous wariness. Jane fell into this category, at least until she was baptised into the faith that exciting night in Ledbury, when she learnt that you could fry an egg directly on the hotplate. By the time the Warburtons came to stay in Manor Cottage, she was one of the hearty enthusiasts who would have been tooting her horn, or at any rate flapping her hotplate lid, on those London–Brighton Aga trips. But she acknowledged one tiny flaw in the system: that if you forget about something you've put in the Aga, there is no smell of burning.

Which brings us back to the unfortunate case of the Warburtons' apple-and-blackberry crumble. Jane's parents were staying with us that weekend, and her mum resourcefully suggested altering the menu, presenting the Warburtons not with 'apple-and-blackberry crumble' but 'Docklow mud pie'. She and Jane then dealt with the crisis by collapsing in laughter so hysterical that it was noiseless, while I wondered whether 'Fawlty' and 'Towers' should be added to the key words on our website. Eventually, with all hands to the pump, not to mention the flour, sugar and butter, we embarked on the construction of a new crumble that was whisked around to Manor Cottage just as the Warburtons were stepping out of their car.

From the start, I got a kick out of being in the hospitality business. Three self-catering holiday cottages didn't exactly make us Conrad and Mrs Hilton, but even so, it was immensely satisfying to feel partly responsible for someone having a successful holiday. The flip side of this, of course, was that not everybody did have a successful holiday. In fact we had to deal with our first complaint barely a week after going into business.

It came from the Farrells, the Liverpool family who had noticed before we did, having been to Docklow several times before on their holidays, that the peacocks had gone. They had forgotten a chequebook but promised to send a cheque when they got home. A day after their departure they phoned to say that the cheque was in the post.

'Thank you very much,' I said. 'Did you have a nice time?'

A long pause. 'Actually,' said Mrs Farrell, 'we were very disappointed.'

My heart sank. This was not a good start to my new career in what my friends glibly called cottaging.

'We found the cottage very dirty,' she said. She pronounced 'dirty' the Scouse way – *dairty*. 'And the sheets were threadbare. I felt ashamed letting my Harry sleep in them sheets. Ashamed!' Mrs Farrell was of the generation who believe that stuff like bedding and towels, even on holiday, are entirely the woman's responsibility. Her gripe was not so much that we had let her down, as that she had let Harry down.

She added that she had not wanted to bother us because she knew we'd only just moved in, and that the condition of the cottage had nothing to do with us. Which was true, although in fairness to Mrs Openshaw, her mind had hardly been on the job either, as she prepared to move out of her home of twenty-three years. And knowing that three of the cottages were about to be sold, I don't suppose she had expended too much energy on keeping them spick and span.

But when we had a proper look round Yewtree Cottage we could see what Mrs Farrell meant. It wasn't the Farrells' fault that they had booked their holiday just as the Openshaws were leaving and we were arriving. We called them back and invited them to take a week at no cost any time in the next twelve months. After all, if the first law of the hospitality business is that customers are always right, the second is this: never give the buggers their money back.

We had ourselves been on the receiving end of this principle. In January 1993, on the first night of our honeymoon, we stayed at the celebrated hotel, the Lygon Arms, in ye olde picture-postcard Cotswolds village of Broadway.

The brochure told us that romantic dinners were served in a great vaulted dining room, but on our single night there, one night being all we could afford, the great vaulted dining room was closed for refurbishment, and a humdrum unvaulted dining room pressed into action. Now, you might think that a honeymooning couple should have things on their minds other than dinner, but for Jane and me, hardly anything takes precedence over dinner. It wasn't just the substitute dining room that riled us, the service was slipshod too. Our food took ages to arrive, whereas, by stark contrast, the wine waiter seemed attached to our table by a strong length of elastic, twanging back to fill my glass after every sip. He also took the entire duration of a very long meal to compute the fact that Jane was not drinking wine, on account of being – oh, the shame – three months pregnant.

That wasn't all. We had a car filled with wedding-presents, and asked the receptionist to ensure that the presents were delivered to our room. They weren't. We ended up carting them ourselves. So for these various reasons I wrote a businesslike letter when I got home, detailing our grievances, and in due course got a brisk reply offering us two nights' complimentary bed-and-breakfast by way of compensation. We never took up the offer. For one thing, dinner-for-two alone would have made it an expensive weekend. For another, we didn't feel inclined to revisit a hotel that had been such a disappointment – although here I should add, in fairness to the Lygon Arms, that I know some people who have never had such disappointments and think it quite splendid.

The point is that this is standard practice across the industry, from the Ritz to the most humble B&B. If someone lodges a justifiable complaint, invite them back to demonstrate that you can do things properly. They may not want to come, but at least you have offered suitable compensation, and you might just turn an unhappy customer into a loyal one.

With Mrs Stonehouse, however, there was more chance of turning cowpats into caviar. The Stonehouses came a month or so after the Farrells, and stayed for a week in Woodlands Cottage. They came from Renfrewshire and Mrs Stonehouse looked like she'd been sucking lemons all the way. She was a tall, thin woman with sharp, pinched features, which seemed to get sharper and more pinched by the minute. It took her twenty-five minutes to register the first complaint. Mrs Stonehouse did not like the old wooden shutters, she wanted curtains. So Jane put curtains up. Mrs Stonehouse then spotted a cobweb. Jane got rid of it. Mrs Stonehouse regarded the toilet-flush as too stiff. We got the plumber to loosen it. Mrs Stonehouse – this was my favourite – thought the duvets too warm. We told her to fuck off.

We didn't, actually, but we fantasised about it. In fact, we stayed calm and polite in the teeth of considerable provocation, an essential faculty in the hospitality business. We knew that our cottages were still a bit frayed round the edges, but we felt that was reflected in the price: £350 for a week in a three-bedroomed cottage sleeping six people, at the height of summer, seemed pretty reasonable. The Farrells had certainly had a case for complaint, compensation even, but the Stonehouses, we felt, didn't. Yet everyone who has ever owned a holiday cottage, or a hotel or a guesthouse, has encountered a Mrs Stonehouse. For Basil Fawlty, you'll recall, it was stone-deaf Mrs Richards, wonderfully played by the late Joan Sanderson. For the manager of the Lygon Arms, who knows, maybe it was us.

Even satisfied customers sometimes leave a wholly unreasonable complaint; I know of a successful holiday cottage enterprise in Cornwall where someone wrote in the comments book: 'Thank you very much, we've had a wonderful holiday, and the cottage is beautiful. Only one disappointment, not enough cake tins!!!'

The fact that there was deemed not to be enough cake tins suggests that there was at least one, but it is the holiday cottage owner's destiny never to please all of the people, all of the time. You think, 'I know, I'll put a cake tin in the cupboard, just in case anyone needs it', and you congratulate yourself for being professional and thorough, only to discover that you have somehow failed by not making the kitchen ready for Jane Asher.

Mrs Openshaw, who in Docklow Grange's prime as a business had run eleven holiday cottages, told us that she had once attended a tourist-board conference at which it was asserted that 95 per cent of guests are very nice, 4 per cent can have niceness forced upon them, and 1 per cent are impossible to please. The 1 per cent was the reason we decided early on not to put a comments book in our cottages, although it wasn't just the negative comments we wanted to eliminate, it was the wrong sort of positive ones, too. A few years earlier Jane and I had stayed in a smart country hotel, in which each room was named after an aristocrat who had stayed in the house when it was still a private home. We spent the night in the Duchess of Somerset, as it were. And leafing through the Duchess of Somerset comments book we found the following, written by someone who'd occupied her a week before us: 'Great room, great hotel. Wonderful rumpy-pumpy in the Canadian hot tub!!!'

Note the three exclamation marks. When people see comments books, they obviously see an opportunity for getting all those pent-up exclamation marks out of their systems. But worse than that was the idea that we were sleeping in the same bed as people who used the expression rumpy-pumpy. And worse than that was the thought of what might be floating around in the Canadian hot tub. Accordingly, we gave it a wide berth, and decided that the people who'd had rumpy-pumpy in such a public arena could not possibly have been English. I mean, dash it all, how many English couples do you know who choose to make love in bubbling water, some distance from their night-clothes, when there is a perfectly serviceable half-tester bed at their disposal, with a light-switch at arm's length? Quite.

Besides, if we had had a comments book, heaven knows what Mrs Stonehouse would have written in it. She probably would have filled it with very small, sloping writing in green ink, and then asked for another one. For unlike the people in Cornwall who mounted the cake-tin protest, Mrs Stonehouse did not have a wonderful holiday.

This was a shame because the sun shone every day, and the Herefordshire countryside was looking its best. Bill Bryson, in *Notes from a Small Country*, records that between 1945 and 1985,

96,000 miles of English hedgerows were destroyed, enough to girdle the earth nearly four times. But the forces of destruction did not appear to have visited Herefordshire. There are lots of regions of England which local folk like to call 'God's own country'. But this, we decided, really was. As we wrote in our brochures, with not the slightest degree of hyperbole, 'this is a truly unspoilt part of rural England, an England of hop fields and apple orchards, of rolling hills, ancient timbered villages and centuries-old churches'. All of which, it has to be said, lost some of its charm in the pissing rain. But when the weather was benign, I honestly couldn't imagine anywhere more idyllic.

Mrs Stonehouse could. For seven whole days she looked as if she'd be happier holidaying in the Gaza Strip. Acidly, she noted that the website had promised table tennis in a lofty barn, yet the table-tennis table was in the garden. What kind of two-bit operation was this? I calmly explained that at the time she had booked, there had indeed been a table-tennis table in a lofty barn. But the lofty barn was now a lofty five-bedroomed house belonging to the Openshaws, with a lofty fitted kitchen where the table-tennis table had been.

'I'm sorry,' I said. 'But there are things that weren't on the website that your children seem to have enjoyed, like the trampoline.'

We had bought a giant trampoline soon after moving in. Like all these things, it came in a flat pack and took us three days, two nervous breakdowns and a blazing row to assemble, but once it was up it quickly proved to be a wonderful recreational resource for our children, their friends and guests' children. It was also a good source of exercise for adults, although Jane counselled other women, especially women who had had babies, to empty their bladders before bouncing. Otherwise, she assured them from uncomfortable personal experience, their pelvic floors might not stand up to the strain.

Mrs Stonehouse wouldn't have gone on the trampoline if she'd had a parquet pelvic floor, but her children had happily bounced on it for hours. So, no table tennis in a lofty barn, but a trampoline in a sun-dappled garden. A reasonable swap, surely?

Her expression softened. She no longer looked like someone who could turn champagne into vinegar at a glance, just milk into yoghurt. She acknowledged that the trampoline had, indeed, been an unexpected extra, but it was not one, she intimated, that made up for such hardships as uncomfortably warm duvets. Moreover, my admission that the website had not yet been brought fully up to date, and that there were things described by the Openshaws which were no longer available, gave her all the ammunition she needed.

About three weeks after they left, we got a letter from Mrs Stonehouse chronicling her grievances in extraordinary, not to say obsessive, detail. We considered most of these unreasonable, but there were one or two which had substance. The Openshaws' website had stated that 'care has been taken in the selection of furnishings and peaceful fabrics to create an atmosphere of peaceful harmony'. Mrs Stonehouse retorted that 'there was no evidence of carefully selected furnishings and fabrics, nothing matched or created harmony'. We could only agree; we didn't much like the furnishings or peaceful fabrics either, which is why many of them ended up being carted off by the Cheap Skip Company.

We therefore wrote back with a variation on the old Lygon Arms principle, offering the Stonehouse family a week's stay at half-price anytime in the following twelve months. It seemed the right sort of gesture. We didn't want them back in our property, but looking on the positive side, we could always cover the toilet bowl with clingfilm.

Her reply was swift. The offer was inadequate, especially as it related to a week she had no intention of taking. What she wanted was her money back. 'I am surprised and dismayed that your offer does not recompense us for the week's holiday for which we have already paid,' she wrote. 'Surely it is normal practice when goods fail to meet anticipated requirements that their cost is refunded or appropriately discounted, and not that of a future purchase.' She acknowledged that we had not owned the cottages for long, and 'may already have made some improvements and plan further refurbishment [but] this unfortunately has no bearing on the circumstances or conditions of our booking'. She concluded that her solicitor had advised her that she was entitled to all her money back. With the generosity of spirit for which she was doubtless famed throughout Renfrewshire, she said she would instead settle for half.

Her solicitor? This was getting nasty. I talked to a cousin of mine, also a solicitor. 'You need to get her out of your hair,' he said. 'So offer her a small sum as a settlement, seventy-five or a hundred quid, and tell her that it is not negotiable. She can take it and agree that your differences have been resolved, or you can tell her that you'll see her in court.'

I'd always wanted to say to someone 'I'll see you in court.' Almost as much as I'd wanted to climb into the back of a London taxi and say 'Follow that car.' But decent advice though it doubtless was, I couldn't bring myself to improve Mrs Stonehouse's day even slightly by sending her a cheque of any size. Reckoning that she was probably bluffing about a solicitor, I called the bluff, writing back to say that I too had taken legal advice, and had been advised that because she had at no point during her stay asked for her money back (which was true), and because she and her family had stayed for the entire week (also true), we would stick by our original offer of a half-price week and go no further. She never replied.

I can be cheerful about it now, frivolous even, but at the time it troubled us. We had been in the holiday cottage business for scarcely two months and already we'd been threatened, however insincerely, with legal action. Despite Mrs Openshaw's warning, we had not thought much about the prospect of dissatisfied customers. We wanted everyone to enjoy Docklow Grange and its environs as much as we did, to which end we added all sorts of touches to the cottages: welcome hampers full of local produce, fresh cut flowers, smart toiletries.

It was all Jane could do to stop me folding over the ends of the toilet rolls into a neat point. There's no better use for a bit of basic origami, I often think. And despite having studied the works of Mr Origami himself, Robert J. Harbin, in the mid-1970s, basic is all I can do. Mr Harbin could turn a sheet of A4 paper into a Chinese lantern in thirty seconds, and into Sydney Opera House in sixty. But who needs a Chinese lantern anyway? A neatly folded toilet roll is so much more worthwhile. I always think it demonstrates that the management really care when they show they have thought about the bottom-wiping experience.

In a way it was useful to have the encounter with Mrs Stonehouse early on. It showed us that this cottage rental lark was vulnerable to all the foibles of human nature, our own as well as our customers'. Our three cottages were not perfect, and we were not perfect at running them. I'd always thought that all hoteliers and bed-and-breakfast proprietors should make a point of sleeping in every one of their rooms at least once, to get the experience from the customers' point of view. I still think that. But somehow I never quite got round to it myself. If the beds were too hard, or too soft, or the plumbing too loud, or the kitchen scissors not sharp enough, the only means we had of knowing was if someone told us. And if someone told us, then it was a complaint. And if someone complained, however constructively, then we couldn't help feeling slightly defensive.

But we quickly realised that we could engage Harrods to furnish the cottages, and offer every customer a complimentary bottle of single malt, and there would still be people who would arrive with demands and leave with grievances that could not be resolved by anything short of a personality transplant.

Much later, in June 2003, a couple arrived who made the Stonehouses look like Terry and June. The Prices were from Australia and had booked to stay for a month in Yewtree Cottage. Mrs Price told us on the phone that they used to run an art gallery in Alice Springs but had sold up and were kind of itinerant. 'We've got rellies in Worcester,' she said. 'But we don't want to stay with them. They'd drive us mad.'

It was a great booking, but we regretted it the instant we met them. They arrived late one Saturday afternoon. We had left the key in the lock and they had let themselves in. I knocked and called out a cheery hello. Mrs Price came to the door. She was short, in her late fifties, and had hair an unnerving shade of sunset-pink. 'This place is freezing,' she said, without so much as a hello in return.

It was a beautiful early summer's day and Yewtree Cottage was looking lovely. Sunshine flooded through the windows. Not even a native of the South American rainforest could have called it freezing. On the other side of the old cider press, the elderly couple staying in Manor Cottage, Mr and Mrs Shearer from

Bromsgrove, were sitting outside, in the shade, enjoying a glass of wine. Obviously Bromsgrove wasn't Alice Springs, but even so.

'I'm sorry,' I said. 'We do have storage heaters upstairs which will come on overnight.' I gestured towards a small fan heater. 'And we have several more of those. I can bring them all round, if you like. They're actually very effective.'

'Oh, those won't do it for us,' she said. 'We come from the tropics.'

Wondering what Basil Fawlty might have said in these slightly challenging circumstances, I continued trying to be as helpful as possible. 'I could also light the wood-burning stove for you.'

'Messy, dirty things,' said Mrs Price. 'I was brought up with them. I don't want to have to deal with that.'

At this point Mr Price came down the stairs. He didn't say anything, just stood there in what seemed to be physical pain. 'My husband likes the warmth,' explained Mrs Price. 'But it is warm,' I wanted to scream, but didn't. I looked at Mr Price. He was short too, with a goatee beard a disappointingly mundane shade of grey. On a string around his neck he wore what appeared to be a dead mouse; probably some sort of charm to ward off the cold. 'I'm terribly sorry if you're uncomfortable,' I said. 'I can supply more heaters.'

'No, you see, we're from the tropics,' said Mrs Price again, raising her voice, as though she was addressing a moron. 'I guess it's unseasonably cold here at the moment.'

The temperature was in the low seventies, fahrenheit. 'No,' I said. 'This actually qualifies as quite a nice English summer's day.'

Mr Price gave a sniff. Mrs Price changed tack. 'Where do you go walking round here?' she asked. 'I'm a very keen walker.'

'There's thirty miles of unbroken countryside between us and the Welsh border,' I said brightly. 'You can climb over the stile at the side of our house, and set off through the fields.'

'I don't have the right footwear for walking through mud,' said Mrs Price.

'There is very little mud at the moment,' I said. 'We haven't had much rain.'

'Yes, but I prefer to walk along roads,' she said. 'And I noticed that the road out there doesn't have a pavement. Will I be safe from the traffic?'

I hope not, I thought. 'Oh yes,' I said. 'And you won't have to walk for long along the main road. There are lots of quiet country lanes round here.'

She looked doubtful. 'Where can we buy a newspaper?' she said, in another abrupt change of tack.

'We'll deliver it to your front door,' I said. 'Part of the service.'

'Tomorrow we'd like the *Sunday Telegraph*,' she said.

'Well, it's normally a case of seeing what they have on the van,' I said. 'They might not have a spare *Sunday Telegraph*.'

'Will they have a *Sunday Times*?'

'I should think so.'

'Well, we'll have that, if they don't have a *Sunday Telegraph*.'

'Of course.'

'But make sure all the bits are inside it. The television listings and all that. What's television reception like round here? Not very good, I suppose?'

And so it went on, with me feeling increasingly nostalgic for the relative wit and charm of Mrs Stonehouse. I also felt a surge of warmth towards the Prices' 'rellies' in Worcester. Anyone who could drive these people mad was a friend of mine, not that the Prices had all that far to go to reach madness. As I walked back to the sanctuary of our kitchen, Mr and Mrs Shearer, who'd overheard the entire exchange, gave me a sympathetic smile. 'We love it here,' said Mrs Shearer. 'Couldn't be nicer,' added Mr Shearer. I could have hugged them.

When Jane came home an hour later I warned her that the guests from hell had arrived. In fact, maybe that explained why they were so bloody cold; they were used to furnaces being energetically stoked by demons. I then went upstairs to work and after a few moments heard the sound of raised voices. Jane had committed the holiday cottage proprietor's ultimate sin and lost her rag with a guest. I didn't blame her one bit.

Apparently, Jane had gone to the cottage and found the fan heater on full blast. It was so hot she could hardly breathe. Yet Mrs Price had resumed the offensive, complaining that it was too cold. Jane had reiterated what I'd said about the fan heaters and the wood-burning stove, but Mrs Price had rejected both options. 'Then wear more clothes,' said Jane, loudly. 'Or better still, maybe you should find somewhere else to stay. I'm not asking you to leave, but we'll happily give you your cheque back. We don't want you here if you're not comfortable.'

Slightly gallingly, the Prices seemed to regard this as a gesture of huge magnanimity. Jane thought she had been unequivocally sharp with them; they thought she had been terribly sweet. A little something is often lost in translation in dialogue between English people and Australians, I have found. What to us sounds slightly on the brusque side – like 'Get stuffed, you mad old cow' – sounds friendly to them. We'd had other Aussie visitors who also seemed a bit snippy at first, yet turned out to be warm-hearted, altogether delightful folk.

There was nothing warm about the Prices, except Yewtree Cottage, which after twenty-four hours of fan heaters going full blast, felt positively equatorial. Yet they still found it uncomfortably chilly. They left two days later. Their £1200 went with them, and Yewtree Cottage remained empty for the next four weeks, in lovely weather at the height of the season. We had turned down lots of potential bookings on the basis that it would be full for a month, and it was income we could hardly afford to lose. But it was still worth every penny not to have Mr and Mrs Price shivering on our doorstep. If they had returned ten minutes later, then, like Kitty and Malcolm Muggeridge, they would have found us performing the 'They've gone, they've gone, they've gone!' jig.

Still, by the time the Prices arrived, and departed, we were confident in our ability to run holiday cottages properly. Had they arrived hard on the heels of the Stonehouses we might have thrown in the towel. Happily, for every Mrs Stonehouse there were lots of customers who liked what they found. Some of them came across us on the internet, others in the pages of *Ariel*, the BBC magazine, in which we advertised our cottages as 'run by former BBC producer'. At least that was a way for Jane to console herself that her career in radio was still of some tangible benefit in her life; 'run by former BBC producer' suggests a place where no detail is overlooked, where reliability is the watchword, where the finest virtues of Britishness are upheld. To people who work for the BBC it does, anyway.

We also advertised in a magazine called *Choice*, aimed at the over-sixty-fives. In marketing-speak, this is targeting 'the grey pound'. But the grey pound is damnably difficult to prise from grey wallets. We became used to hearing clicks on our answering machine, rather than messages. The readers of *Choice* didn't like talking to answering machines. When we did answer the phone to a *Choice* reader, we soon realised that we had made a mistake by advertising before we'd had our brochures printed. The conversation invariably went as follows:

'Hello, Docklow Grange.'

A hesitant, shaky voice. 'Oh, hello, please could you send us one of your colour brochures.'

'I'm afraid we're still waiting for them to come back from the printers. But we can send you a print-out from the internet, which will tell you everything about us.'

A slight note of panic. 'No, I haven't got internet.' For some reason, the readers of *Choice* always referred to the internet without the definite article. British expatriates refer to their homeland in the same peculiar manner, I have noticed. 'What's the news from UK?' Or, 'We left UK twenty years ago. Don't miss it a bit.' Or, 'An aunt of mine sends out baked beans and marmalade from UK.'

We tried to reassure the *Choice* readers that they didn't need the internet. 'It's all right, we just print it out and send it to you. Can I take your address?'

A greater note of panic. 'No, no, we don't have internet. Thank you very much. Goodbye.'

Bless 'em. And I don't mean to sound patronising. I know that I'm going to be exactly that sort of senior citizen, befuddled by the modern world, intimidated by anything new and complicated. Come to think of it, I'm a bit like that already, and always have been. Cashpoint machines were introduced around the time I went to university, but I shied away from them for my entire four years as an undergraduate, terrified of pressing the wrong buttons or getting my coat sleeve caught in the money dispenser or something. I could have written a PhD in the time I would have saved by making withdrawals from the Clydesdale Bank cashpoint in South Street, St Andrews, instead of standing in interminable queues to cash a cheque for £5.

With the zeal of the converted, however, I later became a

cashpoint devotee, hardly able to pass the things without withdrawing £20 or checking the balance of our current account. But that stopped soon after we moved to Docklow. It was too depressing. We were spending money that wasn't ours on a house that wouldn't have been ours, had we taken the most basic financial advice. Accordingly, we badly needed the income from the cottages, and Jane, in particular, got morose when one, two or all three of the cottages lay empty, especially during periods of good weather. That happened a lot in the Indian summer of 2002; we hadn't been marketing them for long enough and could hardly expect full occupancy, but even so, it was frustrating.

One Saturday morning, as I lay in bed treasuring a rare lie-in until getting on for eight o'clock, I heard a bloodcurdling cry, followed by sustained sobbing. With impressive agility I leapt out of bed in forty-five seconds flat and rushed downstairs. Jane had opened the heavy door of the butler's silver safe – which is where we kept valuables such as pet food – and trapped her bare foot between the door and the floor. But it wasn't just the pain that made her cry, it was the accumulated anxiety about whether we would ever make money from the cottages, how we would pay for the upkeep of the house even if we did, and indeed why we had left our nice, comfortable home in Crouch End, and all our cherished friends, to come and live in the middle of nowhere, in a house with a sodding butler's sodding silver safe, as if we sodding needed one.

'Because we love it here,' I suggested, gently. 'Because the kids have fields and woods to play in. Because they can grow up with a dog, and cats, and chickens, and rabbits.'

'Yeah, and who's the sucker who usually ends up mucking them all out, up to her elbows in chicken shit?' she replied, between sobs. I had no answer to that.

The animals had not stopped with Milo the golden retriever. Although it had always been our intention to buy a dog, we hadn't envisaged becoming owners of chickens. But by October, after we had been living in Docklow for three months, we had begun to feel awkward about buying our eggs at Safeway when there was extensive farmland all around us. At the same time, if we were going to keep chickens, we wanted nice decorative ones. So we drove up to the Wernlas Collection in Onibury, Shropshire, which proudly proclaims itself 'the UK's leading conservation centre for rare and traditional breeds of chicken'.

Ali and Chris and family, our friends from Crouch End, were staying that weekend and came with us. It must have tickled them to see us going native by becoming poultry-keepers. Not far from where we had lived in London there was a comedy club called the Hen and Chickens. For eight years, if ever I had asked someone if they were interested in a Hen and Chickens outing, it meant I was proposing an evening of stand-up comedy. But now I was suggesting a Hen and Chickens outing and thinking not of Eddie Izzard or Jo Brand, but of hens and chickens.

Off we went to Onibury, which is just north of Ludlow (which someone told me is itself the town, coincidentally, where Jo Brand's mum lives). Before we bought any livestock, we needed some serious advice. My ignorance of the fowl world was just about total, in fact I wasn't even sure whether there was a difference between a hen and a chicken. I asked Chris whether he knew. 'A hen is a young chicken,' he said confidently. Chris is a chap whose every utterance carries fierce conviction, and his breadth of knowledge of the world is indeed impressive, but just occasionally the facts he dispenses with such certitude turn out to be well-concealed guesses. This was such an occasion. 'A chicken is the generic term for the domestic fowl, embracing pullets, which are hens under a year old, hens and cockerels,' explained the nice man in the Wernlas Collection shop.

I had posed the question with slight apprehension; after all, imagine if you went to a showroom to buy a car and started by asking whether there was a difference between manual cars and automatics, and if so, what was it? You'd be laughed off the forecourt. It's the sort of question a child might ask.

But then self-respecting newspapermen should never be scared to ask humbling and potentially embarrassing questions. One of the privileges thus far of my career as a journalist was to spend the best part of an afternoon interviewing another journalist, the late, indubitably great Alistair Cooke. I sat in the study of his apartment overlooking Central Park in Manhattan, grappling with the absurdly large whisky he had poured me, and interrupting his effortless monologue with just eight questions in three hours. One of them was: what can Britain learn from America?

'You know,' he said, in that comforting mid-Atlantic drawl, 'that's a very good question. If you'll excuse the expression, it's a childlike question. I learnt on the road that the great questions in journalism are. Don't pretend to know anything, ask the questions a child would.'

Cooke told me that during World War Two he had travelled around the United States reporting for *The Times* and the BBC. He had to write about the 'Big Inch' pipeline, which President Roosevelt was having built to supply oil for the war effort in Europe. But Cooke knew nothing about oil and most oilmen he spoke to scoffed at his ignorance. Eventually, however, he heard about an old Scotsman called McLaren who had lived in Austin for fifty years and was generally considered to know more about oil than anyone in Texas. So he went to Austin. 'What do you know about oil?' said McLaren. 'As far as I'm concerned it grows on trees,' Cooke said. And McLaren said, 'Fine, how long have you got?'

'I said that I had as long as it took,' Cooke recalled, 'and it took two days. He gave me a private seminar and accepted the fact that to get to know anything I had to be a child. The first-rate people always do accept that. It's only second-rate people who say "you're wasting my time".'

I'm pleased to say that I have never forgotten that lesson, which is why I cheerfully asked the man at the Wernlas Collection to explain the difference between a hen and a chicken. And being a first-rate person, he cheerfully supplied the answer. Although frankly, he could have told me that a hen was a chicken that had been circumcised, and I would have nodded solemnly.

Anyway, armed with this new knowledge that all hens are chickens, but not all chickens are hens, plus a neat little booklet explaining the differences between breeds, we went to choose.

We greatly admired the Appenzeller Spitzhaubens, which the booklet informed us were hardy birds with distinctive horn-shaped combs, and consistently good layers of small, white eggs, their name deriving from the similarity of their crests to the lace bonnets worn by women of the Appenzell region. 'They're a bit pecky, aren't they,' sniffed Ali, who had already admitted to preferring chickens with piecrust round the outside.

Undeterred by Ali's poultryism, Jane and I carried on looking. We were quite taken with the handsome white Sultans which appeared to be wearing legwarmers and were first imported in 1854 from Constantinople. But they are rotten layers, apparently.

We also liked the white-crested Polands, one of the oldest breeds on record, the booklet informed me, depicted in many seventeenth-century Dutch paintings. But we didn't want only one breed, and the nice man in the shop advised us not to stick Polands in with other kinds, because other chickens are fascinated by their magnificent top-knots, and harass them terribly. Just as Hitler picked on Poland, so do most chickens. Which might well be the first time that seventeenth-century Dutch paintings, Hitler and chickens have ever featured in the same paragraph, although actually there is a faint whiff of the Third Reich about chickens, I have since discovered, as well as the stronger whiff of chicken shit, in that they very much prefer living with their own type. They are innately prejudiced.

As a poultry-keeper of more than two years' standing, I now feel able to make such pronouncements. But at the Wernlas Collection that day we were clueless, and eventually plumped on purely aesthetic grounds for three Buff Rock bantams and a Gold Sebright. Joseph, then aged seven, was inconsolable. 'I wanted a weird one,' he wailed, pointing at a Transylvanian Naked Neck.

We couldn't take the Buff Rocks and the Sebright home, for the fairly sound reason that they hadn't yet been hatched; the ones we saw were for display only. In any case, like parents-to-be, we needed to prepare for their arrival. The very next day, the *Rothmans Football Yearbook* was supplanted on my bedside table by Dr Geoffrey Eley's definitive text, *Home Poultry Keeping*. Lying in bed, while Jane tried to read the latest Margaret Forster novel, I kept interrupting her with valuable titbits, such as that if an eggbound bird is given olive oil, she will usually expel the egg within a couple of hours. Whether ordinary olive oil or extra virgin, Dr Eley did not say. Either way, I was taking my forthcoming responsibilities very seriously. As a consequence, Jane was not making much progress with Margaret Forster.

On the third Sunday in October, we drove back to Onibury to collect our little brood. The children had decided that they wanted to see them before giving them names, but squabbled the entire journey home over whether they were to be called Amber, Babs, Bunty, Edwina, Ruby, Poppy, Daffodil, Ginger, Treasure or Marigold. They were all hens, but had we bought a cockerel I would have pressed strongly for Egbert. Shortly after we moved into Docklow Grange, we had all become extremely fond of the venerable Muscovy duck who waddled imperiously – if a waddle can ever truly be described as imperious – around the old cider press outside the back door. The kids christened him Egbert, which I thought was a wonderful name. But one day I found myself chatting to Mr Openshaw when Egbert waddled by. We both looked at him fondly. 'The children call him Egbert,' I said. Mr Openshaw's smile froze, and his face took on a slightly pained expression. 'His name is Desmond,' he said.

So the name Egbert was still going spare, but the Wernlas Collection man had strongly advised that, being novices, we should stick with hens for the time being. In the end the children agreed on Babs, Ginger, and Ruby for the Buff Rocks – all names lifted from the excellent, not to say seminal film *Chicken Run* – and Marigold for the Sebright.

Advice on chickens came raining in. One veteran poultry-keeper told us that we would become complacent about foxes at our peril. 'The fox only has to be lucky once, but you have to be lucky every time,' he said gravely, invoking the spirit of Clint Eastwood. If we were to keep Babs, Ginger, Ruby and Marigold completely safe, obviously we would have to bring in Dirty Harry. Otherwise we'd take our chances, but to lose even one of them would be expensive as well as heartbreaking. We had paid £15.90 each for Babs, Ginger and Ruby, and £18.70 for Marigold.

This expenditure caused great hilarity in the King's Head, when I made the mistake of mentioning it to Georgie, one of the Trueloves' farm hands. 'Hey, Owen,' he cried. 'Brian here's just paid over sixty quid for four chickens, look.'

Appending the word 'look' to a sentence was a Herefordshire quirk that we had come to enjoy, incidentally. Another was the habit of giving genders to objects, in the French manner. Our odd-job man, Ted, was once repairing some guttering for us, and had brought his ageing father to help. I went out to see how they were getting on. 'I'm afraid he's absolutely knackered,' said Ted. I tutted sympathetically. It was quite a warm day. 'He looks to me,' added Ted, 'like he's going to need replacing.' It was only gradually that I realised he was talking about the guttering, not about his old dad. In the course of familiarising ourselves with the local argot, we had notched up some memorable misunderstandings, although there was nothing to misunderstand about this exchange with Georgie and Owen. They were taking the mickey, royally.

Owen was a farm labourer from Pudleston, in his sixties. He was short, with cropped grey hair, a large bulldog tattoo on his left forearm, and the broadest shoulders I had ever seen. His claim to local fame was that years earlier he'd come second in the Strongest Man in Herefordshire competition and would have come first but for the fact that his false teeth were dislodged when he deployed them to drag a tractor at the end of a tow rope. At the news that we'd spent over £60 on four bantams he threw back his head and laughed the laugh of a man who had just had all his prejudices confirmed about silly-bastard city types who come to live in the country with more money in their wallets than brain cells in their heads. 'I've got four you could 'ave 'ad for 50p each,' he roared.

I wondered whether to point out that I considered £18.70 really quite a bargain for a sweet little creature with golden-brown plumage gorgeously edged with black, reminiscent of the sort of plumped-up cushion you might find in a just-so town house, but decided better of it. Instead I roared with laughter too, and bought them each another pint of Dorothy Goodbody's bitter in a possibly vain attempt to demonstrate that even silly-bastard city types had some redeeming qualities. I certainly didn't add that we had also paid £248.50 for a henhouse from Forsham Cottage Arks in Tenbury Wells, and that it had a stair-case because the man there had told us that 'banties like going upstairs to bed'. Owen would have wet himself.

5

Reclassified Flapjacks

Although a poultry-keeper, clearly I could not yet consider myself a fully fledged countryman. As far as Owen and Georgie were concerned, I would probably never become one. But at least, in September, I had gone on the Countryside Alliance's Liberty and Livelihood march through central London, admittedly propelled not by a burning sense of injustice but by the news desk of the *Independent*, where it was thought that, as the author of a column called 'Tales of the Country', I ought to be in Hyde Park filing a colourful report for the following day's paper.

Far from burning, my sense of injustice about issues such as the proposed ban on fox-hunting was not even warming up in the bottom oven of the Aga. I wasn't really sure what I felt about hunting, but I needed to formulate an opinion, because the Master of the North Herefordshire Hunt had traditionally requested permission to cross our land, and the Openshaws had traditionally said he could do so.

One afternoon I got home from a trip to London to find a note slipped under the door from the Master of the Hunt, Philip Borthwick-Jones. It gave details of a forthcoming hunt and said 'we will be mounted and may wish to visit your land'. Cleverly, a phone number was included that we were to ring only if this was not convenient, like those tiny boxes in communications from book clubs that say tick here if you do not wish to receive an entire set of the *Encyclopaedia Britannica* bound in 100 per cent genuine leather.

What was I to do? I didn't particularly want the North Herefordshire Hunt thundering over my precious few acres, but to refuse would have seemed unfriendly and reinforced my status as a newcomer from the city with no idea of countryside practices. In the end I did nothing, not least because I was sidetracked by some flights of fancy inspired by a marvellous typographical error at the top of the note. 'Autumn hinting has recently started,' it declared.

Now there, it struck me, was a leisure activity that everyone could enjoy, without fear of protest or prohibition.

'Are you, er, planning to pick all those apples in your orchard?'

'Goodness' (looking at watch while simultaneously yawning), 'is that the time?'

'Erm' (loaded cough), 'whose round is it?'

I decided that autumn hinting could definitely catch on, and that if nobody else wanted to be the Master of the North Herefordshire Hint, then, ahem (modest glance at shoes), I wouldn't necessarily be averse myself.

But this was no matter for frivolity. I hadn't been living in the countryside for long enough to develop any strong feelings, yet in the weeks leading up to the Liberty and Livelihood march I felt as though I were excluded from some sort of club. Hardly a day went by without someone saying to me, 'Are you marching?'

Significantly, nobody ever said 'Are you marching to save countryside pursuits?' or 'Are you marching for liberty and live-lihood?' They just said, 'Are you marching?' No further elaboration was needed, which reminded me of some of the old civil rights heroes I met when I lived in Atlanta, Georgia, in the mid-1980s. Those people talked in the same way. They didn't march for civil rights, they just marched. Or in the case of Xernona Clayton, didn't. I got to know Xernona while working as a student intern for Ted Turner's twenty-four-hour news net-work CNN. She was a senior vice-president of CNN, and, while it's true that everyone who rises above the position of janitor in an American corporation sooner or later gets to be called senior vice-president, Xernona was truly exalted. She was Ted Turner's right-hand woman just as, in a previous life, she had once been right-hand woman to Martin Luther King. She it was, indeed, who drove him to Atlanta airport to catch a flight to Memphis, the trip from which he returned in a coffin. 'But I never marched,' she told me. 'I was the bail bondsman. I used to get Dr King and the others out of jail. All the others marched, but not me.'

It might seem daft to compare the Countryside Alliance in 2002 with American civil rights in the 1960s, and so it is, but it didn't seem daft to those who saw it as a cause worth marching for. And although they were characterised in the liberal press as a bunch of unreconstructed, waxed-jacketed toffs with the scent of terrified foxes in their nostrils – not least by Jane's old boss

Rod Liddle, the editor of Radio 4's *Today* programme, who lost his BBC job after suggesting in the *Guardian* that anyone who had forgotten why they had voted Labour in 1997 needed only a glimpse of the forces supporting the Countryside Alliance to be reminded – I came to see that as no less gross a simplification as the portrayal in the right-wing press a few months later of the Stop the War marchers as so many sandal-wearing lefties with the scent of joss sticks in their nostrils.

Both generalisations were prejudiced and ill-informed, which is not, of course, to say that there weren't plenty of unreconstructed toffs on the first march, and lots of lefties in sandals on the second.

A few days before the Liberty and Livelihood march we were invited to dinner by Louise and Rupert Anton, who had become steadfast friends and generously kept introducing us to their mates in the hope that it would help us to assimilate into Herefordshire society. Through them we had met Frank and Fenella, an altogether delightful couple who became good friends also, and who, partly on our recommendation, made arrangements to send their daughter Millie to Stamford Heath school.

Most of the Antons' friends sent their children to expensive fee-paying schools and had themselves attended some of England's more famous boarding schools, which by no means meant that they weren't charming people well worth getting to know, but did mean a few blank looks when we said that our kids attended a Church of England primary, and would have generated even blanker looks if Jane had embarked on a few anecdotes from her schooldays at Kirk Balk Comprehensive near Barnsley. It wasn't that they were too grand for us, or that we were too plebeian for them, just that they didn't seem entirely like kindred spirits.

Before dinner, Rupert introduced me to an engagingly garru-
lous Old Etonian called Nick. 'Are you marching?' said Nick. I
explained that I wasn't, as I just couldn't get worked up about
fox-hunting. 'Ah,' he said. 'But I'm not marching about fox-
hunting. I'm marching in protest at the Government's inept
handling of foot-and-mouth.'

When I replied that, saddened as I had been by the foot-and-
mouth crisis two years earlier, I didn't have desperately strong
feelings about that either, Nick looked at me as though I'd passed
the port in the wrong direction. I realised at that moment that
Nick, the Old Etonian, and Owen, the farm labourer from the
King's Head, had far more in common with each other than I had
with either of them. They were true countrymen, albeit of different hues, while to both of them I was an arriviste without
nearly enough mud on my wellies. I gave myself until the next
dinner party to develop a vehement opinion about a rural issue,
although my worry was that I would choose something that
nobody else gave a toss about, and that I would start hammering
on the table in indignation at the really quite appalling practice of
stapling labels to bullocks' ears, bearing an impersonal number
like 244 rather than a nice name like Bartholomew. The table
would then fall silent, and everyone would stare at me in bewil-
derment, before turning to their neighbour and saying, 'So, did
you march?'

Still, having told people that I had no intention of marching,
there I was on 22 September, alighting from the tube at
Knightsbridge Underground Station and narrowly avoiding
being disembowelled by a woman grappling with a 'Rural
Britain, the New Ethnic Minority' sign that seemed, physically if
not philosophically, a bit too heavy for her.

In Hyde Park, tens of thousands of people were already

gathered, and the entrepreneurs were out in force. I talked to a chap called David Jennet, who was selling whistles at £1 each. He'd arrived at Hyde Park Corner at 9 a.m. and by 10.45 had sold almost his entire consignment of 500. I asked him whether he agreed with the grievances of those marching.

'I don't know nothin' about it, mate,' he said. 'I'm from Southend-on-Sea.'

Jim, in an ice-cream van opposite Knightsbridge Barracks, was a little more clued-up. 'It's about the right to hunt, innit,' he said, handing a 99 to a girl in jodhpurs. 'Which as I see it, is no different to my right to sell ice creams.' His face darkened at the idea that someone might threaten to confiscate his hundreds and thousands, while for some reason I was reminded of the old joke about the ice-cream man who was found dead in his van with raspberry syrup trickling down his face, hundreds and thousands in his hair and a flake in his mouth. A friend commented sadly that he'd done what he'd always been threatening to do, and topped himself.

Of the hundreds and thousands pouring into Hyde Park, many held placards which showed that the right to hunt was but one of dozens of issues on their minds. One man waved a placard which read 'Ban Golf!' Being fairly keen on that royal and ancient game, I asked him to explain the significance of his message. Why ban golf? 'Why not ban golf?' he said. Because unlike fox-hunting, it could not possibly be construed as cruel. 'Yes, but it requires nitrates to be put into the soil, people are passionate about it, let's ban it. You can find an argument for banning anything.'

I took his point, although I wasn't sure that irony that needs an explanation is irony that works. At least it was an original sign, among all those which thundered 'Blair Is Vermin!' Another original one likened the Prime Minister to the Zimbabwean president Robert Mugabe. 'Blair – UK's Magabe,' it proclaimed. I gently pointed out the spelling error. 'Oh no,' wailed John East-Rigby, from the New Forest. 'And I looked it up on the internet last night.'

I was happy to have an opportunity to share with him my technique of never misspelling Mugabe, explaining that backwards it reads 'e ba gum'. Mr East-Rigby and his wife, Cherry, listened politely. I wasn't sure that they had ever heard the expression 'e ba gum'. 'I'm afraid John is dyslexic,' said Cherry, with an apologetic smile.

I continued wandering through a forest of corduroy and brogues. Rod Liddle was wrong to jump to a single conclusion about so many people, but had he stood in Hyde Park for half an hour that Sunday morning, he would not necessarily have been parted from his opinions. As I scribbled my observations, I tried to see myself, in a year or two, with a placard rather than a notebook in my hand. I couldn't quite visualise it. But I had no doubt that the longer I lived in the countryside, the more I would understand, and perhaps come to share, the grievances of ordinary countryfolk.

The problem I had, however, and for that matter still have, is with taking part in a protest encompassing so many grievances that you can get lumped in with causes you don't much care for. Or worse, that you despise.

Outside the Mandarin Oriental Hyde Park Hotel I noticed several well-groomed young men handing out copies of a newspaper called *The Countrysider*. At first glance it seemed innocuous. A cute squirrel adorned the masthead. I took one, and flicked through it. There was an editorial under the headline 'Countryside under Threat from White Flight', which opined that 'prime farmland and priceless wildlife habitats are being destroyed by housing developments, and those moving in are mostly white, middle-class city folk – ordinary people who, in the main, are sick to death of living in our increasingly alien, cosmopolitan, overcrowded, congested, polluted, crime-infested urban centres . . . they are people who see rural Britain as a refuge, a place to make a fresh start'.

I must have been having a slow-witted day. It wasn't until I saw the adjective 'cosmopolitan' used pejoratively – an adjective Jane and I had used in the 'reasons to stay' column during all the late nights of agonising over whether or not to leave London – that darker thoughts than squirrel welfare came to mind. And sure enough, on the very next page was an application to join the British National Party (family membership a bargainous £35 a year).

Even though the vast majority of marchers would have disassociated themselves entirely from the repugnant views of the Far Right, I could see why the BNP had recognised a potential recruiting ground. I had the same misgivings about the Stop the War march the following spring, which I again covered for the *Independent*. I felt an affinity with the people who opposed the invasion of Iraq, but none at all with those who lionised Palestinian suicide-bombers.

How many people, I later wondered, went on both marches? Few, I would guess, even though there must have been plenty who opposed both the bombing of Baghdad and the banning of fox-hunting, if only because the prospect of that war (to say nothing of the brutal reality and then the horrible aftermath of it) showed the absurdity of so many people getting their knickers into such a twist about the rights of foxes.

As one of the few people not in the Metropolitan Police to be present on both occasions, I found it pleasing that the two enormous marches, which between them mobilised over 2 million people, were almost perfect mirror images of one another. If Liddle was not completely wide of the mark to suggest that the tweedy stalwarts of the Countryside Alliance offered a reminder to those who had started to forget just why they voted Labour back into power, a sizeable number of Stop the War marchers, carrying Socialist Workers Party placards bearing photographs of a benignly smiling Yasser Arafat, offered a similarly potent reminder of why Labour had been out of power for so long in the first place.

Is this getting too political for you? It's starting to get too political for me. All I'll add is that one march was multi-racial and the other overwhelmingly mono-racial, and that the day when stewards at a march in support of countryside interests have 'In the name of Allah the most beneficent, the most merciful' printed on the backs of their jackets, as did many of the Stop the War marchers, will be the day Britain comes of age as a healthy, polytheistic society.

There was one other notable difference between the Countryside Alliance march and the Stop the War march: food. At the latter there were no signs of the hamburger and hot-dog stalls hastily erected in readiness for the former. Maybe London's hamburger merchants took the view that there would be too many vegetarians, although I personally could have murdered one. A hamburger, that is. I wouldn't murder a vegetarian. Just a spot of gentle torture is quite enough.

For the anti-war battalions mustering in Hyde Park, by contrast with their pro-countryside counterparts, the food-and-drink stalls sold only herbal tea – peppermint, camomile, or apple and ginger – and flapjacks. The flapjacks cost £1, except for the 'reclassified' flapjacks which cost £1.50 and had cannabis baked into them. It occurred to me on the train journey home – after I had filed my report, alas – that there would have been a fabulous melee on both occasions if the caterers had got the dates of their marches mixed up. Then we would have seen right-on vegans protecting their children from the abhorrent sight and smell of burgers, and ruddy-faced country squires stoned out of their heads, after complaining that the flapjacks tasted a bit damn iffy.

But for all I know, some ruddy-faced country squires might enjoy the odd spliff. There's certainly plenty of time for all sorts of recreational activities on those long rural winter evenings, as the following month we found out practically overnight, when balmy autumn turned to punishing winter. Ever since we had moved from London, people had been issuing dire warnings about the Herefordshire winters. It was like one of those fairy tales by the Brothers Grimm, in which a woodsman and his wife move to a new forest and are jolly and contented, but everyone tells them to beware the horrid troll who lives under the old stone bridge. Except they grow so jolly and contented that they clean forget about the horrid troll, until one night he comes and eats them up. That's kind of how it was with winter in Herefordshire. Suddenly it was upon us, and by the time we remembered all those warnings, it was too late. Not that there was much we could have done.

The county that we had moved to in July now seemed more like another country. Even the mice came in from the cold; one night, we heard what sounded like dozens of them enjoying a ceilidh in the pantry.

And the power cuts started, rendering the long winter evenings a sight longer. In all the detailed conversations we'd had with those friends, and friends of friends, who were former city-dwellers, relentlessly quizzing them about what we might expect when we moved to the country, none of them mentioned power cuts. Maybe north Herefordshire was unusually vulnerable. We certainly didn't seem to be quite plugged in properly to the National Grid.

It seemed that almost every time there were high winds, or persistently heavy rain, we would lose electricity without so much as a phut. In my garret I became a neurotic wreck, pressing the 'save' button on my computer keyboard after practically every word. I've just done it now. And again now. Sometimes the loss of power would last for only a second or two, which was maddening, because the central-heating timer in the cellar needed resetting every time. But towards the end of October we had a truly epic blackout.

It started with gales that swept across western England killing six people, which put our discomfort into perspective. But after the first eight hours we had stopped counting our blessings and started counting our candles. The power stopped at 8.32 on Sunday morning and had not been restored by four that afternoon, even though the gales had abated. We phoned our electricity supplier, Powergen, to see what was going on. The cables were down, they said, which funnily enough I'd already sussed for myself. Although a company which sponsors the rugby league cup final can't be entirely bad, I didn't have much faith in Powergen. Only a week earlier I had received a letter addressed to Mr Viner at U Tree Cotage, and even if I could forgive them the Cotage, any outfit that thought Yewtree might be spelt U Tree was not one I especially wanted powering my microwave. U Bend Cottage, on the other hand, might have fitted nicely, given the recurring problems we were having with the bloody cistern.

133

Powergen did not know when the fault would be corrected, so Jane managed to dig out about a thousand tea lights – or T lights, for those who work in the accounts department at Powergen. To the great amusement of the children – not to mention our friends Howie and Bel who had been staying with us for the weekend, and whose appreciation of candlelit bedtimes in Herefordshire was doubtless intensified by the impending prospect of a drive home to fully electrified East Dulwich – the place took on a distinct Hammer House of Horror look. I kept walking up the stairs fully expecting to bump into Vincent Price on his way down.

The following morning, the power was still off. We phoned Powergen again and heard that 120,000 households had originally been affected, but 60,000 had been reconnected. This was of little consolation to Jane who had waited three months for our new John Lewis of Hungerford kitchen to be fitted. Monday, 28 October, was D-Day (or dee-day if you're from Powergen accounts), but when the kitchen-fitters arrived and found there was no electricity, they turned tail and went home to Hungerford. Jane watched them go with tears in her eyes. She was less sorry to watch me go, for I had been harrumphing all morning that I had two newspaper columns and a 2000-word feature to write and couldn't do it without being able to plug in a computer. That afternoon I drove to the motorway and checked into the first hotel I saw, turning that week's 'Tales of the Country' into 'Tales of the Bromsgrove Hilton'.

There, I wrote my stuff and watched *Coronation Street* with a twenty-four-watt pang of guilt. The next afternoon I drove home. The electricity was still off. It was finally restored at 9.28 that evening; the power cut had lasted 60 hours and 56 minutes. It seemed bizarre that in an age when space shuttles could orbit the earth, an electricity company was powerless – pun forcefully intended – to do anything for days on end about a few overhead cables brought down by storms. It wasn't as though we lived on an Orkney island.

Some folk had it worse, though. In particular, of course, the six who died. But the rest of us were gripped by the spirit of Monty Python's 'Four Yorkshiremen' sketch, as we compared the extent of the inconvenience.

'We were cut off until Tuesday night and lost the contents of our freezer!'

'That's nothing, we didn't get our power back until Wednesday afternoon, everything in the freezer was ruined, and we can't turn the burglar alarm off!!'

'Pah! You think that's bad? We were off until Friday morning, the entire contents of the freezer were written off, we can't stop the bloody burglar alarm ringing, and we lost grandma, who was on a life-support machine in the attic!!!'

But the loss of grandma was less traumatic than the tribulations of our painter-decorator, Brian. We'd had Brian in for three weeks already, decorating the kitchen in readiness for the new fittings. The previous kitchen at Docklow Grange, as the Openshaws readily admitted, had been far too small for a house of its size. We'd had an internal wall ripped out, and with all the consequent upheaval had been living without a kitchen for nearly a month. I know there are books written by people who have been taken hostage in the Middle East and chained to radiators for five years, so existing for almost twenty-eight days with no fridge and only sporadic access to a kitchen sink can't necessarily be called hardship. However, with three permanently hungry children to feed, it was a situation which had, on occasion, verged on the trying. It was exciting to be within sight of the finishing-line, which is why it had been so frustrating to watch the kitchen-fitters push their van into reverse.

At least we had Brian to entertain us. Brian was a tall, athletically built man in, I would guess, his mid-fifties. He came from the charmingly named Herefordshire village of Stoke Bliss, and lived on the estate of Lord Darnley, for whom his wife was housekeeper. For the first few days he scarcely said a word, and we had him earmarked as the strong, silent, serious type. Gradually, however, it became clear that Brian was a man from whom Eddie Izzard might take lessons in comic timing, leaving an hour for Jack Dee to study the nuances of his hangdog delivery. Partly, it was his broad Herefordshire accent that made him so funny. But mostly, it was the fact that he was so funny that made him so funny.

Brian excelled even himself in that week of the sixty-hour power cut, when he recounted what life had been like at home in Stoke Bliss after dark. Without any source of light, he and his wife were finally forced to deploy the cute snowman candle that had stood proudly on their sideboard, wick unlit, every Christmas Day for the previous twelve years. 'When I brought him out he had a little smile on his face, thinking it was Christmas again,' said Brian, looking forlorn. 'But then he saw the dreaded box of matches. I blame the wife. Because I go to bed early. But she stayed up, and the next morning he was just a bowl of wax. I think we might just leave him in a saucer, look, like some people leave ashes in an urn.'

By now weeping with laughter, I told Brian that I would look in every fancy gift shop, when I was next in Covent Garden or somewhere like it, until I found another snowman candle. 'Oh, it wouldn't be the same,' he said, mournfully. 'It would be like trying to replace a dog.'

Brian and I were not the only Brians about the place. The man who serviced the Aga was a Brian, and the locksmith, who came to fix window-locks that would satisfy the insurance company, was a Brian, too. Most confusingly, Brian the painter-decorator's boss was another painter-decorator called Brian, although rather oddly he kept calling me David. Perhaps it was more than he could bear to have another Brian to deal with. Whatever, my name, the bane of my life when I was a child in the heyday of the *Magic Roundabout*, was an unexpected asset when it came to assimilating in the Welsh Marches. If Herefordshire was full of anything at all, other than sheep, cattle and apples, it was full of Brians.

But I couldn't just rely on my suddenly ubiquitous name. We had to keep making an effort to meet people, especially people in and around Docklow. Our social life was evolving through Stamford Heath school; we had become fairly friendly with two or three other sets of parents. But we also needed to make friends on our doorstep, or as close to our doorstep as we could find people.

In fact, we did have fairly immediate neighbours. Four of the eleven cottages surrounding Docklow Grange, all of which the Openshaws had originally run as holiday lets, were now owner-occupied all year round.

One of our neighbours was Will, a wildlife consultant in his mid forties whose job it was to tell property developers that they couldn't build a shopping-centre on this or that field because it would be awfully upsetting for a colony of great crested newts. In my book this made Will something of a hero, but he was an unlikely hero, a kindly but diffident man who reminded me powerfully of Mr Allen, my kindly but diffident chemistry teacher at King George V School from 1973 to the joyous day in

1978 when I completed my chemistry O-Level, in which I scraped a U, and was able to contemplate a future in which the mystifying Periodic Table would never again play a part. Mr Allen rejoiced in the nickname of Tog. That was because his car registration started with the letters TOG; I sometimes wonder whether schoolboys are as boundlessly inventive now as they were thirty years ago.

Will did not have much idea of how to deal with children, something else which reminded me of Tog. But that didn't matter because his enthusiasms were their enthusiasms. Scarcely had we moved in than Will was at the back door wondering whether the children might, er, like to go with him to check out bats with his new bat-meter. Would they? Were daffodils yellow? Was Tinky-Winky a Teletubbie?

Will enriched our lives considerably, albeit in some strange ways. He would suddenly appear at our back door with the news that he had some slowworms round for afternoon tea, or at least a man who had brought some slowworms, and would we like to meet them? On another occasion it was a moth man. Will's friend, a moth expert, had set up a trap in Will's garden to see how many species of moth were knocking around, and there were twenty-six. Joseph and Jacob went to have a look and, slightly disconcertingly, came back full of fervour for moths.

For a few nights, *A Complete Guide to British Moths*, by the estimable Margaret Brooks, became Joseph's bedtime reading matter. And when I could prise it from Joseph's grasp I found it fascinating, too. I'd always thought of moths as mildly annoying creatures which chew holes in favourite jumpers and bang around stupidly against the insides of light shades, good only for the old joke about the man who knocks on the door of a psychiatrist at midnight and says to him 'Can you help me, I think I'm a moth.'

'But what brings you to my house at this late hour?' asks the psychiatrist. 'Your light was on,' says the man.

But I now regarded moths with new respect, and told anyone who was interested – which admittedly was hardly anyone, except Joseph and Jacob who knew already – what absolutely marvellous names moths have. There are exotically named moths (Merveille du Jour, Feathered Ranunculus, Jersey Tiger) and grand-sounding moths (Plumed Prominent, Varied Coronet, White Ermine) and moths you might find holding doors open for the Plumed Prominent (Red-Necked Footman, Dingy Footman, Speckled Footman) and moths even the Red-Necked Footman might look down on (Chimney Sweeper, Ground Lackey, Pigmy Footman).

There are moths you wouldn't want to meet in a back alley (Death's-Head Hawk, Dark Dagger, Satyr Pug) and moths you really wouldn't mind meeting in a back alley (Belted Beauty, Straw Belle, Maiden's Blush) and annoyingly successful moths (Ruddy Highflyer) and religious moths (Small Quaker, Hebrew Character) and nearly religious moths (Muslin Footman) and even moths which aren't quite sure what sort of moths they are (Confused, Uncertain). You can pass a happy twenty minutes on the toilet by reading only the index of *A Complete Guide to British Moths*, and that's just what I did. But I also delved into the book proper, and decided that I would be mildly disappointed if my life never threw up a social situation in which I could casually let slip that the Lobster moth has no anal claspers.

Among the many other interesting people to whom Will introduced us was Roger Plant, who was a dab hand, possibly the only hand, at making twig pencils. Big, little, knotty, smooth, gnarled, oak, maple, birch – rare was the twig from which Roger could not make a handsome pencil, into which he would then tastefully sear the owner's name. What a lovely way to make a living. He made some for our kids who treasured them for the best part of an hour, which for kids isn't bad going. At least it would take a long time before they were worn into stubs. Roger also made us some twig pencils which just had 'Docklow Grange' seared into them, which occasionally we handed out to people staying in our cottages. You didn't have to go to hotel-keeping school to know that little things like that can lift your establishment above the ordinary, a strategy which, I can report, has also dawned on the proprietors of the Launceston Hotel in Blackpool, who proudly display a local newspaper cutting on their forecourt, memorably headlined 'Muesli for breakfast keeps B&B ahead of the rest'.

Our other permanent neighbours were Tracey and Dave, Maurice and Margaret, and Annie. Annie was a cheerful, lively, attractive woman of, if she will forgive me, fairly mature years, who had moved to Docklow from Birmingham. She had a wonderful Brummie accent – not an oxymoron, in my book – which turned Milo into Marlow. Or even Marlowe. One week we had a charming woman staying in Yewtree Cottage, a Shakespearean scholar heavily involved with the Royal Shakespeare Company at Stratford-upon-Avon, and she and her husband were thrilled to hear Annie calling our dog Marlowe; I didn't have the heart to tell them that it was Milo, and that he was named not after a sixteenth-century dramatist but after a twenty-first century Tweenie.

Maurice and Margaret lived next door to Annie and were the sweetest old couple you could ever hope to encounter outside a storybook. If it wasn't for the fact that Jane's mum and dad visited us frequently, Maurice and Margaret would have made marvellous surrogate grandparents for our kids.

And then there were Tracey and Dave, a couple in their thirties, who had not always enjoyed the most cordial of relations with the Openshaws. A feud, in fact, is what you might call it, involving fences and hedges, trees and drains, those traditional ingredients in an English suburban feud, even if Docklow was anything but suburbia. We hoped that we would not inherit this uncomfortable relationship and we didn't; we got on well with Tracey and Dave, just as we got on with the Openshaws, although we could understand how the problems had arisen. It was the responsibility of Docklow Grange to maintain the long drive, the drains, the septic tank, the small car park and everything else that belonged to the house but was used communally. In return, the occupants of the cottages paid an annual service charge. Where neighbour A has responsibilities and neighbour B is obliged to hand over money, difficulties inevitably arise. All we could strive to be was fair, and dutiful, and hope that the arrival of our boisterous children did not puncture the serenity of what Annie, with her Birmingham vowels, called 'fearyland'.

To us, if not to our neighbours, the absence of children other than our own in the immediate vicinity was a source of regret. When Jane had her periodic bouts of gloom, such as the one occasioned by the accident with the heavy safe door, the scarcity of other kids always came up. It was certainly a contrast with life down Park Avenue South, where most of Eleanor and Joseph's social life had unfolded on the pavement.

If one day encapsulated this contrast, it was Hallowe'en. In Crouch End, Hallowe'en had been a riot, almost literally. And the kids were so disappointed by the prospect of missing a Crouch End Hallowe'en that Jane, with some misgivings, decided to take them back for it. I stayed in Docklow, where the Openshaws conspicuously failed to turn up at the front door wearing Wicked Witch of the West masks. I did not need to dispense a single fun-sized Snickers bar to a 6-year-old wearing green face paint and a tall pointy hat, let alone the bucketful that we had kept by the front door in London every 31 October. And I can't say I missed it. For some years in Crouch End, Hallowe'en had been more of a trial than a trick or a treat. The only laugh I could remember having was when Eleanor, then five, told my mother, whose hearing was in the process of deserting her, that before she went trick-or-treating she was going to a Hallowe'en party. 'A which party, dear?' said Grandma, turning up her hearing aid. 'Yes,' said Eleanor, excitedly.

So there I was on my own in Docklow, while in Crouch End mobs of kids, including my own, rampaged the streets like eighteenth-century press gangs, the difference being that the press gangs were more decorously behaved. The new trend among the older children, Jane reported the following day, was to hurl eggs at any house not displaying pumpkin lanterns.

The next night, with her and the kids making a weekend of it in London, I went on my own to a curry evening in aid of Docklow church. I had never thought of myself as the sort of chap who attends church socials on his own – or at all, come to that – but then I'd never expected myself to wind up living in the sticks, either.

The curry evening took place at the home of Eddie Crowley, the auctioneer at the harvest auction who'd mistaken the large beetroot for a vast radish, and his wife, Debbie. The Crowleys lived about a dozen fields away, which round here counts as practically cheek-by-jowl. They, too, were incomers, although of much longer standing. They had come from Liverpool, and were typical of the warm, witty, gregarious, big-hearted people in which that most maligned of cities specialises. We had lived in

Docklow Grange for less than a week when Eddie came round to tell us that he was an electrician by trade, and that if ever we needed some emergency electrical work carried out at a time of day or night when it would be difficult to find somebody, we shouldn't hesitate to call him. That was one of the many occasions when I felt faintly inadequate being a writer. What could I say in return? That he should similarly feel free to call me if at 4 a.m. he felt the need to construct a perfectly formed sentence?

The second of the Crowleys' three children, 17-year-old Amy, was our children's much-loved babysitter. Amy's rites of passage became almost as significant to us as they were to her and her family. That's what happens when you live in the country, with a supply of babysitters effectively limited to one. When Amy passed her driving test, we exulted. When she started making plans to go travelling, we mourned. I told her there was no need to see the world, she could just read lots of travel books; I had an almost complete set of *Rough Guides*, which she was welcome to borrow at any time.

Devastated as we and the children would be to lose her babysitting skills, which on one occasion involved the four of them trampolining until 11 p.m., we realised that Amy wouldn't be living in Docklow for ever. The same, we knew, would in due course apply to our own children. Such is the paradox faced by people who leave the city to bring up their family in the country. If they do a good job, their children will probably grow up with the enterprise and ambition to move to the city.

Eddie and Debbie had manifestly done a good job with all three of their kids, as indeed they seemed to make a good job of most things, if not, perhaps, the identification of root vegetables. They certainly made a good job of cooking a vat of lamb biryani in the name of the Church of England, and, better still, sat me next to Trish, an effervescent woman from Bromyard who gently berated me when, well before midnight, I got up to leave, citing some writing that had to be finished. 'But you'll be missing all the excitement,' said Trish. 'What excitement?' I asked.

'Well, it will start with me doing some belly dancing, and end up with car-keys in the middle of the table. You know what we're like in the country. You come without a wife and leave with one.'

I laughed nervously, and checked deep in my pocket for the keys to my shabby Volkswagen Polo. Looking around at the Docklow church elders, whose swinging days on the whole appeared to be behind them, I felt fairly certain that Trish was joking. But I stayed a little while longer, engaging her in an entirely hypothetical conversation about wife-swapping parties. I had always thought it was a suburban phenomenon, but evidently not. 'Oh no,' she said, eyes twinkling. 'In the country there's a sign to show people you're a swinger, and that's by planting pampas grass in your front garden.'

I told her that we had some pampas grass in the garden at Docklow Grange, but it was at the back of the house rather than the front. What might be the significance of that, I wondered. She was just about to tell me when Fran Tandy, the church warden, stood up to call the raffle. Regrettably, I never found out.

The following week I wrote about my pampas grass discovery in my 'Tales of the Country' column, and for several days afterwards was bombarded with e-mails from *Independent* readers, many of them expressing concern about the conspicuous clumps of pampas grass in their own front gardens. One letter was published in the paper, from a reader suggesting that *Kniphofia caulescens*, or red-hot pokers, would surely be a more reliable indication that the residents of a house were, as it were, up for it.

This correspondence was typical of the Great British Public. If I have learnt anything from being a national newspaper columnist, it is that the most frivolous subjects excite the keenest response. In August 2002, I was inundated with letters and e-mails after I wrote about the toilets at Reading station.

It is extraordinary how toilet-related matters move people to pick up not just paper, but a pen, too. I suppose that, although my correspondents recognised that the toilets at Reading station were not a subject of earth-shattering importance, they also realised that if you happened to be changing trains in Reading bursting for the loo, then hardly anything could seem more earth-shatteringly important. And that was the pressing situation in which I found myself one day on the way back to Worcester Shrub Hill, when I was excited to find that the gents loo at Reading station was not only spotlessly clean, but was suffused in a soft blue lighting that would not have disgraced a nightclub. You could have held a twenty-first-birthday party there without any qualms.

Moreover, the cubicle lock worked like a dream, and there was not a single felt-tip willy on the wall. There was also an entry charge of 20p through a little turnstile, which raised interesting civil liberties questions. Should a person without 20p to spend be denied the use of a clean toilet? Whatever, there seemed to be a clear-cut case of cause-and-effect linking the 20p to the cleanliness. As for the subdued blue lighting, my illusions that it had been installed by the Reading station mandarins to create a charming ambience for urinating, took a bit of a knock when I phoned the Great Western Railway head office and was told that the lighting was designed to discourage heroin users, who can't find their veins in such conditions.

All the same, I wrote a paean to the Reading station toilet. I also included an anecdote about the five minutes or so I once spent in a toilet cubicle at Watford Gap services. Eleanor was three months old at the time, and I took her, fast asleep in her car seat, into the cubicle with me. After a few moments she opened her eyes. 'Hello, little sausage,' I cooed. 'Have you woken up?' You'll recall that my propensity for calling my children 'sausage' had led to misunderstandings in a playground in Muswell Hill. So it was at Watford Gap services. I became aware of the man in the adjoining cubicle leaving hurriedly, although I didn't make the connection until later.

You don't need to be George Michael to have a public toilet story, and you don't need to be my brother-in-law Tony to have a corporate toilet story, although he has one of the best. Tony used to have a colleague who intimidated everyone in the firm by flossing his teeth at the same time as having a pee. They were intimidated because a man that good at multitasking was obviously destined to become chief executive. And so he did, in due course.

For about a week after my column, toilet stories rained in. One reader, Mike Arnott, recalled a story his uncle used to tell about arriving at Victoria station on a train with no toilets, and being desperate to go. At Victoria, Uncle Arnott rushed to the gents and dived into a cubicle. But such was his haste that as he dropped his trousers everything fell out his pockets, including a penknife, keys and lots of loose change. He then realised that the adjoining cubicle was occupied, when a frightfully posh voice said, 'Good God, man, what have you been eating?'

Other readers addressed the question I had raised about the 20p charge being a civil liberties issue. Not that it was ever an issue in the land of *liberté*, *egalité* and *fraternité*. I lived in Paris for a year when I was nineteen, and hurdling the little Reading turnstile would have been a sight easier than trying to slip without paying past those fierce old crones who used to sit behind saucers full of 10 franc coins, guarding restaurant toilets in bars on the Champs-Elysées. The patron saint of Parisian toilet attendants was obviously Cerberus, the terrifying fifty-headed dog who guarded the underworld in Greek legend.

But even for an impecunious hotel porter, which I then was, 10 francs for a visit to a proper toilet was preferable to a stand-up job for free. That year I became far more acquainted than I would have liked with that strange squatting arrangement that prevails, or did in 1981, in so many Parisian bars and cafés. In fact, I developed a theory that hours spent in those toilets had given the French fantastic thigh muscles, which was why they were so good at skiing. Because, fundamentally, skiing required the same posture. If in using those toilets I'd imagined that I was wearing skis and sitting on a drag-lift, I might have been better at it.

While my mind is across the Channel, as it were, one more toilet story occurs. I'm on what you might call a toilet roll. When I was about twenty-five, I was invited for Christmas to the Provençal farmhouse of my then-girlfriend's aunt and uncle. The party included the aunt and uncle and their two young daughters, my girlfriend's mother, father and younger sister, my girlfriend and me. I was the only non-family member, which made it all the more appalling that I went down with a dose of diarrhoea worse than any I had had before, or have had since. Feel free to skip the next few paragraphs here, by the way, especially if you're eating.

The layout of the house was such that my girlfriend, her sister and I shared a room off her parents' bedroom, through which we had to pad quietly if, in the dead of night, we needed the loo. But there was nothing dead about this one particular night, when I needed the loo about thirty-seven times. If you've ever tried to pad quietly when you have diarrhoea, you'll know that it verges on the impossible. Worse, the toilet was located about a metre from my girlfriend's parents' bed. Mercifully there was an intervening wall, but it was on the uncomfortably thin side. I knew her folks pretty well by then, but this was a measure of intimacy that all three of us could have done without.

The following morning I felt marginally better, but not confident enough with the state of my fundament to go on the proposed walk. So I stayed in the farmhouse while everyone else went out, and then, lulled into a false sense of security by the slight improvement in my condition, had a disaster. A disaster which sealed the sad demise of a pair of M&S Y-fronts. But how to get rid of them? I couldn't conceal them in my case, certainly couldn't jettison them in an indoor bin, and there were no outdoor bins anywhere to be seen. Nothing in life had prepared me for this predicament.

Eventually, I gingerly dropped them into a Boots polythene bag that I happened to have with me, then ventured outside and found a few small stones. I dropped the stones into the bag, tied it up tightly, and walked over to the edge of a deep thicket. Like one of those South American bolas-throwers, I then whirled the bag round my head a couple of times, before letting it fly into the heart of the deep thicket, never to be found.

By the time everyone returned from the walk, I was back in the house. They were all extremely solicitous but, in any case, by the evening I was pretty much back to normal, able to enjoy food again. After a delicious and convivial dinner, the conversation turned to my girlfriend's Uncle Leon's future plans for the house and grounds. 'Well,' said Uncle Leon, in his magnificently fruity voice, 'the next thing I intend to do is to cut that deep thicket right back.'

Now, there was a reason I got bogged down in toilet-related matters, and here it is. When we took over the cottages from the Openshaws, Mrs O. told us that she made it clear to every incoming guest, or at any rate those of the relevant age and gender, that they should not flush used sanitary towels down the loo. She strongly recommended that we did the same, because the septic tank was easily blocked and the ramifications of a blocked septic tank could be messy, smelly and expensive. She also had a sign up in each cottage exhorting customers to 'please put towels in the bin provided'.

But Jane and I felt that such a sign wasn't quite us. And I was doubly sure that asking women what not to do with their sanitary towels wasn't quite me. It's a subject nine out of ten Englishmen are awkward with, and I, emphatically, was one of those nine. Obviously we did need a sign in the cottages, but we didn't want it to be too po-faced and formal. We had once seen a sign in a holiday property we stayed in ourselves which requested that NOTHING AT ALL be flushed down the toilet. That seemed to be pitching it a bit strong. On the other hand, we didn't want a sign that was too larky. A reader recommended the message put up by her friends in rural France: 'Please do not put anything down this toilet unless you have eaten it first.' I quite liked that. But was it a bit twee?

While we were grappling with this problem, one night I even dreamt about sanitary towels, a dream mixed up with Peter Kay, the comedian. Which must sound bizarre, although there was an explanation. At the beginning of his television career, long before he became the multimillionaire he is now, I got quite friendly with Peter. As the *Mail on Sunday*'s television critic I had written a glowing review of a programme he had made for a slot admirably designed by Channel 4 to showcase new talent. Less admirably the series was transmitted at about 11.55 p.m. on a Tuesday night. But Peter's programme, *The Services*, in which he played many of the staff and customers at a service station on the M61, was utterly brilliant and deserving of a much bigger audience than the few insomniacs it got. I wrote as much, and predicted that this roly-poly young comic from Bolton would become a big star. I wish somebody had offered me shares in him.

Anyway, Peter had the decency to ring me up and thank me for my review, and we arranged to meet for lunch. We had quite a few lunches before his career went into orbit and we lost touch, and they always ended with me practically having an asthma attack from laughing so much. He used to tell me about the holiday jobs he'd had in his teens, one of which was in the box office at the Odeon in Bolton, where he worked alongside two young women in their early twenties called Michelle and Marie.

There was one slightly eccentric regular who had a bit of a soft spot for Marie, but when he arrived one afternoon to watch *Back to the Future*, she was in the ladies' loo changing the roller-towel. 'Where's Marie this afternoon,' said this guy. 'She's in t' toilet changing t' towel,' said Michelle. The man recoiled. 'That's more information than I needed, thank you,' he said, and stomped off. I hope that's even 25 per cent as funny written down as it was to hear Peter telling it.

Not, of course, that it's a subject to joke about. In any case, by November there was hardly anyone staying in the cottages for us to worry about what they might or might not be flushing down the loo. Obviously we knew that it was a seasonal business, but even so, it was frustrating to have them sitting empty, especially as we were still spending the bank's money on our kitchen. The latest project was the floor, being laid by two rather pukka brothers-in-law, Jerry and Stephen of County Tiles in Ludlow. They were great to have around; charming, dedicated, highly efficient, punctual, nice to the dog, and they laughed at my jokes. They were also the first upper-middle-class English people I had ever met who were unfamiliar with London. They had just completed a big job in Islington, and had been loaned a flat on the Holloway Road for the duration. It was, quite literally, an eye-opener.

'There were police cars racing up and down at five in the morning,' said Jerry, incredulously.

'One night we looked out and saw a helicopter chasing some cars down the A1,' added Stephen.

'We couldn't park our car anywhere near the flat,' said Jerry.

'Yes,' said Stephen. 'We had to keep moving it to avoid getting a parking ticket.'

'There were tramps outside our door every single day,' said Jerry, shaking his head.

'We had five hundred pounds' worth of tools stolen,' said Stephen.

'We kept seeing the same guys begging for money,' said Jerry.

'People's faces were so miserable,' said Stephen.

'And the tube was just awful,' said Jerry.

'But we did go to some fantastic restaurants,' said Stephen.

'Oh, yes, we really enjoyed ourselves,' said Jerry, as though anyone could ever have doubted it.

In their guileless double-act, I suppose, lay a neat synopsis of city life. Dirty, busy, polluted, crime-ridden, yet full of pleasures. A world apart from Ludlow, anyway, despite its proud standing as second only to London in the number of Michelin-starred restaurants it could boast.

Jane and I had been keen to visit Ludlow long before we ever imagined that we might end up living a mere twenty-five-minute drive from its manifold charms. We had read great things about its restaurants, above all the Merchant House, run by Shaun Hill and his wife, Anja. We knew it had a medieval castle, that it was surrounded by A. E. Housman's blue remembered hills, and that it was said to be one of the prettiest market towns in England. Why we never got there from London I'm not sure. I suppose the arrival of children put the kibosh on weekend visits to anywhere that wasn't by the sea or near a wildlife park. Had we known that kids can climb the castle ramparts, paddle in the impossibly picturesque River Teme below, and then stuff themselves with cream cakes in the delightful 1950s time capsule that is De Grey's tearoom just at the top of Broad Street on the right as you head up the hill, not that the management need reward me for such a plug with a free vanilla slice next time I go in, we'd have visited much sooner.

However – and this is a big however – people who live in Herefordshire and Shropshire are always waxing lyrical about Ludlow. Which is fair enough, for it is a place that inspires lyricism. But amid all the fanfare over Ludlow, the poor old town of Leominster, twelve miles south, tends to get overlooked. And that's not fair. Leominster has numerous virtues of its own, as members of the Test Card Circle, assembling at the Royal Oak Hotel, will tell anyone who cares to listen. They will also tell you that the girl with her toy clown playing noughts and crosses, in the most famous test card image of all, was called Carol Hersee, and was the daughter of George Hersee, a BBC sound engineer. The Test Card Circle have invited her to their conventions, but she keeps declining. The last they heard of her, she was a costumier on *Miss Saigon*. And the last time that particular test card was transmitted, I can tell you with authority, was a Saturday morning in October 2002, between 4 and 5 a.m. How about that?

6

The Siberian Hamster

In the sixth century, there was a tiny settlement where Leominster is now called Llanleini, a Welsh name meaning 'church in the swampy area'. By the seventh century, the settlement was known by the Anglo-Saxons as Leon minster. This, too, meant 'church in the swampy area'. The two conclusions that local historians have drawn from this, after considerable discussion and hundreds of custard creams, is that the area was a touch on the swampy side, and that there was a church there.

By 1025 there was a nunnery, too, endowed by Leofric, the Earl of Coventry. His wife was Lady Godiva, Britain's first and still most famous streaker. Apparently, the reason Lady Godiva rode her horse naked through the streets of Coventry was to persuade Leofric to reduce his punitive taxes on the townsfolk. He surely would have given in to her demands if he'd realised that her courageous stunt would make it his destiny for at least the next thousand years to be less famous than his wife, and by some distance. In which respect, nothing much has changed. Who can name the partner of Erica Roe, who bared her breasts at Twickenham?

Incidentally, I recently read a newspaper article about the demands made by the Hollywood actress Sharon Stone as she prepared to make *Basic Instinct II*. Apparently, a clause in her contract stated that: 'No nudity, other than as exists in the current approved screenplay, without express written consent in the form of Sharon's full nudity rider, and no use of a body double without express written consent.' It occurred to me that a full nudity rider, whatever exactly that is, should be known as a Lady Godiva.

Anyway, in 1046 a terrible scandal engulfed the nunnery, when Sweyn Godwinson – the younger brother of Harold Godwinson who became King Harold and twenty years later got it in the eye at the Battle of Hastings – took a strong fancy to the abbess, Edgiva. Downright smitten in fact, and not used to being denied, Sweyn abducted her and forced her to become his sexual plaything. Edgiva then managed to contact Max of Clifford, an eleventh-century PR man, and got her own back by dragging Sweyn's name through the *News of the (Known) World*. There was quite a brouhaha, at any rate. And it spelt the end of not just Edgiva's nunnery, but also the village around it. By 1086, when the Domesday Book was compiled, Leominster was no longer considered important enough to merit a mention.

But it wasn't long before Leominster's fortunes changed again, with the decision of King Henry I, in 1123, to build a

Benedictine priory there. Henry I built priories all over the place, in an attempt to expiate the grief he felt at the drowning of his one legitimate son (and quite a few illegitimate ones) in a shipwreck. It didn't work; the poor chap is said never to have smiled again. But it worked for Leominster. The town around the handsome new priory grew and thrived.

It then entered a golden age which lasted quite a few centuries, largely on the back of the lucrative wool trade. There was not just a weekday market but also a Saturday market, the mark of a town that was going places. Such was Leominster's growing prosperity, indeed, that it began to rival that of the nearby cathedral cities of Hereford and Worcester. So in the fourteenth century the worthies of Hereford and Worcester, feeling threatened, got together and successfully petitioned Parliament to ban Leominster's Saturday market. Leominster's halcyon phase more or less ended there, which seems to me a good enough reason now not to patronise the much finer shopping centres of Hereford or Worcester when I can get what I need in Leominster: I like the idea of sustaining a 600-year-old grudge.

But it was really the Industrial Revolution which did for Leominster, as prosperity moved northwards and eastwards. Even by the early seventeenth century it was still a monied place, the townsfolk commissioning the distinguished Marches architect John Abel to build an extravagant market hall, which still stands today, albeit not in its original location.

In a fit of planning madness the Victorian town fathers took down the market hall, but it was bought by Richard Arkwright, a local benefactor and direct descendant of the chap who invented the spinning jenny. To my eternal shame I've never been sure what a spinning jenny is – I often get it mixed up with the lazy susan, but I think that's the revolving plate in the middle of a table and the spinning jenny is something to do with cotton. Or is it the other way round?

Either way, Arkwright sensibly tried to have the market hall erected in the market square but after four years of trying got tired of dealing with self-important petty bureaucrats, who, hard as it might be to believe if you've recently made a planning application to your local council, have never been more self-important than in Victorian times. Instead, Arkwright sited the market hall near the priory, in an area called the grange, which is where, magnificently, it remains.

These days it houses the offices of Leominster Council, which I like to think would have tickled old Arkwright. And should you ever be passing, look for the inscription in gold lettering which reads: 'The just man shall be in everlasting remembrance.' This was a reference by John Abel, the architect, to a Catholic martyr called Roger Cadwallader.

Poor Cadwallader, who came from Stretton Sugwas near Hereford, had trained in a French seminary, and then returned to Herefordshire where he conducted secret masses for closet Catholics. It was the time of the Gunpowder Plot; no time, even in secret, to be a Catholic in England. In 1610 Cadwallader was betrayed and captured. He was meant to be tried in Hereford, but the plague was passing through at the time, so instead he was tried in Leominster, and in 1612, after an impeccably fair trial presided over by a scrupulously impartial judge, was sentenced to be hanged, drawn and quartered. It was a kind of seventeenth-century Hutton Report.

Being hanged, drawn and quartered, you might reasonably think, is about as unlucky as a man can get. But for Cadwallader things got worse. The usual hangman couldn't make it for the big day, so a couple of local stonemasons were engaged instead, and made a terrible hash of the drawing and quartering. Instead of only a moderately prolonged and agonising death, Cadwallader's death was excessively drawn-out and desperately painful. And when his head was finally held up for the crowd to see, instead of the usual cheer there was resounding silence. Partly because they were appalled by what they had witnessed, and partly because a lot of them were themselves secret Catholics. As, indeed, was John Abel. So when he designed the market hall in 1633, he stuck in a reference to brave old Roger Cadwallader.

At the time we arrived to live in Herefordshire we knew nothing of Leominster's colourful history. It was pronounced Lemster, that was about all we knew. But of all the things there were to know about Leominster, that was probably the most useful. To give it the full Leo-minster treatment was to reveal oneself as unequivocally an outsider. In fact, Leominster was actually spelt Lemster until the Ordnance Survey came along in the nineteenth-century and restored its rightful name. The Victorians were used to place names being changed. In a fleeting burst of francophilia, they also changed the name of Hampton Wafer, the next village along from Docklow, to Hampton Wafre. Strange lot, the Victorians.

When I had asked Mr Openshaw what Leominster was like, shortly before we moved in, he said 'Leominster? Oh, it's black and white.' Jane and I nodded solemnly, while wondering what the hell he meant. We knew he couldn't possibly be talking about the town's racial mix, but decided, on balance, that he was probably referring to Leominster's honest, uncomplicated vibe, what you see is what you get, folk who call a spade a spade, that sort of thing.

While there is indeed that kind of vibe about Leominster, he was being more literal than that. Leominster stands at the beginning of the so-called black-and-white trail of villages full of ancient black-and-white timbered houses and pubs. Some are Tudor, but some are much earlier. And the prettiest of those villages, such as Pembridge and Weobley, are more than a match, aesthetically speaking, for even the most chocolate-boxy sweep of the Cotswolds.

Just as Leominster tends to get eclipsed by Ludlow, so the Welsh Marches are eclipsed by the Cotswolds. I really don't know why. I can't understand why there aren't parties of chattering Japanese tourists being disgorged every other hour into the middle of Weobley. Or at the very least, into the middle of Hereford. But I'm glad there aren't. It is not just the Herefordshire scenery that makes it, in my totally unbiased view, England's finest county. It is also that it remains so relatively undiscovered. If this book only sells eleven copies then that will be my consolation, that nobody can blame me for ruining the secret. On the other hand, Herefordshire deserves wider appreciation. Its orchards somehow seem more orchardy, its churches more churchy, its villages more villagey, than anywhere else I know. And its cider, of course, is very much more cidery.

Fortuitously, our first trip into Leominster as Herefordshire residents was the day of the monthly Farmers' Market in Corn Square. The square was bathed in sunshine; farmers' wives, broad of bottom and ruddy of cheek, dispensed organic vegetables and good cheer; all seemed right with the world. And just to intensify my sense of arriving in an England that in many fundamental ways had changed little in 150-odd years, I read that Leominster's stocks had last been used in 1848, here in Corn Square, when a man called Thomas Morgan was publicly ridiculed for being drunk and disorderly. The stocks hadn't been used for a while, so more than 2000 people turned up to cheer, so inconveniencing the traders that they paid Morgan's fine and he was set free. I had a bet with myself that some of the traders now selling me olive ciabatta, that great Herefordshire delicacy, were descendants of those who had paid Thomas Morgan's fine.

In my column I registered my growing admiration for Leominster, only for an acquaintance, who lived locally and read the *Independent*, to tell me wryly that his wife had said, 'It's all very well forming an opinion of Leominster in the summer; just wait until it's November and piddling with rain and the only people he sees walking around are old women holding the hands of their simple fifty-year-old sons.'

I reported this observation in 'Tales of the Country' and within a few days wished I hadn't. It had evolved like a Chinese whisper, becoming a more robust opinion and worse, becoming my opinion. Even two months later, once the children were happily settled at Stamford Heath School, another mum said to Jane, 'You know, Brian shouldn't have written in the paper that Leominster is full of mentally handicapped people.'

Jane was aghast. 'Did you actually read what he wrote?' she asked.

'No,' said the other mum, 'but somebody told me.'

It was undoubtedly true that, by November, Leominster was a less captivating place than it had been four months earlier. But then driving rain and bitter cold does nothing for Padua, either, or Avignon or Bruges. Or Ludlow, come to that. However, it is also true that in the first flush of enthusiasm we had overlooked some of Leominster's deficiencies. It maddened me that many of the shops seemed to close by three on a Saturday afternoon. I drove in one Saturday to buy tomatoes, and not a single tomato could I find, except in Somerfield or Safeway. I don't like buying prepackaged tomatoes in supermarkets. Call me old-fashioned, but I don't like buying tomatoes in shops where I can also have my photographs developed and my trousers dry-cleaned. There had apparently been great consternation among the independent traders when Safeway opened on the edge of town, but they didn't seem to be offering much competition.

Nor could we find a family-friendly café that we liked. In Crouch End there were hundreds. Within seconds of us walking into Pizza Bella on Crouch End Broadway, the waitress was dishing out balloons and crayons and puzzle sheets featuring mazes and word searches. It is true that our children became so familiar with these puzzle sheets that they could find all the words – pizza, bella, pasta and, this being Crouch End, cappuccino – in about twenty-five unchallenging seconds, but at least Jane and I had twenty-five seconds in which to enjoy uninterrupted conversation.

Naturally, we couldn't expect Leominster to have anywhere quite like that. Crouch End, after all, was absolutely stuffed with children. It was like Hamelin before the Pied Piper arrived. A similar enterprise in Leominster would have ended up with the waitresses handing balloons and crayons to customers of all ages, just to reduce the stockpile. But nor did we expect to find a café in Leominster in which there was open antagonism towards children. Yet there was one in the middle of town in which customers with children were 'requested' not to sit at tables in the window, obviously because the proprietor thought King Herod might peer in and decide to get his cheese toastie elsewhere.

In the same café one day, Joseph politely asked if, instead of the advertised full English breakfast of eggs, bacon, mushrooms, tomatoes, sausages, black pudding, potato cakes and essence of kitchen sink, he could just have eggs, sausages and baked beans. The waitress reacted as though he'd asked her to do the splits.

But grudgingly she trudged off to ask the chef if he could oblige. Jane heard his brusque reply. 'If they want that sort of thing there's plenty of other places in town.'

Several months later, as a short aside, I found myself on a press trip to the West Indies. Many people who spend long enough in journalism sooner or later get invited on one or more press trips organised by immensely glamorous and usually rather Sloaney women representing blue-chip travel companies. For quite a few years after it started, the *Independent*, unlike all other newspapers, virtuously declined such offers on its journalists' behalf. The reasoning went that a writer invited on a freebie would have his or her critical faculties clouded by too many complimentary cocktails, and that the reader would therefore be poorly served. As an ethical stance, it was entirely beyond reproach. And to this day the paper's excellent travel supremo, Simon Calder, bills himself as 'the man who pays his way'. But, as I understand it, someone eventually realised that if the travel pages were to feature articles about fabulous, exotic locations, then, happily for those aforementioned journalists, some degree of freebie-taking was unavoidable.

Not being a dedicated travel writer, I hadn't been on many such trips. But this one was a doozy, two days at a swish villa on a promontory in Antigua, followed by two more on a sleek motor-launch in the British Virgin Islands. It wasn't the kind of journalistic assignment that was going to win me the Pulitzer Prize I had fantasised about when I started off in the profession, but when you've got a rum punch in front of you and a view of the sun setting over the Caribbean, a Pulitzer Prize can wait.

Just as I drained my rum punch, my mobile phone rang. It was Jane. She sounded excited. My two fellow journalists and Mel, the (immensely glamorous) PR woman, could not help but overhear my side of the conversation. 'Really?' I said. 'That's fantastic! . . . Brilliant! . . . And have you . . . Oh, wow! . . . Did you? . . . Yes, yes, I can imagine . . . What great news! . . . Yes, I'm fine . . . Just drinking a rum punch looking at an exquisite sunset, but tell me more . . . Really?! . . . Gosh . . . Yeah, I can't wait . . . OK, love to the kids, bye.'

My colleagues looked at me expectantly. Was it a lottery win? Had a close relative been offered a peerage? 'That was my wife,' I told them. 'Apparently, a new café has just opened in Leominster.'

They looked blankly at me. I explained about the whole business of moving out of London, and that, although there were sweet tearooms aplenty in Leominster, and one decidedly hip place called the Blue Note Café which had live music in the evenings, the town had badly lacked somewhere spacious with lots of pizazz and no lace doilies. Until now. Jane had been in the market square that day and had spotted a new café called the Flying Dutchman. It was rigged out in gleaming steel and burnished wood, and the food was just great. It was exactly what Leominster needed. At any rate, it was exactly what we needed. Not because we were café junkies, which might be the impression I am giving here, but because we didn't want to feel entirely severed from our former life. And the Flying Dutchman was the sort of place that would have looked perfectly at home in north London. Even if months passed between visits, it was nice to know it was there.

And yet, the Flying Dutchman notwithstanding, we slowly began to realise that we couldn't apply London values to Leominster. We began to value Leominster for what it was, and stopped resenting it because it wasn't always what we wanted it to be. I think this is an experience common among people who leave big cities and start relying on small towns. They gradually realise that it is they who must adapt to the small town, not the small town to them.

After a while, we began to like the fact that so many of Leominster's shops closed by mid-afternoon on Saturday. It was the shopkeepers' weekend too, after all. Why should they be slaving behind a busy counter when they could be weeding the garden or walking the dog? So we would buy our tomatoes on Saturday morning, or even sometime on a Friday. It wasn't the greatest inconvenience in the world.

Rural England, we began to appreciate, operates on a different time scale to urban England. Never mind British Summer Time and Greenwich Mean Time, there should be British City Time and British Country Time. For one thing, everything in the country happens so much more slowly. I began to formulate a theory not unlike the jet-lag theory, which holds that for every hour's time difference between countries, a day of adjustment is required. Thus, if one flies to Australia where they are ten hours ahead, it will take ten days to adjust. That's the rule as applied in professional sport, anyway. England's Test cricketers, when they head Down Under for an Ashes series, are told that they can expect not to feel themselves until they have been there for ten or eleven days. And you need to feel yourself when you're being bombarded by Australian quick bowlers, if only to make sure that all your bits and pieces are still in place.

A phenomenon not unrelated to jet lag applies when you move from the city to the country. Maybe I should patent it as Viner's Law; holding that for every year you have lived in the city, you can expect a month of disorientation in the country. I think that ratio is about right. On which basis, having lived in London since 1987, I could expect it to take me well over a year to get used to the different pace of life in Herefordshire.

But it is not just a different pace of life, it is also a different interpretation of the day. Herefordshire is England's most agricultural county, and agriculture starts earlier than industry and commerce. That's why towns like Leominster start winding down by mid-afternoon, because ever since the abbess Edgiva tried to fight off randy Sweyn Godwinson and doubtless for some years before that, people have done their chores in the morning. Once you begin to relate that way of life to a thousand years of history, instead of comparing it unfavourably with places where you can buy a book or a doughnut or an electrical device well into the evening, then you're on the way to overcoming your city lag.

But at the end of the day – or round here, at the beginning of the day – ways of life are about people, not places. According to the person we were dealing with, the Herefordshire way of doing things could be either beguiling or, that regrettably underused word, nettlesome. Just after ten o'clock one winter's morning, Jane went into a bakery in the high street in Bromyard, and asked for a white sliced-loaf. 'We've completely sold out of bread,' said the plump young woman behind the counter, cheerfully. 'It's brilliant.'

Jane looked at her bemusedly. 'It's not brilliant for me,' she said.

This was the point at which even the most complacent of shop-assistants might be expected to say, 'No, sorry, you're right.' But not this shop assistant.

'Well, it's brilliant for me,' she said heatedly.

'Well actually it's not,' said Jane, 'because if you'd made a bit more, you'd have sold a bit more.'

They probably could have continued like that for hours, building up to a duel like the one Benny Hill sang about, in which

Ernie the milkman's love rival, Ted the baker, reached for his bun. But instead of biting the dust after being hit in the eye by the concrete-hardened crust of a stale pork pie, which as you will remember was poor Ernie's fate, Jane left and went to another bakery up the road.

I duly wrote about this episode in the *Independent*, venturing the theory that customer service in rural England is often exceptionally good and sometimes exceptionally poor. In cities, I asserted, standards of service tend to fall somewhere between these two extremes. Shop staff are usually polite, usually efficient, but rarely effusive. They don't often put themselves out for customers, largely because there's not enough time. In the remoter provinces there's more time and fewer people. As a rule service is smilier and more personal, which in itself can be frustrating, as you stand behind another customer who is being engaged, by the woman behind the till, in an in-depth conversation about delphiniums or *EastEnders* or her recent holiday in Tenby. But in the sticks, by the same token, I have encountered PhD-level surliness in shops, cafés and even pubs, as opposed to the basic GCSE stuff you get in London.

Gratifyingly, my column about varying standards of service received another load of e-mails, one from a chap who reported that he'd been into a greengrocer's in Bromyard and asked for flat-leaf parsley, to be told that the shop had run out but if he cared to walk along the pavement for twenty yards, then turn left into an alley, turn right at the end of the alley and walk for maybe 100 yards, then he could help himself from the grocer's front garden. In that delightful respect, small-town or country life in England has much less in common with life in London or Birmingham or Manchester than with life in rural France or Spain or Italy.

But let's get back, the eleven miles or so, to Leominster. Although we lived nearly as close to Bromyard, Leominster was where we usually did our shopping, where we took the children to the library, where we registered with a doctor.

Even the experience of visiting the doctor's surgery contrasted markedly with London. At Crouch End Health Centre, our family GP had been Dr Williamson, a woman of irreproachable professionalism and competence, but whose style was most politely described as no-nonsense.

When Eleanor was three, she needed a routine hearing test. At the same time, Jane needed a routine smear test. So she asked Dr Williamson whether she could get both jobs done in the same visit. As far as Eleanor knew, the sole purpose of the visit was to have her hearing tested, but she sat in the corner of the room and didn't bat an eyelid when the doctor invited Jane to lie down on the couch. Eleanor watched with interest as Dr Williamson poked around Jane's insides with a speculum, and then, when the poking was over and Jane was told to get her clothes back on, she asked, in a faintly anxious voice: 'Are my ears all right, Mummy?' That had been the hearing test as far as she was concerned, which struck Jane as uproariously funny. Not Dr Williamson. 'I haven't tested your ears yet, Eleanor,' she said curtly.

I suppose curtness was the best way of dealing with the sometimes barely tolerable demands on a busy London medical centre. If ever we rang to make an appointment for one of the children on, say, a Tuesday, we would be lucky to get an appointment by the end of the week. If we thought the child needed attention fairly urgently, we were advised to take him or her to see the duty doctor, which meant sitting around for up to two hours in a kind of sitcom waiting room, with sniffles and snuffles and snorts on all sides. I always went in the hope of seeing a little boy with his head stuck in a saucepan, but disappointingly never did.

The first time I phoned the surgery in Leominster, to make an appointment for Joseph who was coughing badly during the night, I was asked: 'Would you prefer this morning or this afternoon?' Our doctor was a gently spoken Scotsman in his thirties, Dr Senior, who struck me as just the sort of chap who might have helped Dr Finlay out with his Casebook. He had the same air of professionalism as Dr Williamson but oodles more charm. I don't suppose that's because he worked in Leominster and she in London; it might just as easily have been the other way round. But it certainly seemed as though the National Health Service was functioning more cheerfully and, indeed, more efficiently in the Marches.

On the night in London that Eleanor was born, we were advised not to go into hospital – St Mary's, Paddington – until Jane's contractions were two minutes apart. We did as we were told and Eleanor was born within half-an-hour of us arriving in hospital. Eight hours later Jane was discharged, such was the desperate need for beds. On the same frantic night, one woman gave birth to her baby in a hospital corridor.

Admittedly it was an unusually busy few hours for childbirth at St Mary's. For some reason waters were breaking all over west London that night; it was like living in the Ruhr Valley on the night 617 Squadron came over. But we couldn't help thinking back to that experience when our friend Kate later gave birth to her fourth child, Freya, at Ludlow Community Hospital, staying in for four days and commending the excellent food. Apparently, in the fairly recent past, women with newborn babies had even been encouraged to go out for dinner with their partners on their last night in hospital, while the Ludlow midwives babysat. Had the same facility been available at the Whittington Hospital, Highgate, where Joseph was born, the woman in the bed next to Jane's would have jumped at it. As it was, she couldn't jump anywhere. She was an inmate at Holloway Prison, handcuffed to the bedpost.

Of course, for every aspect of life in Herefordshire that seemed better than it had been in London, there was another that was manifestly worse. Our reliance on the car had become absolute. Our children could not walk to their friends' houses, at least not in less than a week. And it was now early December, and the mice were arriving at our house on full-board package deals, inclusive of Safeway's Belgian truffles on arrival.

Our carpenter, Alan Gwilliam, recommended propping up a milk bottle baited with chocolate. Apparently the little blighters could get in but they couldn't get out. Alan had put one down in his loft, with a bit of chocolate pinched from his young son's Advent calendar. 'Works a treat,' he said.

We considered following Alan's advice, not least because he was just about the most capable man we had ever met. He wasn't rib-achingly funny like Brian the painter-decorator, who had finished painting the kitchen some weeks earlier, filling me with the rare sensation of regret that a decorating job had not carried on for longer than the original assessment. But Alan was worth his weight in MDF, all the same. What he couldn't do with a spirit level and a plank just wasn't worth doing.

Alan was building some benching for the conservatory and while I was away in London for three days one week, Jane said that if I didn't hurry back I might find that she had married him. He certainly had an aura of calm that was reassuring, not to say indispensable, in a house that not only had mice running around like headless chickens, and every possibility of genuine headless chickens if the foxes were as hungry as the mice seemed to be, but also a regiment of electricians traipsing all over the place doing the rewiring. Jane was making so many mugs of tea containing so much sugar that she imagined people from the financial division at Tetley's and Tate & Lyle poring over graphs and trying to work out why sales seemed to have entered such a steep and sudden incline. Why *do* tradesmen take so much sugar with their tea? One of the electricians asked for four-and-a-half spoonfuls, which filled almost half the mug. But Alan, of course, took tea with no sugar. He was easy to cater for. That was another reason she liked him enough to elope with him.

'As long as I can be best man I'll be delighted for you,' I said. When a chap was as capable as Alan, and you had his mobile phone number, it was important to keep him onside.

However, in the end we didn't go down Alan's baited milk-bottle route. Our neighbour Will, the wildlife consultant, lent us two humane traps which we placed in the pantry, and by the next morning both were occupied. It was Will who identified them as yellow-necked mice. He seemed quite excited with his find. And in truth, they were sweet little things, with big black eyes and pointed snouts.

'I don't particularly want them scurrying around the kitchen at night, but I wouldn't mind keeping one as a pet,' I told Will.

He gave me a sympathetic smile. It was the sympathy of one who knows about wildlife matters, addressing one who does not.

'I think it would be a high-maintenance pet,' he said. 'They have very fast metabolisms.'

I must have looked unusually blank, even for me. 'They tend to pee and poo a lot,' he explained.

So instead we set them free at the end of the drive, and continued the exercise for a week, gradually emptying the house of yellow-necked mice, until it dawned on me that we were almost certainly catching the same pair every night. In fact, judging by the amusement in their black eyes, they seemed to regard it as a bit of a lark. I was being had, by the French and Saunders of the yellow-necked mice world.

Sterner measures were called for, so we phoned Leo Pest Control in Leominster, and the next day answered the door to a ruddy-cheeked man of sixty-odd wearing a blue boiler suit. This was the first of many times that we would set eyes on Maurice O'Grady, not merely the guru of pest control, but the Maharishi. We soon came to realise that Maurice exuded wisdom, not to mention witty anecdotal evidence in favour of storing chicken feed in a metal rather than a plastic dustbin.

What Maurice didn't know about pest control you could write with a marker-pen on the back of a stamp. That's what Jane's Auntie Jose, queen of imagery, would have said, anyway. And Maurice would have agreed. Maurice was not short of self-confidence in matters pertaining to mice, rats, moles, flies, woodworm, deathwatch beetle and all other pests, but then his high opinion of his own professional expertise was shared by people all over the county.

Maurice and his van were a familiar sight around Herefordshire, partly because his number plate was L77 RAT. 'It only cost me £280,' he told me with pride, as he stood on the doorstep of Docklow Grange that cold December morning. 'Nobody else wanted it.'

I couldn't help thinking of my old schoolfriend, Andy Coughlan, six-foot-three and built like a brick outbuilding. While studying veterinary science at Liverpool University in the early 1980s, Andy had created an alter ego for himself, whom he called Rodentman. Rodentman was a self-styled superhero who used to patrol the streets of Toxteth doing good deeds, at a time when the streets of Toxteth were not the genteel boulevards they are now. He had furry rat ears and a giant R on his chest, and naturally he wore a pair of Y-fronts over his tights. I'm not making this up, honestly. For months on end Rodentman used to wander the streets helping little old ladies across the road, and giving harassed mums a hand lifting pushchairs up flights of steps. Once, at my university digs hundreds of miles away, during a birthday party Andy had said he couldn't attend, Rodentman clambered in through an upstairs window, saying he'd heard there was a light bulb that needed changing. How we laughed.

What Andy would have given for L77 RAT. More than Maurice would have given for Andy's furry ears, anyway. In Maurice's book, vermin were not to be taken lightly. They were enemies worthy of respect. It wouldn't have surprised me if Maurice had kept a photograph of a common brown rat next to his bed, as Montgomery kept a photograph of Rommel, looking into the eyes of his deadliest foe first thing in the morning and last thing at night.

But that is not to say that Maurice took his job too seriously. No sooner had he crossed the threshold, having known us for all of two minutes, than he was sitting at the kitchen table telling us about the day he drove home, late at night, after a day shooting rabbits and foxes on his wife's family's farm in Wales.

'They'd given me a dead calf to provide meat for my dogs,' he said. 'But I couldn't get him in the boot, look. The only place I could get him was propped up on the front seat, and I had to put the seat belt around him to keep him up.'

You can guess what happened next in this real-life Far Side cartoon. It was well after midnight, and just over the English border Maurice was stopped by the West Mercia police. One of the officers walked round the front of his car with a torch, to check his tax disc, but when the beam of his torch illuminated the calf in the passenger seat, he nearly keeled over in fright. For all anyone knows he's still having counselling to deal with post-traumatic stress disorder.

Tales such as this were to become a regular source of entertainment over the following months, as Maurice single-handedly revived a dying social convention: the pop-in. On the whole, people don't pop in any more. When I was a child, friends and neighbours were forever popping in. Now, the pop-in seems to be a relic of the past. These days, coffee and biscuits with a friend or neighbour is almost always prefaced by a phone call, if not by several phone calls and hieroglyphics in three different-coloured pens on the kitchen calendar.

Even in London, when we lived within walking distance of many of our friends, we didn't get many pop-ins. In the country the lack of spontaneity was easier to understand; it's hard to pop in when the person you're visiting lives at the end of eight miles of narrow lanes, and a further mile of rough track. Especially if you finally pop in to find that she's popped out. But some of my happier mornings at Docklow Grange came to revolve around Maurice popping in. Jane called me down from my office with the welcome news that 'Maurice is here' and I pushed back a deadline an hour or so in favour of sitting round the kitchen table listening to Maurice's latest tales of rat, mole and badger infestation. It was safe to say that *The Wind in the Willows* was not his favourite book; the notion of a rat, a mole and a badger punting insouciantly along a river was Maurice's idea of a pest-control problem that needed tackling urgently. A nightmarish situation. If I'd asked him who wrote it, he'd probably have said Stephen King.

But all that was in the future as we explained our yellow-necked mouse problem. Maurice listened carefully, and casually told us that if you could push a Biro through a gap in the woodwork, then a mouse could get through, too. This was alarming, given that there were gaps in our woodwork through which we could push a bicycle. He put poison down, along with doses of the deliciously named Rodent Deodorant, which he told us would get rid of the whiff of decomposing mice.

But mice were not our only rodent problem. Eleanor had come tearing down the stairs a few days earlier claiming that a furry creature with a long tail had fearlessly eyeballed her while she was sitting on the loo, and that if it had been a mouse, it was an unusually large one. 'I think,' she said with a quavering voice, 'that it may have been a rat.' Remembering my *Fawlty Towers*, I told her that it was probably a Siberian hamster. She didn't seem convinced.

Mercifully, Maurice seemed fairly sure that there were no rats at large in the house. Clearly, Eleanor's visitor *had* been a Siberian hamster. But we had two cellars and there was clear evidence of rats in both of them. With just a smidgen more relish than I would have liked, Maurice showed us a fresh set of ratty footprints.

'I'll look after them for you,' he said. 'But rats are not as easy to poison as mice. They're neophobic, see, which means they hate change. Mice are different. They're very inquisitive, and if they see something that wasn't there the night before, they'll head for it first. They'll try anything once, that's their downfall. Rats are harder to deal with.'

The Montgomery and Rommel analogy came back into my head as we waved Maurice off. This was clearly a battle he was going to enjoy. For us, however, with the Christmas holidays approaching, a rodent problem was the last thing we needed. Anyone with a rambling old house in the country would have told us that rats and mice were more likely to visit than any maiden aunt, but we hadn't yet been living there for six months. Viner's Law held true. We were not ready to shake off our townie sensibilities.

A week later Maurice came back and checked whether the mice had taken the poisoned bait. They had. And some of the rat poison had gone too. But there was another problem we wanted Maurice to deal with: the 800,000 flies. Until the weather had started to get colder, living in Docklow Grange had been like living a couple of miles from a motor-racing circuit staging a never-ending Formula One Grand Prix. There was a constant drone, now loud, now soft, but always there.

Towards the end of October the Grand Prix had finally stopped, obviously won by the fly world's answer to Michael Schumacher. Sorry as we were to see the end of the Indian summer, we decided that the swollen rain clouds gathering over the Black Mountains had silver linings, and that the change in the weather might spell an end to the battalions of flies. I had started to hit the trigger of the fly spray like a man bent on vengeance in a Sam Peckinpah western. The floor and windowsills in my office were littered with dozens of fly corpses, although flies zapped with fly spray do not expire quietly, but whizz round and round like souped-up break dancers. The noise was no longer Formula One, more like motocross.

Moreover, despite wiping out thousands of the buggers, it wasn't long before twice as many of them revved back into action. The notion that flies were a summer and autumn phe-nomenon was, we realised, misplaced. Maurice told us that they were cluster flies, which lay eggs in the soil and live on worms, rather than blowflies, which live off the carcasses of dead animals. Which by the sound of it was something to be grateful for. He said he would smoke them out, but as in the case of the rats, he had a predator's respect for his prey. He fixed me with a look that suggested I was unaware of the enemy's fire power. 'They know this property much better than you do,' he said, ominously.

So did Mr Openshaw. Five months in Docklow Grange had done little to help us understand the mysterious workings of the house: why there was a deep well under the kitchen floor, how there came to be four fireplaces yet only three chimneys, why there was a wall, with a window in it, dividing the landing in half. But Mr Openshaw had lived in the house for over twenty years and, better still, was an architect. He seemed more than happy to answer my recurrent questions about the Grange's arcane plumbing system; his happiness, perhaps, something to do with the fact that he and Mrs O. were now living not 300 yards away in a modern barn conversion, enjoying plumbing devoid of little eccentricities, such as occasional bursts of yellowy-brown water.

Still, if the internal organs of the house remained a mystery despite Mr Openshaw's efforts to unravel them for us, we were at least getting to know more about its history. In mid-December we took a booking for Manor Cottage from Mr and Mrs Goodfellow, an elderly couple from Sutton Coldfield. They had seen our advert in *Choice* magazine and Mrs Goodfellow phoned to ask if they could come for a long weekend.

'Is this the same Docklow Grange that has a big Victorian conservatory,' she asked. She sounded excited. I said it was. 'In that case,' she said, 'my late mother was the nanny there in the 1920s. She left in 1931 to get married, and I was taken there myself in about 1935, to meet her old employers. I'll look forward to seeing it again. And I'll bring some photographs.'

Mrs Goodfellow turned out to be a lovely old dear, who grew quite emotional when we showed her the conservatory. 'It's funny,' she said, wiping away a tear. 'It's big but it's nothing like as big as I remembered it, I suppose because I was a tiny child at the time.'

We showed Mrs Goodfellow all round the house, including the old servants' quarters. As the nanny, and therefore neither quite below-stairs nor quite part of the family, her mother had lived in the servants' quarters yet had had servants of her own. It was fascinating stuff, real social history, although our interest in what she had to tell us seemed to leave her husband somewhat disgruntled. When we quizzed her about her childhood memories of Docklow Grange, and her mother's nannying experiences, he kept butting in with memories of his own.

'I must have been three or four when I was brought here,' said Mrs Goodfellow. 'And I can remember very clearly that there was an old grandmother who sat on a wicker chair in the conservatory and used to get visiting children to walk backwards until they fell in the pond. She did it to me, even though my mother was there, and roared with laughter.'

Jane and I were agog. 'I grew up in Leicestershire myself,' added Mr Goodfellow. 'Now, I can remember the milk being delivered by pony and trap. Mr Devlin, the milkman's name was. Irish fellow. Huge nose. Had twin daughters about my age, called Mary and Joan.'

And so it went on, with Mrs Goodfellow titillating us with snatches of information about our house and the people who lived there, and Mr Goodfellow weighing in with arbitrary details of his own childhood. From the expression on her face, Mrs Goodfellow was at least as exasperated as we were, but we all listened politely. And at least he wasn't able to whip out his own photographs when she showed us hers.

They were curling, faded snapshots of a very different era and yet a very familiar house. In one of them, we could see the old stone font in the middle of the lawn. We knew it had been carted over from the church – presumably when the elders decided to splash out, as it were, on a new one. And now we at least knew that the font predated 1928, the date of the photograph. Another photo showed Mrs Goodfellow's mother and a couple of maids larking around in finery 'borrowed' from the lady of the house while she was in Scotland on a shooting-party. Our odd-jobman, Ted, was convinced that Docklow Grange had spirits. At least we could tell him they were high ones. And if that didn't interest him, then we could tell him that, as a 7-year-old, Mr Goodfellow had broken his arm falling out of a tree on a farm just outside Melton Mowbray.

We were sorry to see Mrs Goodfellow leave. She was a lovely woman and we felt sure we could have dredged her memory further. But now we had other fish to fry, and turkeys to roast. It would be Christmas in a week's time, and the cottages would all be full again.

We also had pheasants to casserole. Robert Hanson, the affable chairman of the parish council, had turned up one frosty morning with three brace of them, shot the day before. When we lived in London we had scoffed at our friend Biddy, who had moved to Somerset and was forever interrupting her phone calls saying things like 'Must dash, my neighbour from down the lane has just dropped by with some freshly picked doodleberries' or 'Have to go, Mrs Puddleduck is here with some nettle, borage and hedge-clippings soup.' It sounded to us, bitter and twisted urbanites that we were, as though she was trying too hard to make things sound idyllic. But living in the country, we had found, really could be like that. Frequent was the day when we would turn up at the front door to find some damsons from this neighbour, or some parsnips from that one. Likewise Rob Hanson's pheasants.

The weekend before Christmas, Jane's old university friend Cathy came to stay, with her husband, Pete, and their boys Jack, Sam and Ben. Just as we sat down with them to eat Rob's casseroled pheasants, there was a distant sound like a chorus of angels. Had I died and gone to heaven? It was a not-impossible scenario, given those little gullet-sized bones you get in pheasant casseroles. But no, it was carol singers, at least twenty of them, which represented a sizeable percentage of the population of downtown Docklow. They had probably been outside Eddie and Debbie's house, halfway through 'God Rest Ye Merry Gentlemen', before they realised that Eddie and Debbie were at the back, singing.

It was a joy to open the door to row upon row – two and a half rows, anyway – of shining faces, belting out 'Once in Royal David's City'. I couldn't remember the last time we'd been visited by carol singers. In London, for some reason, the best we'd had was a couple of sullen youths who probably wished that they were having it away in a manger, rather than singing about one. Yet I thought back to Hallowe'en, and reflected on how quiet that had been in Docklow, by contrast with the hullabaloo in Crouch End.

What significance was there in this? I supposed it meant that old English traditions were faring better in the countryside than in the city, where they were being supplanted, certainly in the case of trick-or-bloody-treating, by Americana. But such suppositions led me towards dodgy territory, the kind of territory where I might find myself rubbing shoulders with the BNP. They, and their revolting freesheet *The Countrysider*, which I'd picked up at the Liberty and Livelihood march, claimed that Englishness was more alive in the countryside as a result of 'white flight' from the cities. They would have seized on our twenty-odd carol singers as evidence of Englishness thriving in the sticks. But what was Englishness, exactly? And did it diminish that Englishness to live among a mix of faiths and cultures? Hardly. So here in the countryside we were richer in one sense, I concluded, yet poorer in another, all of which heavy-duty philosophising lasted the exact duration of 'Silent Night'.

We encouraged the carol singers to take their charity buckets to our three cottages, which by now were fully occupied. We could have filled each of them twenty times over for Christmas and New Year, which was frustrating, because apart from the Goodfellows' stay they had been empty since October half-term.

Another *Choice* reader had phoned up expressing interest in a three-day break in Manor Cottage at the beginning of December, however. First of all she asked for a description of the cottage and the grounds. 'Oh yes, that sounds perfect,' she said, when I filled her in. 'And how far is it from Birmingham?'

'About an hour's drive,' I said.

'Oh, yes, that's ideal,' she said.

'And with a three-day break in low season we are offering a complimentary dinner for two,' I added.

'Oh, reeaaally,' she said. 'What sort of dinners do you cook?'

'Oh, beef or venison casseroles, or braised chicken, followed by apple or rhubarb crumble, or sticky toffee pudding, that sort of thing.'

'That sounds absolutely smashing,' she said. 'How much would it be to rent your lovely cottage for three nights?'

'Manor Cottage, three-night break, low season, that will be one hundred and fifty pounds,' I said, checking the tariff.

'Mmmm,' she said. 'No thank you very much.' Click.

I didn't know whether she thought £150 too steep, or even too cheap. If five months in the cottage rental business had taught me anything, it was that, as Thora Hird once said in the under-rated sitcom *In Loving Memory*, there's nowt so queer as girt folk up a snickert. I was also reminded of an exchange I'd once had at a car-boot sale in London, a fund-raising event for St Mary's School. I was selling a multicoloured velvet cushion and it caught the eye of a woman in a flowery smock, something of an ageing hippy, who admired it vociferously.

'Now that,' she said loudly, 'is gorgeous. Gorgeous! Those colours are beautiful. Jenny, come and look at this cushion.'

Jenny came over. 'Gorgeous,' she agreed.

'Wouldn't those colours look absolutely divine in my sitting room.'

'Divine,' concurred Jenny.

'And it's velvet, too,' said the woman in the smock. 'Feel it, Jenny. Isn't it soft?'

'Gorgeously soft,' said Jenny.

The woman turned to me. 'How much do you want for it?' she asked. Well, it was by now ten to three. The sale was supposed to finish at three. I was ready to go home. 'That'll be 10p,' I said. The woman looked at the cushion again. 'Naah,' she said, and walked away.

Of course, it was one thing having a cushion rejected in a car-boot sale; losing a potential paying guest was altogether different. I found an empathy for all those proprietors of restaurants on Greek waterfronts who stand outside their establishments des-perately trying to tempt the punters in. It was all I could do not to stand on the A44 saying 'Very good stifado' and 'You like octopus? How about red mullet?'

At any rate, we needed to rethink our marketing strategy. We renewed the idea of launching a 'celebration package', which would entail the same extended party renting all three cottages for two nights, and coming into our house on one of the nights for a slap-up four-course dinner. Especially now that she had mastered the Aga, Jane could easily cook four excellent courses for ten or twelve people. And I looked forward to a spot of maître d'ing, calling on the experience I had gained as a waiter at Roundtrees Restaurant in Southport when I was seventeen. I would even be able to emulate the Roundtrees maître d', Emile, by patting the cook's bottom every now and then. With the pertinent difference that the cook at Roundtrees whose bottom Emile liked to pat was a hairy Corsican called George.

I don't how Emile got his exotic name, as he came from a lot closer to Ormskirk than the Auvergne. He was camper than Larry Grayson and, to the tremendous amusement of the gentlefolk of Southport, had a habit of crying 'Ooh, I'm having a hot flush' as he scurried through the restaurant delivering meals and taking orders. He had also taught me how to carry five plates at a time, although I realised later – too late, some might say – that the cocked little finger and the mincing walk were not strictly necessary. Whatever, I felt that I was equipped with the essential maître d'ing arts if our celebration idea came off.

Then there was the recitals idea which I had broached with Vanessa Redgrave. I still had her e-mail address, although every time I read about her she was on stage in New York or filming in Romania. I didn't think she'd quite have time to revisit Bromyard and, besides, she would have clean forgotten who I was.

Never mind. We could come back to that. For now we busied ourselves with preparing for Christmas. Docklow Grange was the perfect house for Christmas, with its ivy-clad exterior and open fireplaces and chimneys comfortably big enough to accommodate Santa Claus. Not to mention Ken Dodd. With working chimneys we needed a chimney sweep and there was one in the local *Yellow Pages* called Ken Dodd. We had an American friend staying with us when Ken came to sweep the chimneys and he was visibly disappointed; he'd expected an English chimney sweep to be twelve years old and wearing a battered top hat. Nor, of course, did he appreciate the significance of the name Ken Dodd. But I thought it was about the most perfect name imaginable for a chimney sweep – who, after all, carries a tickling stick of sorts – at least until my friend Mary Rose told me that hers was called Mr Bristley.

Happily, the cottages were all booked for the festive period. A vicar and his family had taken Yewtree for Christmas, which seemed a little strange. A vicar going on holiday at Christmas was like Tim Henman spending Wimbledon fortnight on the Costa Brava. But that was no business of ours.

In Manor Cottage we had an elderly couple from nearby Worcester. Bless them, they wanted to get away from home but couldn't face a long journey, so they chose somewhere half an hour's drive away. They had asked if we would supply them with lunch on Christmas Day. Jane, who already had nine to feed – the five of us plus her sister and family – gently tried to put them off, by explaining that lunch wouldn't be ready until four o'clock, and that for three courses it would cost £20 per head. 'That's very reasonable,' they said. 'And four o'clock will be perfect.'

So at five to four on Christmas Day my sister-in-law Jackie and I, half-cut after several glasses of champagne, loaded a tray with two piled platefuls of Christmas lunch and strode, with the studied purposefulness of the half-cut, towards Manor Cottage. Just before we got there we realised that we had left the gravy behind. Giggling helplessly, we turned back, crying 'Gravy!' This was not a catering operation of which Gordon Ramsay would have approved, but if the spirit of Michelin was missing, at least we could offer boundless spirit of the festive variety. Not that Mr and Mrs Beetham especially needed our help. When finally we delivered the tray, they were sitting on the sofa wearing paper hats and holding hands. They had a blazing fire going in the wood-burning stove. I almost asked if I could join them.

Not for the first time, I wondered if I had missed my vocation. Satisfying as it was to think of people reading my newspaper and magazine articles and perhaps even enjoying them, it gave me even more satisfaction to see contented guests. Not long after we had moved in, I happened to be passing a Homebase store, and on a whim bought a wrought-iron table and chairs to stick outside Manor Cottage, which otherwise had no garden. A few days later the people staying in Manor Cottage were sitting at my table, bathed in early-morning sunshine, drinking coffee and eating toast made with the bread that we had left for them in their welcome hamper. It sounds absurd, I know, but that spectacle gave me more pleasure than almost anything else I had done professionally. Especially as I had converted the chairs and table myself from fiendish flat-pack form, and they showed no imminent signs of collapsing.

Two days before Christmas, however, an even more impressive feat of tabular construction had taken place. Since my early teens I had longed for my own snooker table. My schoolfriend Bill Birtles had had a half-sized one, and among the fondest memories of my teenage years was of long weekday afternoons at Bill's house, playing snooker instead of revising for my O-Levels. The result of this was a very ordinary set of O-Level results, but an enduring ability to exert sidespin on the cue ball, and, while I wouldn't want to share this observation with my children as they head towards their teens, I've never been given much reason to believe that I got my priorities wrong.

Until we moved to Docklow I had never lived anywhere remotely big enough for even a half-sized snooker table. But the grange had a huge, rather gloomy room about the size of a small village hall, which the Openshaws had used as their dining room. When I casually mentioned to Mr Openshaw that I was thinking of putting a dining table in their old sitting room, and a snooker table in their dining room, he said, 'Well, it's your house now.' But his disapproval was plain enough. If I'd suggested having the 1850s exterior stone-cladded, and perhaps faux-Victorian street-lamps all the way up the drive, he could not have made it plainer.

More problematically, Jane disapproved too. She was quite properly worried that we couldn't afford it, but also, although she was not normally a snob, she thought that a snooker table was 'very *Footballers' Wives*'. This latter concern was not exactly allayed by a man called Andy Williams, who had been selling and fitting snooker tables since 1963. Naturally, as soon as I met Andy I made a joke about him not being the other Andy Williams, who had enjoyed a 1973 hit with 'Solitaire'. I couldn't imagine anyone having had the wit to say anything like that to him before, yet he responded as though it was an unoriginal observation, which seemed strange. I had found him by phoning a snooker-loving mate, Clive, who lived not far away in Warwickshire and had recommended Andy's shop, A&D Billiards, in Birmingham.

Andy, it transpired, had fitted snooker tables in the past for Gary Lineker, footballer, Mark Lawrenson, footballer, and Jasper Carrott, comedian. This information did nothing to dispel Jane's '*Footballers' Wives*' preconception of a snooker room. 'At least Jasper Carrott's not a footballer,' I said weakly. Moreover, the

Linekers, I pointed out, were a pretty classy couple. Jane agreed that they were, and conceded that there was no other obvious permanent use for the room, which the children had been using as a skateboarding park for the last five months. 'But if you're going to buy a snooker table I don't want one of those nasty light things with funny fringes hanging over it,' she said. I agreed to find some other form of lighting.

So off I went to A&D Billiards. The shop was in Bournville, home of Cadbury's, which seemed apt, because like Charlie Bucket when he finally got into Willie Wonka's chocolate factory, I wandered around Andy's workshops for an hour in a state of awestruck happiness.

Did I want a newer table, its cloth laid on Italian slate, or an older one on Welsh slate? Fully reconditioned or part reconditioned? Turned legs or square legs? Oak or mahogany? West of England cloth or Hainsworth cloth? Every time I made a decision, with the help of Andy's expert advice, there was another one to make. It reminded me of that *Two Ronnies* sketch in which one of them ordered a glass of milk in a café, and was offered more and more choices until it came down to Daisy or Mildred, and then to which of Daisy's teats.

Finally, I chose a handsome table made in 1910 by the highly reputable company of Burroughs and Watts. It had turned mahogany legs, which struck me as being at least as beautiful as the legs of Nicole Kidman or Cameron Diaz, and Andy's price seemed reasonable. The bank would pay, and the children would not have to go without new winter coats.

I shook hands on the deal with Andy, paid him a deposit, and made my way back to Bournville station, as giddily excited as a child on Christmas Eve. It had been an ambition since I was fifteen to own my own snooker table. At university I had played in the student union with my friend Dom – the man who would later form a fierce passion for Agas – just about every lunch time. But I hadn't played regularly since I graduated (with merely a 2:1 in Modern History, but a first in getting the cue ball safely back to baulk). If ever I fancied a frame or two when we lived in London, I had to venture along to a dodgy snooker hall in Finsbury Park where you paid your entrance money to a Desperate Dan looka-like behind reinforced glass. Hilda, I think her name was.

The table was installed a week later by Andy and two of his assistants. It took the three of them more than two hours, but by then I'd already waited more than twenty-five years. All I needed now was somebody to have a regular game with. Jacob, who showed the greatest interest in daddy's new toy, could barely see over the top of the table. I wondered whether to invite Georgie and Owen, and some of the other farm hands from the King's Head, who were still unhappy about Roger and Jean's decision to get rid of the pool table. But that might have seemed like a bla-tant attempt to win their friendship and, besides, I didn't want to come over all lord-of-the-manor.

Over Christmas and New Year there would be no difficulty in finding snooker partners; we had many of our old friends from Crouch End coming up for New Year's Eve. They were people, we knew, who would be precious friends at least until we all had our bus passes. But at the same time we couldn't keep looking in life's rear-view mirror. We had entered 2002 as Londoners. We were entering 2003 as country folk. And by 2004 we hoped that we would have put down serious roots in Herefordshire with or without a bag of ericaceous compost – and I say that because I don't want you to think that I have lived all this time in the country without getting to know a thing or two about gardening.

7

Looking for Ingrid Bergman

I started the New Year with my usual set of resolutions, which by the second week in January had, as usual, fallen by the wayside. Except one. I had resolved to take our golden retriever Milo to dog-obedience classes. Not because he was especially disobedient, in fact for a seven-month-old puppy he was remarkably biddable, but there were times when he would go tanking after the herds of deer that roamed Mortimer Forest near Ludlow, and refuse to come to heel.

He also had that unfortunate doggie habit of trying to hump people's legs, which was particularly untimely in the case of the woman from the Heart of England Tourist Board, who came to decide how many stars our cottages merited. She gave us three and told us they would be secured as soon as we could provide a toast rack for each cottage, a butter dish, a torch, a headboard for every bed, and enough cutlery to set the table for a three-course meal without necessitating the long twenty-five-inch trudge back to the cutlery drawer. She omitted to add that it would probably improve the quality of our guests' stay if our dog didn't try to shag them. But we were more or less aware of that already.

Just to dwell for a moment longer on the requirements of the Heart of England Tourist Board. We had chucked out some rather nasty headboards in dark-brown velour which had been in the cottages when we took them over. We had then had all the bedrooms painted and bought some jolly white-and-blue bed linen. Yet we would have been better off, in terms of star ratings, had we kept the brown velour headboards. Does that seem odd to you? It does to me. Not that I begrudge these people their clip-boards and checklists. They do a fine, worthwhile job, and don't deserve to be assaulted by randy golden retrievers.

It was on a damp Monday night in January that I went with Milo to the West Mercian Dog Training Class at Leominster Community Hall. On the way, my mobile phone rang. It was my old friend Pete, the guy who'd unwittingly put me off moving to Cheshire by singing the praises of the marvellous retail parks that were springing up there. I hadn't spoken to Pete since we'd moved to Docklow. 'Whereabouts are you?' he asked. 'On my way to a dog-obedience class,' I said. 'Oh,' he said. A pause. 'Have you got a dog?'

It struck me that it would have been humiliating turning up to dog-obedience classes without a dog. It was humiliating enough turning up with one, being commanded to trot round and round in anticlockwise and then clockwise circles.

There were nine other owners there, with a range of dogs and a range of behavioural problems. Milo, I soon realised, was the class goody-goody. Whereas Archie, half terrier, half juvenile delinquent, was the class tearaway.

Our teacher was Stuart Brace, a barrel-chested former dog-handler with the West Mercia Constabulary. Latterly he had worked in drug detection and was the sort of man who would have had Fluffy, the savage beast in *Harry Potter and the Philosopher's Stone*, sitting up and begging for a Bonio. He was a no-nonsense guy with a no-nonsense moustache. And Archie, he told us, was a thoroughly bad lot. We were not to let our dogs go head to head with Archie. Archie had had a terrible start in life, although he would be all right in the end. He just needed to be taught how to socialise with other animals.

Stuart was clearly a tough cookie, although I sensed that he had a bark worse than his bite. 'Aaaaaiieee!' cried Archie's owner, a short, pale man with wispy red hair. 'Archie bit me again!' Archie evidently had a bite worse than his bark.

When Archie's owner pulled up his trouser leg to inspect his latest wound, Stuart could not resist poking fun. He clearly thought that Archie's owner was making an unnecessary fuss. 'Shall we all bare our left legs?' he said, rolling up his trousers. Archie's timid owner looked him straight in the moustache. 'Why? It's not a masonic lodge meeting,' he said bravely. I applauded, albeit inwardly. He was, fleetingly, the Chihuahua that Roared.

Dog-training classes in Leominster: all human life was there. As well as all canine life, obviously. Milo and I never went again (another New Year's resolution up in smoke) but I learnt enough in that two hours at least to curb his less appealing enthusiasms, if not get rid of them altogether. As for Milo, he had a ball that night. Mercifully it wasn't Archie's.

It also occurred to me – as Milo and I trotted round in yet another circle, hard on the heels of the comely owner of Tally, a Staffordshire bull terrier – that for anyone single the classes would provide an excellent opportunity to meet a compatible spirit. All you needed was a dog, although you could always invent one, like the character in Nick Hornby's novel *About a Boy*, who pretended to have a son so that he could meet some available young mums at a single parents' group.

You could say that you'd left your boxer puppy at home because he wasn't yet ready to be introduced into doggie society, and that you'd just come along to pick up tips. You'd have a hot date in no time. In my bachelor days I would definitely have been interested in becoming further acquainted with Tally's owner. We had already established something of a bond as a result of our dogs getting to know one another, and I should think that the leap to a fulfilling sexual relationship between two humans is that little bit shorter once their dogs have energetically sniffed each other's bottoms. Just think of Roger and Anita in *A Hundred and One Dalmations*.

And while you're doing that, let me bring up the TV gardener Monty Don, or more accurately his lovely wife, Sarah, to whom the subject of bottom-sniffing inexorably leads.

I'd better explain. Soon after we moved to Docklow, somebody mentioned that Monty Don lived nearby. Although I knew next to nothing about gardening, I had read and enjoyed his column in the *Observer*, so I got his number from a mutual friend and phoned to introduce myself. He in turn, as it happened, had read my column in the *Independent*. So he knew who I was. 'Come over for a cup of tea,' he said.

In terms of *The Good Life*, if Jane and I were Margo and Jerry aspiring to be Tom and Barbara, Monty and Sarah made Tom and Barbara look like Margo and Jerry. They had built their home from medieval remains, and created a remarkable garden out of featureless fields. There seemed to be no vegetable they didn't grow. They even grew ten different types of chicory, for heaven's sake, which to a chap who had never grown so much as a tomato under his own steam (which might have been the problem: too much steam) was pretty damn awe-inspiring.

After Monty had shown me the garden, Sarah made tea. She had baked a cake made with their own eggs and their own raspberries, and if she had told me that the sugar came from their own organic sugar cane and had been refined by them using a pestle and mortar they had made themselves with some Roman marble they had excavated, plus an old sieve and a ball of homemade twine, I shouldn't have been in the least surprised. All this, good looks, obvious mutual devotion, three healthy kids and a healthy income, too. 'Some people have it all,' I thought, admiringly. Sarah even had an enviable way with words. 'We must get together again,' she said, as I reluctantly left with half of the cake remaining. 'Now that we've sniffed each other's bottoms.'

On the way home I considered what a perfect metaphor this was for an initially tentative encounter between human beings. And what a perfect life they seemed to have. But as I got to know them a little better – with the bottom-sniffing behind us, so to speak – I found that things had not always been so splendiferously rosy in their garden. In the 1980s they had run a successful costume jewellery company in London, but had overextended their borrowings and gone bankrupt. And the house they had bought in Herefordshire, which was to have been the family home, was repossessed by the bank.

As a consequence Monty had had a nervous breakdown. It seemed hard to believe of this immensely capable man, so urbane and natural in front of a television camera. And yet he had been unable to work for more than a year, and was reduced to maintaining the graveyard of a church in Leominster. As the old joke goes, that was one way of landing a job with 500 people under him, but, of course, it was no joke. That he and Sarah emerged from all that as contented, well balanced and successful as they now seemed, and with ten different types of chicory to pick as well, testified to the strength of the human spirit. Their human spirit, anyway. It also proved that nobody's life ever progresses as smoothly as it might appear from the outside. It is often said that envy is a destructive emotion. Worse than that, it is invariably misplaced.

The Dons' story encapsulated another truth about our move to the countryside. All that fretting about whether we would find people like us had been a waste of good fretting time. We were actually befriending people who weren't like us, which was much more life-enhancing.

This was never truer than in the case of the Snells. As a keen fan of *The Archers*, Jane had been tickled to be introduced to a Mrs Snell at the Docklow church fete, but Shelagh Snell of Docklow proved to be nothing like Linda Snell of Ambridge. Shelagh was a gregarious, infinitely kind-hearted woman pushing seventy, from my own old stamping ground of Merseyside. Her husband, Jim, a retired architect, was a sweetheart.

They were *Independent* readers, too, card-carrying liberals, a breed we had expected to be hard to find in the country. In London, the liberal middle classes fall broadly into three categories regarding the country. There are those who truly yearn to sell up and move to a thatched idyll; those who would quite like to but don't either because of work commitments or because they can't quite bring themselves to give up the benefits of city life; and there are those who wouldn't touch the country with a bargepole. Indeed, wouldn't touch a bargepole. But what many of these people have in common is the conviction that in the country, minds get narrower by roughly one neuro-watt – or however one measures breadth of mind – per mile beyond the M25. The word 'parochial' is not their only euphemism for narrow-mindedness. They have another: Middle England.

Well, here we were in the middle of Middle England and the Snells were about to introduce us to some of the most broad-minded people we had ever met. Not that we anticipated it on the Friday in January that we went to have lunch with them. They wanted us to meet some of their best friends and contemporaries, and much as we liked Shelagh and Jim, we went along thinking that lunch with a bunch of septuagenarians was a far and poignant cry from the lively social life we had enjoyed in Crouch End.

The condescension and stark, stupid naivety behind this notion became clear in no time. The Snells' friends, John, John and Nancy, were captivating company; they made us feel dull by comparison. In fact they helped us to realise that our topics of conversation at N8 gatherings had perhaps been on the limited side – football, secondary schooling and vasectomies predominating. At the Snells, apart from anything else, it was nice to have a vasectomy-free meal.

I don't suppose John and John had ever given much thought to the snip. They were a couple, and had been for well over thirty years. The older John was an ordained minister in the Church of England, and a raconteur at least as fine as the late Peter Ustinov. His career serving the Almighty, and his deftness with an anecdote, was a happy combination, generating a series of stories that remain among the funniest I have ever heard. I have often thought that the producer or host of a television talk show should be brave enough occasionally to break with convention, and feature not a celebrity but an ordinary person who has great stories to tell and tells them superbly. Would that not make better telly than a soap star talking about her rebellious teen years in Ramsgate? A celebrity or two could be invited on the same show, just to secure the viewing figures. But John would have gone down a storm on *Parkinson*.

Befriending the Snells, and the Johns and Nancy, and for that matter Sarah and Monty Don, illustrated another truth about moving to the countryside. Or moving anywhere, I suppose. When you have a shared history with people, as we did with the Crouch End mob, and even more so with our school and university friends, you rarely get to know much about them beyond that shared history. You tend to talk about things you have done together, or of people you know in common, rather than of anything deeper in the past, or anything particularly meaningful about the present.

There is comfort in that shared history, of course. On 6 January 2003, a week before lunch at the Snells, 4-year-old Jacob, our baby, went to school for the first time. Previously he had been at a pre-school nursery in Stamford Heath, but now he was going to school proper, with a little red uniform, and for Jane, in particular, it was an emotional moment. Her new friends among the other Stamford Heath mums understood those emotions, but the people she wanted around her that morning were those who had known little Jakey all his life: the Crouch Enders Kim, Ali, Rebecca, Jacky. At that moment, more than any other moment since we had driven away, she missed north London terribly.

But as I say, a shared history could be inhibiting. When you get to know people long after the really significant events in your life have taken place, such as marriage and having kids, they tell you all about themselves in a rush. Thus it was with the Johns, of whom we became deeply fond very quickly. And what a lot there was to tell. In 1966, John senior had been vicar of a church in Amblecote near Stourbridge, a job which came with a lovely house attached. John – young, attractive, still single, charismatic, and with excellent living quarters – was highly eligible. He was also, of course, gay. But that was entirely beyond the ken of the man from the diocesan magazine who came to interview him. 'I don't understand, Father, why you aren't married,' he said. 'I'm sure you're looking out for a wife. Do tell me what you look for in a prospective wife.'

John smiled, and made no attempt to dodge the question. 'I would want someone who liked dogs and looked like Ingrid Bergman,' he said.

It was an innocuous enough remark, but from the diocesan magazine it was picked up by the local newspaper, then by several national newspapers, and then, indeed, by the international press. 'English Vicar Seeks Wife' was the headline in the *Toronto Star*. 'In the leafy English hamlet of Amblecote,' began the story in the *New York Times*, causing great mirth in Amblecote, which was one of the centres of the Midlands glass-making industry. In the *Sunday Express*, a Giles cartoon featured a vicar's housekeeper telling him that Ingrid Bergman was on the phone. For three or four days, John was world-famous.

Our lunches with the Johns, and the Snells, and Nancy – a recently widowed bluestocking in her mid-seventies, with an irresistible twinkle and a zest for life, despite losing her beloved Donald not long before we met, that we had rarely seen in people half her age – became semi-regular occasions. With a surprising stolidity for so unstolid a group, we called ourselves the Friday

197

luncheon club, and took it in turns to host lunch every couple of months. The highlight of most luncheon club meetings was an anecdote from the older John, which the younger John had doubtless heard several hundred times before, although being without a shadow of a doubt the nicest, kindest man in the world, he generally responded as though he was hearing it afresh.

One of my favourites among John's many stories concerned an incident that he said had befallen him before he moved to Amblecote, when he was a young curate in Pershore, coincidentally the town in which we had come within a Toyah Wilcox of making our home. Summoned one day to the handsome house of a very grand lady, he was appalled to find, as he wheeled his bicycle up her path, a fierce Alsatian blocking his way. The beast was barking ferociously at him with what seemed like murderous intent, and John was wondering whether to back off, or whether to put his fate in the hands of the Lord and plough intrepidly on.

At this point an upstairs window opened and the grand old lady looked out.

'Kick his balls,' she commanded, in an imperious voice. John looked at her in disbelief, then nervously eyed the dog.

'They're at the back,' she added. 'Go on! He enjoys it.'

Hesitantly, John shaped up to do as he had been bidden. 'What on earth are you doing?' she called. 'I said kick his balls! They're at the back of the lawn.'

I thought that was a hilarious story, especially the way John told it, and I included it in my 'Tales of the Country' column the following week. Yet by some cosmically unfortunate coincidence, it turned out that the very same story had appeared in the *Independent*'s property supplement the day before, related by an estate agent as having happened to him. Not in Pershore, though. That would have been too much.

I had not the slightest doubt that the incident really had befallen John, and that the estate agent had appropriated it. After all, even urban or semi-rural myths have to start somewhere. But I got lots of letters and e-mails, including one with the following withering observation: 'I could enjoy a most convivial evening at the pub, given a pint for every inspector in the life-and-pensions office I worked for who told the tale of the fierce dog and his balls in posh ladies' gardens.'

Most readers pointed out the duplication of stories good-naturedly. Some accused me of not reading my own newspaper, although I was at least able to say that as I had filed my column two days in advance, I had no way of knowing that I would be beaten by twenty-four hours to the same anecdote.

The cattiest letter was written anonymously, as catty letters generally are. Thankfully I don't get much hate mail, I suppose because I tend not to write about things which incite hatred, with the obvious exception of septic tanks. A brave and esteemed colleague on the *Independent*, Yasmin Alibhai-Brown, once wrote a column purely about the appalling letters and e-mails she had received as a result of her thoughtful pieces about the difficulties of being a Muslim in modern Britain. I was shocked. Compared with the abuse she got, mine hardly registered.

But I got a few, and one of the most hysterical, in both senses of the word, was from someone who claimed to have been at school with me. The writer asserted that as a child I had been, among other unenviable things, 'gauche'. This greatly tickled my friend Craig, who advised me that I probably didn't need round-the-clock protection from someone who would send hate mail containing the word 'gauche'. The writer, obviously enraged by what he had seen of my accounts of family life in the country, added that he wasn't interested in me or my 'hideous sprogs', which was a perfectly reasonable sentiment, even if it begged the question, why had he bothered to write? 'If I thought you had the balls to reply I'd sign this letter,' he concluded. 'Oh yeah,' I thought. 'Just which of us is the one with no balls?'

The catty response to my story about John contained my column, cut out and paperclipped to the relevant 'Confessions of an Estate Agent'. There was an arrow pointing at my head, and a single word, the old Herefordshire expression 'twazzock'. Which tickled Jane almost as much as John's anecdote had. The children were greatly taken with it, too. Twazzock duly became something of a favourite family word.

Meanwhile, beyond these entertaining diversions, the hard Herefordshire winter wore on. The warnings had not been exaggerated, and our alarmingly high consumption of petrol was matched by our consumption of oil, which fired both the central-heating system and the Aga. But even with the radiators on full throttle, it was impossible to keep Docklow Grange warm. I had always taken a curious pride in the fact that I slept naked even through the winter, but the sub-zero temperature in our bedroom finally wore me down, until I started going to bed looking like the Michelin Man.

To make matters worse, the oil firing our central-heating system then ran out. Nobody had told us that living in the country would be, to such a large extent, about emptying and filling things. Especially in midwinter. Hardly a day seemed to go by without us making arrangements to have the coal cellar filled or the septic tank emptied or the log shed filled or the storm-water tank emptied or the oil tank filled. You'll have noticed the plethora of tanks in that sentence. We had more tanks than the British army. And the consequences of neglecting our emptying or filling duties were costly.

We had two oil tanks, one connected to the central-heating system, the other to the Aga. In early November we'd had the former refilled, at a cost of £483. On 2 January, the oil ran out, and the heating stopped. So less than two months heating had cost us nearly £500, and of more immediate concern, we were bloody freezing. Even more freezing than usual. Jane and I had a night-time ritual which involved running round the bedroom swatting flies, which just seemed to get bigger and louder as we headed deep into winter. And they always timed their buzzing to start the instant we had settled under the duvet. You could check the bedroom for flies, and find none, and then as soon as you were in bed a noise would commence as if the band of the Grenadier Guards had marched into the room, all playing kazoos. But with no heating, and no company able to supply oil for the best part of a week, we valued the fly-swatting ritual as a means of keeping warm. In the morning we had another ritual, bracing ourselves and then leaping out of bed on the count of three, like *Thelma and Louise.*

Even the short walk to the King's Head became an exercise in survival techniques, but the words 'lamb shank' spurred us on through the cruel westerly wind. Roger and Jean had hired a new chef, Johnny, who had formerly been sous-chef at the Three Crowns in Ullingswick, an excellent gastro-pub which in certain circles of north Herefordshire society was talked about with near-religious reverence.

On the second weekend in January my half-brother Alexander came to stay, with his new girlfriend Amanda. Alexander is an artist living in New York; Amanda is an American child psychologist with bags of Manhattan chic. On the Saturday it was Amanda's birthday, an event normally celebrated at some stylish restaurant in the East Village with friends including, Alexander

quietly told us, the *Sex and the City* actress Sarah Jessica Parker.
We took them to the King's Head, where Amanda ordered the
scampi. And then left the scampi. 'Does it always come with
batter on?' she asked sweetly, with a flash of her gorgeous teeth,
pulling her pashmina a little tighter round her shoulders. We
realised that pub grub in Docklow had not passed muster with a
woman used to clinking Cosmopolitans with Carrie Bradshaw.
But to us, Johnny seemed like a godsend. We started eating at the
King's Head at least a couple of times a week. Quite apart from
the quality of the food, it was a sight warmer than our house.

After what seemed like an aeon – although five days might be
a closer estimate – the Countrywide lorry arrived to refuel our
tanks. Meanwhile, fewer rodents were refuelling in our pantry.
Maurice O'Grady kept dropping by to refresh the bait, which
took five minutes, and tell us his latest infestation stories, which
took an hour and a half. Thanks to him, our house no longer
seemed to be quite as popular with coach parties of yellow-
necked mice, and by mid-February they had stopped altogether.

This might also have had something to do with the arrival of
our cat, Tess.

I was returning from the Stop the War march in London, on
15 February, when Jane called. 'Are you sitting down,' she asked.
I was on a Thames train heading out of Paddington with a thousand weary anti-war campaigners. 'No,' I said. And then,
apprehensively: 'Why?'

'We've got a cat,' she said.

It is always a clever tactic to prepare someone for disastrous
news, and then to hit them with merely terrible news, because
their initial sensation is relief. So it was with me. I didn't like cats
one little bit, but I thought she was going to tell me something
even worse. Maybe her Uncle Gerald was coming to stay.

Compared with that prospect – Uncle Gerald being a man with the capacity to make even corpses yawn with boredom as he embarks for the thirty-fourth time on the story of how he was overtaken on the inside while minding his own business in the middle lane of the M5 – a cat didn't seem so bad.

There were a number of reasons why I didn't like cats. I didn't like the sight, when they raised their tails, of their little round – forgive me, but no other word will do – arseholes. And I didn't think they deserved their reputation for lavatorial fastidiousness. When we lived in London, there was a gang of neighbourhood cats who viewed our front garden as one big litter tray. 'Are you coming to the park,' one would say to another. 'Yeah,' would come the answer. 'But first I've got to crap in the Viners' garden.' 'OK,' the first cat would reply. 'I'll wait for you here. No, sod it, I might as well join you.'

Jane, who did not share my antipathy towards cats, had taken the children that day to Shortwood Family Farm, a petting farm seven or eight miles from us, not far from the charming little market town of Ledbury (if there are any towns in Herefordshire that aren't charming little market towns, I have yet to find them). They had seen some sweet kittens and the woman at the farm said they could have one for £7, which would have given Georgie and Owen in the King's Head another good laugh. 'Now they've gone and paid seven quid for an unwanted farm kitten!' But the children had said 'Oh pleeeeease', and Jane had thought, why not? It could only help with the mouse situation.

Tess, half-white and half-tortoiseshell, quickly made herself at home. I could, of course, have come over like a Victorian father, and refused to countenance the idea of giving house room to a damnable cat, but firstly Jane wasn't likely to respond like a Victorian wife and say 'Yes, dear, if that's your wish'; secondly the children would go hysterically tragic on me; and thirdly I had spent the day with a couple of million people who were trying to persuade the Government not to involve British troops in a disastrous war. It wasn't just the thought of death by Uncle Gerald's anecdotes that put the notion of a pet cat in perspective, it was also the thought of death by bomb and bullet.

So Tess joined Milo, Babs, Ginger, Ruby and Marigold in the menagerie. But what was a house in the country with a dog, four chickens and a cat, but no miniature Shetland pony?

I don't know where the idea to buy a pony came from. Well, I do. It came from Jane, which was perverse, firstly because she already had a house, three cottages, three children and six animals to look after, and secondly because she was worryingly allergic to horse hair. 'But it might actually be therapeutic,' she said, when I raised the possibility of her suffering an eyes, ears, nose and throat trauma on a daily basis. 'A kind of aversion therapy. And don't you think it would be lovely to have a Shetland pony grazing in the orchard? Our kids could ride her, and so could the children of cottage guests. We could put her on the website.'

Eleanor and Joseph had started riding lessons the summer before, but Eleanor, typical of a first-born child, did not like to do anything unless she could do it well. This character trait hadn't caused her too many problems; she was a natural gymnast, had a good eye for a ball, a good ear for music, could turn her hand with impressive speed to most things.

But in Herefordshire lots of children learn to ride almost as soon as they can walk. Turning up at the stables every Saturday morning to find tots half her size on ponies twice as big as hers, began to demoralise her. Jane felt that if Eleanor could ride a Shetland in the privacy of her own garden, it might build up her

confidence. After all, it was Mr Shetland Pony himself, the car-
toonist Norman Thelwell, who said that the breed was 'perfect
for introducing children to the problems of horsemanship'. Did
you know, by the way, that Thelwell, whose very name is syn-
onymous with fat little girls riding fat little ponies in the heart of
the English countryside, came from exceedingly urban
Birkenhead, on the banks of the Mersey? I didn't, until I read his
obituary.

Undoubtedly a Thelwell-style pony would add to the rustic
charm as far as guests were concerned. We would also be provided with plenty of horse muck which even I, though still very
much a beginner in the garden, knew to be fabulous for com-
posting.

I raised a few further objections – chief among them the fact
that we knew diddly-squat about diddly, squat ponies or indeed
any kind of ponies – but it became clear that Jane had, yes, the
bit between her teeth. She took advice from people who did know
about ponies and found that they were creatures which liked
company, so if we bought one we might have to think about
buying a donkey or a goat to live with it. This was getting out of
hand. What if we then found that goats got on well with
Vietnamese pot-bellied pigs? Or alligators?

Undeterred, Jane started looking for Shetland ponies for sale
on the internet, and found one called Zoe, a piebald, who was five
years old, lived in Devon with an experienced Shetland breeder
called Margaret Shillitoe, and could be ours for £400 plus the
cost of transporting her up the M5. Could we justify spending
£400 on a pony? We couldn't, but for a one-off payment we'd
have top-quality manure for years.

Zoe, said Margaret over the phone, was a good-natured, characterful pony. This reminded me of some of the estate agents'

euphemisms we had got to know so well while house-hunting. A 'characterful' house generally meant one in which the front door fell down as soon as you inserted a key. A characterful pony probably meant one that bit like Mike Tyson and kicked like Alan Shearer. But at least we wouldn't have to get back on to the internet to buy company for Zoe, through smellygoat.com. Margaret told us that Zoe was pregnant! We would be getting two ponies for the price of one. She would conveniently produce her own companion, towards the end of May.

And so we became the official owners of a miniature Shetland pony apparently becoming steadily less miniature. It had been a Wednesday when Jane found Zoe on the internet. We bought her the next day, Thursday, and took delivery on the Saturday, a dizzying turn of events.

Zoe arrived in a horsebox driven by Margaret's husband, and seemed surprisingly demure after three hours on the motorway. The children were instantly smitten. My own devotion was going to be a much harder commodity to obtain, but I had to admit that for such a resolutely squat creature she was absurdly pretty, with big black eyes peeping curiously through a thick black fringe, and a swishy tail almost down to the ground. 'Aaaaaaachooooooo!' was Jane's considered assessment of the newcomer. Not for the first time I wondered whether, in trying to embrace country life, we had perhaps shown more passion than was good for us.

One or two horse-loving friends certainly thought so, making no attempt to hide their disapproval that we had bought a pony. 'It's not like buying a hamster, you know,' said one, Jennifer, rather haughtily. If she'd had a mane, she would have tossed it. 'Dang,' I said. 'That must be why she's not running round and round on that wheel we bought for her.'

We didn't know many horse-lovers. Most of our city friends

knew marginally less about ponies than we did, which amounted to almost total ignorance. When Jane told her friend Kim that an excess of grass can bring on a painful disease called laminitis, Kim, who worked in education in the London Borough of Haringey, said it sounded like something she might get in the staff room, brought on by far too much laminating.

That seemed to me like a pretty good joke, but to crack it in the presence of our friends Jennifer or Sophie would have been beyond the pail, if you will. They both had friends – four-legged ones, of course – who'd died from laminitis. The fact that we'd even needed telling about it was confirmation that we were unsuitable people to own a pony.

This disapproval took us by surprise. We'd thought that perhaps Jennifer, Sophie and the other horsey types we knew would welcome us into the horsey community, express solidarity, give us generous helpings of advice and maybe some spare Polo mints, which, after all, is pretty much how it goes when you have your first baby. Nobody says, 'Ooh, you haven't had a baby before, it's not like getting a hamster, you know.' And then mutters to other experienced parents, 'I bet they've never even heard of Calpol.'

But far from them encouraging us, the exact opposite was true. We realised with a jolt that they thought us downright irresponsible. What right did we have to own a pony? What did we know of mucking out or scraping hooves?

Maybe we were irresponsible. Maybe it was unfair to Zoe to take her from an environment geared to the welfare of miniature Shetlands, to one where nobody had quite finished reading the *Ladybird Guide to Ponies*. Margaret Shillitoe hadn't been too perturbed about selling a miniature Shetland to novices, but it certainly took a while before we became confident about handling her, not least because of her inclination to take a friendly bite of whichever part of the human body happened to be at head height, a situation which in my case especially was fraught with peril.

About this time I happened to read in a newspaper that Shetland ponies were going to be trained to guide blind people. It was said that they were more intelligent than dogs and blessed with better memories, which would make them more suitable as companions for the blind.

This provoked many intriguing images, one of the most colourful of which was that a Shetland pony might one day enter Parliament – not, like the Emperor Caligula's beloved stallion Incitatus, as a representative of the people, but as the eyes of David Blunkett, the sightless Home Secretary. I liked the idea of observers in the public gallery asking who that was in the chamber with the twitching nostrils, the barrel chest, the severe fringe and the iffy teeth. 'No, not Ann Widdecombe, on the other side.'

But it was hard to imagine Zoe doing anything for the blind, except biting them, possibly. On the other hand, she seemed to have a keen sense of humour. One afternoon we looked out of the window to see Joseph taking Zoe for a walk. It was a showery spring afternoon but the sun was out and a dazzling rainbow framed the distant Brecon Beacons. The sight of our 8-year-old trotting round the garden, Shetland pony at his side, completed a heart-warming spectacle. Except that Zoe suddenly quickened her pace and pulled Joseph clean off his feet. We had told Joseph that he was on no account to let go of Zoe's lead rein and he obeyed our instructions to the letter, bless him. Clinging on for dear life, he was dragged on his tummy across the wet lawn, looking for all the world like Lee Van Cleef being humiliated in a spaghetti Western.

A few moments later, when Zoe stopped to munch the herbaceous border, Joseph got to his feet, wailing. He had a single muddy stripe from forehead to crotch, and I'm ashamed to say that once we'd established that it was only his pride that had been injured, Jane and I could not stop laughing. The spooky thing is that nor could Zoe. She was quite clearly roaring with laughter.

After the first couple of weeks we all felt a little more at ease with Zoe, and she with us. In due course she became quite a sweet-natured little pony, especially once we'd had her broken in, so that the children could ride her. But we continued to recognise how essentially little we knew about equine needs, for instance when we visited some friends in Shropshire to find one of their two ponies being manipulated by a chiropractor. How do you know when your pony needs to see a chiropractor? And how do you know which chiropractor she needs to see? For this was not a chiropractor specialising in animals, but an ordinary one, who conceivably had spent that morning easing the back pains of a newsagent, a housewife and an accountant in Ludlow, before attending Lulu the pony.

Clearly, in the thinly populated Welsh Marches, those working in the health sector could greatly increase their customer base by treating animals as well as people. This intriguing notion brought to mind another e-mail I had had from Dr Norman Mills, the *Independent* reader who had alerted me to the existence of the hill so fortuitously close to Lord Hereford's Knob: Myarth.

Norman had become a regular correspondent, and frequently sent me anecdotes relating to his career as chief executive of a Welsh hospital. One of his managers was summoned to Outpatients one day to deal with a furious local farmer who had just had an unfortunate altercation with a colorectal specialist. The specialist had been examining the farmer, and at a delicate stage of the examination, while peering as far up his passage as he could, had said, 'I think, Mr Griffiths, that you're going to have to see a vet.'

Enraged by this burst of maladroit humour at such a moment of personal indignity, Mr Griffiths shouted at the specialist to bugger off, got dressed and stormed out, then demanded that he be allowed to make a formal complaint. It took Norman's manager some time to calm him down, and make him realise that the bewildered specialist had in fact been referring to Yvette, the colorectal nurse.

It was a vet rather than Yvette, though, that our pony Zoe needed to see. We called out Mike Devoy, of the Ryelands Clinic in Leominster, and asked him to give her the once-over. We also wanted to know whether her living quarters were suitable. For example, would we need to build her a shelter? Mike made the reassuring point that nature had prepared her to cope with life on a Shetland island, so an orchard in Herefordshire, with a plentiful supply of crunchy carrots, would probably suit her just fine.

Jane was right about the allergy. Slowly but surely it receded, to the point where only by kissing Zoe would she get the itchy eyes and runny nose that previously she would have developed by doing nothing more than watching the *Horse of the Year Show* on TV. So kissing was out. Meanwhile, I slowly conquered my aversion to the cat. As cats went, Tess was a reasonably pleasant creature to have around, not that she was around very much. Having spent her first few months on a farm, Tess liked to get out and about. And meet other cats. We spent a few days feeling proud that Tess was filling out nicely in our care before it became clear that the reason she was filling out had nothing to do with Whiskas sachets of turkey and vegetables in gravy. She, too, was going to be a mum.

A year earlier, I reflected, we had been living in London with no pets and a garden thirty feet square. We'd had a rabbit but it had been eaten by an urban fox, and a guinea pig which had died of shock after being slapped around by our next-door neighbour's tom – another reason I didn't care for cats very much. Now, we had a litter of kittens on the way and a foal due to be born in our orchard. I sometimes felt as though I'd wandered into somebody else's life. Or at the very least into a Sunday evening TV drama, probably starring Pauline Quirke.

Especially as it seemed that I was going to act as midwife in the birth of Zoe's foal. With our friends Ali and Chris we had arranged to rent a villa in Sardinia at the end of May, but increasingly it looked as though I wouldn't be able to afford the time off work. Jane and the kids would have to go without me, leaving me to write hard and look after the animals. And looking after the animals might involve sticking a soapy arm up a pony's orifice, at least if every other episode of *All Creatures Great and Small*, another Sunday evening TV drama, was anything to go by.

I asked the blessedly calm Mike Devoy whether the big event would require any direct input from me, meaning 'direct input' in an all-too literal sense. Mike explained that my arm almost certainly wouldn't be required up any orifice of Zoe's. The birth of her foal would be a straightforward business, he explained, yet dramatic. The word he used, in fact, was 'violent'. Zoe, he said, would fire her foal out like a cannonball, and I would only need to intervene if there were complications, which were unlikely. I smiled the smile of a first-time skydiver who has just been told that his parachute is 95 per cent certain to open. 'And how will I know if there are complications?' I asked.

'Oh, it will be pretty obvious,' said Mike. 'But it wouldn't be a bad idea to spread the placenta out afterwards and check it for tears, just to make sure there's none still in there.'

I looked at Jane, who was making hardly any attempt to stifle her amusement. 'So while you're tucking into a plate of pasta in some Sardinian seaside restaurant, I will be inspecting a Shetland pony's placenta,' I said.

'I'll leave you some carbonara sauce,' she said, unhelpfully. 'I imagine that would be delicious with pony placenta.'

Happily, not all our animals were producing offspring; our hens were producing something even more exciting. On Monday, 10 March, at 6.03 p.m. (I checked, because historic moments such as this need recording), I heard a terrific squawking and flapping coming from the direction of the chicken house. It was Jane. She had found an egg.

We had now had Ruby, Babs, Ginger and Marigold for four months, with nothing to show for their presence except an awful lot of droppings. So the inaugural egg caused intense excitement, and even phone calls to family and friends, as on the occasion of childbirth. We were tempted to send out little pink-edged cards, with a photograph of the egg and details of the time of delivery, weight, star sign etc. But we didn't. Apart from anything else, we didn't know whether it was Ruby, Babs, Ginger or Marigold we should be congratulating.

The egg was perfect, although tiny, about the dimensions of a large, slightly squashed grape. It was a charming shade of off-white, what the paintmakers Farrow & Ball call Dimity, for curious reasons of their own. It is not entirely fanciful, by the way, to bring paint into a paragraph about eggs. Both have an eggshell finish, after all, with some eggs inclining to matt, others to gloss. And we had a friend who in a slightly bonkers middle-class bohemian way had carefully chosen her six chickens according to the varying colour of their eggs, ranging from pure white to off-white to cream to pale brown to hazelnut to dark brown, just so they looked lovely in her pantry. Like the spectrum of a Farrow & Ball colour chart, indeed.

We weren't going to go down that eccentric route, but we did accord our first egg a certain amount of veneration. Instead of a christening we had a ceremonial frying, and, like Loyd Grossman on *Masterchef*, divided the perfect little fried egg five ways. But Joseph declined his taste of history. 'No, yuck, it dropped out of a hen's bottom,' he said.

'And the other thousand eggs you've eaten were all laid by cardboard boxes, I suppose?' I said. Heavy sarcasm is wasted on children. 'Don't know,' he said. 'But I'm not eating that one.'

After a day or two, when the other three hens had started laying as well, Joseph conquered his qualms, and actually became chief consumer of our little bantam eggs. We were some distance from being self-sufficient, still more Margo and Jerry than Barbara and Tom, but it was immensely pleasing to have something yolky for all our outlay. Later, indeed, we would add another six hens to our brood, and catch ourselves talking enthusiastically to fellow poultry-keepers about the exciting garden eco-system in which hens can play such an important part. You feed them vegetable peelings and leftover scraps from the kitchen, and then you collect their eggs. The eggshells and the hen droppings are added to the compost, which in turn enriches the soil in which you grow vegetables, the peelings from which go back to the hens. As do the crumbs from the toast soldiers you made to eat with their eggs in the first place. I can think of nothing more satisfying, and I write as a man who once, in a tennis pro-am, placed a drop shot just out of the reach of John Patrick McEnroe, albeit flukily.

By March, this renewed enthusiasm for country living was beginning to eclipse the gloom that had set in once we realised that winters in Docklow could be just as cold inside as out, especially during those interminable evenings without the benefit of electricity.

Now, in the fields and hedgerows around us, and along our drive, the snowdrops were out and some early daffodils were starting to bloom. It was our first Docklow spring and although I remembered how exasperated I had been as Londoner when people who had moved to that hinterland beyond the M25 started wittering on about the thrill of watching the changing of the seasons, I now knew what they meant.

The English countryside in early spring is surely the best place in the world to find Mother Nature with her pinny on, getting down to a hard day's graft. At the Trueloves' farm there were 750 ewes in various stages of lambing, and in the King's Head one night, Roger Truelove, Martin's brother, kindly offered to let the children see a lamb being born. He said he'd call us the following morning when a birth seemed imminent, and at 11 a.m. the phone rang.

'You'd better get round here quick,' said Roger. Before he had quite finished the word 'quick' we were in the car. If Detective Starsky had driven a Volvo, he would have driven it like I did to Roger's barn, where we arrived just in time to see a lamb dropping out in a slithery miracle of blood and goo. 'Yeeucch,' cried the children, as one. I pointed out that their arrival into the world had been no less messy.

In the next half-hour, we watched three more lambs being born, which the children were permitted to feed. Roger also showed us a lamb 'off his legs', unable to stand because of vitamin B12 deficiency. Had it been born outdoors, it would probably have been attacked by carrion crows. Or worse, by ravens, which peck the eyes out of newborn lambs. There's nowhere quite like the English countryside for reminding you that, behind that pinny of hers, Mother Nature is an unsentimental old moo.

But at least we were getting to know her. In the city there had been only two seasons; the one with leaves on the pavements and the one without; the one with the ice-cream van tootling tunefully along the road at quarter past five – very annoyingly for all the mums who didn't particularly want their kids to have a 99 with raspberry sauce before their spaghetti bolognese but couldn't cope with the nuclear fallout if they said no – and the one without. Here, we had seen, smelt and felt winter turning to spring. That, I decided, would be my riposte when the children suddenly realised that there were no ice-cream vans in Docklow. 'But, darling, who needs a Tropical Solero when you've seen a burgeoning forsythia?'

I don't want to get too lyrical about it but each day seemed to bring more colour to the landscape. Each day also brought Will to our back door. Not only was Will a wildlife expert himself, he also counted many among his friends. So at our back door in his engagingly hesitant way he would announce that he had a bat lady or a moth man coming round, and did the children want to look at their wares? One afternoon I looked out of the kitchen window to see four people, wearing an interesting variety of hats, scrutinising our old cider press through magnifying glasses. I went out to see what on earth they were doing.

One of them was Will, and he introduced the others as two distinguished lichenologists and an expert on moss. 'A mossologist?' I ventured. They laughed as I have rarely seen people laugh outside a Peter Kay or Billy Connolly gig, clutching their sides

215

and gasping for air. Eventually they recovered sufficiently to tell me that the study of moss is called bryology.

They found several interesting varieties of lichen on the cider press, and more in the orchard, all of which was dutifully noted down for forwarding to Bradford University's lichen-recording project. The abundance of lichen growing on the fruit trees in the orchard, they told me, meant that the air quality in Docklow was excellent. 'It tells us how things are changing,' said a woman called Joy. 'Politicians can lie, but lichen can't.'

I asked Joy whether there was one particular lichen which, if found in our orchard, would send tremors of excitement through the world of lichenology. She looked delighted with the question. 'Yes, if we found *Lobaria pulmonaria* here then we would be celebrating for years to come,' she said. I loved that image, of perpetually partying lichenologists, with one occasionally standing on a chair and shouting '*Lobaria pulmonaria*', and everyone else whooping and hugging one another. Sadly, our orchard did not offer such riches, but they did find some *Lecanora soralifera* which gave them – and having been infected by their enthusiasm, me too – a little buzz of satisfaction.

Will's own area of expertise was frogs and toads. Will was into amphibians in a big way, to the extent that we had sent him a Christmas card wishing him an 'amphibian-filled new year'. Unfortunately, we had accidentally given Will's card to Malcolm the postman, and Malcolm's to Will, leaving Will wondering why we should be giving him a tenner and thanking him for his excellent service, and Malcolm why we should be wishing him a year filled with amphibians.

Not least of Will's charms was that even though he knew I could barely distinguish between a natterjack and a flapjack, he was eager to embrace me with his enthusiasms. 'I've just come back from the Froglife conference in Edinburgh,' he told me one day, adding, before I could start edging away, that a Swedish academic had delivered a particularly fascinating lecture on deep-sniffing newts.

My instinct to edge away was almost always misplaced. There was always some detail in what Will told me that captured my imagination. On this occasion it was that the Swedish academic had discovered that newts, with some heavy-duty sniffing, could seek from afar which ponds were free of threatening fish. To Will, this was a revelation no less astonishing than, say, the revelation of John Major's affair with Edwina Currie was to the political correspondent, and my own regard for newts increased as well. It was nice to think of the little fellows thoughtfully inhaling the air and then legging it towards a suitable pond. I had a friend who in exactly the same manner – no kidding – could locate a reliable Balti house in an unfamiliar town centre.

One afternoon in early February Will had turned up at the back door scarcely able to contain his excitement. 'The toads are on the move,' he said.

It was a somewhat gnomic declaration, rather evocative, we thought, of wartime. It was not hard to imagine Helmut, a German wireless operator with little round glasses, telling an officer that he had just intercepted an Allied message saying 'The toads are on the move', and to picture the ensuing consternation as they debated whether or not 'toads' was sly British code for the Seventh Armoured Division outside Alamein.

But when Will said toads, he meant, of course, toads. The night of 4 February had been unusually warm, apparently, and had prompted the earliest mass migration of toads on record, offering further evidence of creeping climatic change. Will told

217

us that he had counted fifty toads on their way to nearby Bodenham Lake for their annual bonkfest. 'Unfortunately, thirty-eight of them had been squashed by cars,' he added. If only their mating instincts were matched by an ability to look both ways at the kerb.

Meanwhile, the frogs of Herefordshire were having a more enjoyable spring than their big cousins. On another afternoon, Will called round with a man called John Cancalosi, an American wildlife photographer of considerable renown. John was visiting him because he wanted Will to take him to Tupsley Quarry in Hereford, where Will knew a pond in which hundreds of frogs were frantically mating. They asked if Joseph and I wanted to go with them, which we did, of course. It was a weekday and I had work to do, but the opportunity to watch 900 bonking frogs doesn't come around all that often.

On the way we found out that John had had some extraordinarily exciting assignments, one of which brought him toe to toe with a lion in the African bush. And yet, slightly frustratingly, he didn't really want to tell us about his dangerous missions, he just wanted to hear about mine. The one that particularly captivated him had happened in the February of 2002 when I intrepidly, with hardly any thought for my own physical safety and without so much as a tetanus injection, went to a Valentine's Day party at Hugh Hefner's Playboy Mansion in Los Angeles. I was there on a commission for the *Radio Times*, who wanted me to trail Ruby Wax trailing Hefner. John looked at me wide-eyed when I told him that I had ventured into Hefner's notorious underground grotto, rubbing shoulders with Kevin Spacey on his way out, and there sat down next to two near-naked women who were, as the Americans put it, making out. I whipped out my notebook, but it wasn't my notebook they wanted whipped out. One of them put her hand on my knee and asked if I had ever had 'a mansion experience' and if not, did I want one now?

'My Gaad,' said John. 'And what happened then?'

'We're here,' said Will, who had just pulled up outside Tupsley Quarry, and I think was getting anxious that John was losing his focus. But he didn't have to worry. A truly astonishing spectacle awaited us at the pond, where a regiment of frogs, most of them in the throes of sexual congress, peered at us from just above the water's surface. As we stood there, more and more popped up, until we estimated that there were at least 900 and probably over a thousand.

They were noisy lovers, too. The males emitted a low-pitched call to pull the females, which from so many of them at once sounded oddly like the purring of a giant cat. Mostly the sex was one on one, but here and there we saw small orgies of three or four frogs grappling on blankets of frog spawn. It made Hugh Hefner's Valentine's Day party look like an afternoon in Hereford library.

I found it rather uplifting to be in the presence of so much sex, and would have been even more uplifted had there not been so much litter around. Tupsley Quarry was a nature reserve administered by the council, and the council had been failing dismally in its duty to keep the place clean. But in a way the litter – empty pop bottles, cans, sweet wrappers – gave the spectacle a dash of surrealism. One frog seemed to be entertaining her partner in a fabulous pink boudoir, but on closer inspection it turned out to be an empty packet of prawn cocktail-flavoured crisps.

We stayed for an hour or so, with John snapping furiously and Joseph gradually becoming bored. Had he been a few years older it would have been a useful biology lesson. I could still remember learning from Mr Greenhalgh at King George V how the snail and the octopus do it – although not together, of course. I suppose he chose the snail and the octopus because they have such interesting reproductive methods. Snails, as I recall, fire little arrows at each other, like Robin Hood and the Sheriff of Nottingham, while the male octopus grows an extra tentacle with a sperm sac at the end of it, and none too subtly rams it up his mate. For a class of 14-year-olds – and Mr Greenhalgh too, for that matter – that seemed absolutely hilarious. In fact, Mr Greenhalgh, who was well practised at teaching biology to adolescent boys, even suggested that the octopus might cry 'Whahay!' as he delivered the telling thrust. For a short while, useless as I was at mastering the rudiments of photosynthesis, or understanding the point of an experiment to determine whether something was sucrose or glucose, biology had become my favourite subject. In the Hereford area in early spring, I told Will, all 14-year-olds should be taken to Tupsley Quarry to see frogs having sex. Maybe they already were, which might explain the prawn-cocktail crisp packets and empty bottles of pop.

Back at Docklow Grange, we didn't have anything to rival the love-in at Tupsley Quarry, but different wildlife was beginning to stir and we noticed the birdsong changing. We also started seeing squirrels, presumably just emerged from hibernation. In some cases, they would have been better off turning off the alarm clock and kipping for a bit longer. At the Farmers' Market in Leominster I spotted 'tree rabbit' for sale, while the fishmonger round the corner had dispensed with the politically correct euphemism, and was selling them as plain squirrels.

Shelagh Snell told me she had been in there when a woman bought six squirrels for a curry she was planning to make. I quite liked the idea of turning a garden pest into a tikka massala, and went to investigate. The fishmonger said his squirrels, at £3 apiece, were going like hot cakes, although they tasted more like a cross between rabbit and chicken. Our butcher, Stuart Fletcher of Draper's Lane, snorted when I passed this on. 'Rats with bushy tails,' he said, disdainfully.

If there was one sphere of retailing where Leominster could surpass even the sprauncest parts of London, Knightsbridge or Holland Park, it was butchery. I have come to the conclusion that beef, like Guinness, is ideally consumed close to its place of origin, and Herefordshire beef is, I will hear no dissent, the very best.

Local pigkind is pretty special too. There is a pig farmer near Ludlow called Mr Tudge (all pig farmers should be called Mr Tudge) whose name even pops up on local menus. The Three Crowns at Ullingswick used to serve not belly of pork but Gordon Tudge's belly of pork, which is like the difference between a painting of water lilies and Monet's painting of water lilies. Our luncheon club friend Nancy once planned to roast a pork loin for a Friday gathering, but decided that only Mr Tudge's loin would do. Having lived in Ludlow she knew him and his pork well, but now she lived the other side of Malvern, at least a ninety-minute round trip away from his farm shop. So she phoned Mr Tudge and arranged to meet him in a lay-by on the A44. He drew up at the appointed time and handed over the wrapped loin of pork with what I like to think was a faint air of mystery, making it look, to anyone who might have been watching, like a clandestine collection of MI5 files or top-quality heroin. If there is anything that sums up the pleasure of living in the country and developing a strong relationship with a local food supplier, it is Nancy picking up Mr Tudge's loin in a lay-by.

For lovers of birds, or churches, or flowers, or castles, or fishing, or walking, or any number of other pursuits, there can be few better counties than Herefordshire in which to live. But, it has to be said, it isn't much of a place for vegetarians. Meat looms large, on every menu and in every high street. And in common with every town in the county, Leominster had not one but several fantastic butchers, of whom Stuart Fletcher was our favourite. A well-upholstered man, he had the requisite pork-sausage fingers and looked as though he might have been the model for Mr Bones the Butcher in Happy Families. On his counter he proudly displayed a framed letter from the 'Two Fat Ladies' cook Clarissa Dickson-Wright, who had tasted one of his sausages, or more likely quite a lot more than one, at a friend's house in Gloucestershire, and wanted him to know how splendid she thought they were. Which in turn made me think how splendid Ms Dickson-Wright was; she must have been aware that a note scribbled by her in about thirty seconds would make the day, week and month of an obscure Leominster butcher.

It had taken us eight months or so to decide that Stuart Fletcher was our favourite butcher, and he was pushed all the way to the wire, I should add, by Legges of Bromyard and Griffiths of Ludlow. In that time we had also found our favourite places to buy fruit and veg, to eat out, to walk the dog, to get our hair cut, all of which contributed to the increasing feeling that Herefordshire was home, although actually our favourite hair-cutting joint was in Shropshire, the Gentlemen's Barber in Ludlow, run by an engaging guy called Geraint who had a wonderful manner with the children and fed me fascinating titbits, and sometimes mischievous titbits, for instance that it was a local private school which had the highest incidence of nits.

The only unsettling thing was that Roger and Jean were leaving the King's Head. There had been rumours for weeks that they intended to sell up after scarcely a year, but this was hotly denied by Roger. 'People round here haven't got anything better to talk about,' he muttered darkly, when I told him what I had heard. 'There's absolutely no truth in it at all. If we were going, you'd be the first to know.'

Coming from a landlord with whom I had reached an elbows-on-bar, let's-sort-out-the-world's-problems relationship, this seemed to me pretty unequivocal. I assured those who were peddling the rumour that they had it wrong, yet it turned out that I was the one who was wrong. One evening, Roger sat down with Jane and me as we were tucking into one of his Highly Commended steaks. 'Er, those rumours were actually true,' he said. 'We just didn't want to say anything until it was all done and dusted. But we have sold up and we'll be leaving in a couple of weeks. We're hoping to buy a pub in Chipping Campden.'

In a community the size of Docklow, this news was at least as seismic as the Dudley earthquake had been for people living in Brick Kiln Lane. The local pub changing hands, when there is nowhere to hang out but the local pub, is a momentous event in a small village. Probably irrationally, I felt more than a little betrayed by Roger's secrecy. But he made amends by sharing with me a precious bottle of 1953 cognac, which may or may not have been any good but certainly tasted significant, on their last night at the King's Head.

As for the people who had bought the business, there wasn't much he could tell me, except that they were relatively local and hadn't been in the pub trade before. Would they maintain culinary standards, that was our main concern. Owen, Georgie and the other farm labourers, by stark contrast, didn't give a stuff about pigeon breasts with celeriac mash. They merely hoped that whoever the newcomers were, they might restore the pool table and the dartboard. Bollocks to the celeriac mash. And maybe they were right. Maybe Docklow was no place for a pub with gastronomic pretensions. Anyway, I liked pool and darts as much as the next man. Hell, I might even be accepted into the team.

I liked Owen and Georgie, and there were faint signs that they were beginning to like me. They had at least taken to greeting me with slightly warmer scowls than before, and our growing bond was then cemented, as growing bonds often are, by getting paralytic together. It was a night or two before Roger and Jean's departure, and I popped in for an early-evening pint. Owen and Georgie were already at the bar. 'Do you want a pint, Bri?' asked Owen. Not all Brians like answering to the chummy Bri. It would probably be unwise to try it on with the art critic Brian Sewell, for instance. He does plummy, but not chummy. But I quite liked it; until I moved to Herefordshire only my oldest schoolfriends, Pete and Mike, called me Bri. But not only was there a glut of Brians in this part of the country, they all seemed to have been shortened to Bri.

One pint led to a second and a second somehow led to a seventh, and it was nearly midnight by the time I stumbled home. I had learnt that Owen was a foundling, which sounded impressively Dickensian. He had literally been found, swaddled in a blanket, on the doorstep of a house in Pudleston, sixty-four years earlier. The farmer's wife who found him took him to an orphanage in Birmingham, but stayed in contact and her husband hired him as a labourer when he reached his mid-teens. He had worked for the family ever since and never found out who his parents were, although his theory, aired somewhere between the fifth and sixth pints, was that she was a gypsy girl who'd been impregnated by her father or one of her brothers. 'Christ,' said Georgie, and looked thoughtful. He'd obviously never heard this bit of Owen's story before, and seemed to be reaching for some words to match the poignancy of the moment. 'That must be why you're so bloody daft,' he said.

It was an evening of revelations. I told Owen and Georgie my own story, that I had been adopted as a baby and brought up an only child, and a perfectly happy one, I might add. I was told at the age of nine that I'd been adopted, I suppose when I was considered old enough to understand. I don't remember the news having a particularly devastating effect on me, yet I can still remember exactly where I was at the time, so maybe it did. I was in the back of the car outside Hillside post office in Southport. My father had gone in to buy some stamps or something, and while he was inside my mother broke the news. She always got the tricky jobs.

I never wanted to know who my biological parents were. Although my dad died when I was just fourteen, he remained unarguably my dad. Even when I became a journalist, a profession supposedly propelled by curiosity, I didn't want to know. But it wasn't because I thought I might open a can of worms by finding out – I felt no resentment towards the couple who'd given me up for adoption; on the contrary, when I did think about it I knew they had done me a considerable favour. It was more that I felt settled and secure about who I was and where I came from. Far from feeling that they made an unwanted start in life, adopted children, it has always seemed to me, should draw huge emotional comfort from the knowledge that they were wanted so desperately as to be embraced by a family with whom they had no genetic knot. Can a child be *more* wanted, in fact?

So I made no attempt to trace my biological parents even when we were expecting our own first child, which is the point at which many adopted children start thinking about their genes. Certainly, it was troubling for Jane to be asked those questions about medical history: had there been any Down's syndrome in the family? Any blood disorders? Any heart defects? We only knew 50 per cent of the story.

She gently suggested to me that it might be a good idea to find out, but I resisted. And the situation might have stayed like that except that, unknown to me, my natural mother had been making increasingly strenuous efforts to find me for more than ten years.

One Saturday morning in 1997, when we were living in Crouch End and I was still working for the *Mail on Sunday*, I got a letter on Post-Adoption Society notepaper. Coincidentally, a couple of weeks earlier I had written a review of an edition of the *Vanessa* show, in which Vanessa Feltz and her studio audience had behaved appallingly, I thought, by collectively haranguing a woman who had given up her son for adoption in the early 1960s. That was when I was adopted, too, but don't get excited: it wasn't that much of a coincidence.

To make matters worse, the adopted son then walked on and joined in the harangue. Apparently he had always felt bitter about being given up and this was the first time – on daytime television! – that he'd had a chance to confront his natural mother. It was later found that some of the encounters on Vanessa's show and shows like it were staged, but this one seemed genuine enough. I was outraged, on this poor woman's behalf. But I found that in writing about the programme in the *Mail on Sunday*, I had to declare my personal situation. It would have been disingenuous not to. So I wrote pretty much what you've read above, about how I had no axe to grind with my natural mother, whoever she was, and felt that on top of life's ultimate good turn, giving birth to me, she had done me another fairly big one.

In the ten days or so after that article was published, I got a huge postbag of overwhelmingly supportive letters, many from people who'd been adopted, or were adoptive parents. It was during that period that the letter arrived from the Post-Adoption Society, so when I saw the letterhead I assumed it was just another response to the piece in the *Mail on Sunday*.

But it wasn't. It had been written on behalf of a woman called Doris who had given birth to a boy on 25 October 1961, in the Northern Hospital, Islington. He had initially been called Robin, after his natural father, but had then had his name changed to Brian by his adoptive mother and father, Mr and Mrs Viner. The bit about being called Robin was the only thing my mother had ever told me about the circumstances of my birth. So I knew that the Post-Adoption Society had done their work well, helping Doris to find me. The question was: did I want to meet her?

Not to would have been perverse. So we met, and liked each other. She was an elegant bohemian who smoked cigarettes in a long silver holder and answered to the name of Pip, Dorises being downright uncommon in elegant bohemian circles. She lived in north London, only a few miles from us. And she ran a long-established shop in Islington selling Afghan rugs and objets d'art. Amazingly, my friend Derek, who would later open his own rug shop just round the corner – the one called Tribe which his horrified mother had thought he was going to call Tripe – knew her quite well. 'Do you know a woman called Pip, who has a shop selling Afghan rugs,' I casually enquired one day. 'Yeah,' he said. 'Why do you ask?' 'Oh, no particular reason,' I said. 'Except that she gave birth to me.'

Giving birth to me did not, however, make her my mother.

Not in what I considered to be the proper sense. And in fairness, she was highly sensitive to the emotional nuances of the situation. I had a mother and didn't need another one. But I didn't have brothers. Except that now I did. Thrillingly, Pip had gone on to have two sons, Yoram and Alexander. Just as thrillingly, she was still in touch with my natural father, Robin, who lived in Suffolk with his wife, Jenny, and made pots, dissolving any faint hope I might have nursed that my natural father would turn out to be an oil baron. But in the world of ceramics, he was extremely highly regarded. He had also served in the SAS and had later been squash champion of Suffolk, undefeated for a number of years, so obviously that was where I got my extreme physical fortitude and fantastic deftness on the squash court. Not to mention my fondness for spiral staircases; Robin's forebears, it turned out, had been lighthouse keepers in the Scilly Isles. More excitingly still, Robin had gone on to have two daughters and a son. So suddenly I had five half-siblings, and in due course befriended them all.

For some reason I was especially delighted to find that I had two sisters, the younger of whom, Polly, had three kids the same age as mine. Spooky. Even more spookily, and unluckily for her, Polly resembled me more than she resembled either of her full siblings, Samantha and Marcus. She quickly became very dear to me. And Samantha, who had emigrated to Australia in her teens, I got to know over the course of a long, let's-catch-up-on-what-we've-each-been-doing-for-the-last-forty-years session over a happy weekend in Melbourne, where fortuitously I had been sent by the *Independent* to report on some sporting events. It was great. Five siblings, none of whom had ever screamed at me to get out of the bathroom, or pinched my Clearasil.

That was the story I told Owen and Georgie in the King's

Head, and they responded with appropriate expressions of interest and surprise. 'Well, bugger me', principally. It wasn't as poignant as Owen's tale, but it wasn't bad. With the help of Dorothy Goodbody – the beer, not another character in the story of my adoption – I had stopped being the silly sod from London who'd bought the Openshaws' house for far too much money, and then spent £60-plus on four chickens, but something perilously close to a mate.

8

The Great Magnolia Heist

I knew it would take years for us to assimilate fully in the country, if indeed we ever would, but once you've got hammered with the local farm hands then at least you're on the way. And at least we got our next three chickens for the price of a bottle of wine, which was rather more the way of doing things in Docklow. They came from Debbie Crowley down the road, and were Marans, which according to Francine Raymond's *Big Book of Garden Hens*, a tome as indispensable to the middle-class poultry-fancier as the Kama Sutra is to the sexual athlete, were 'prolific layers of nice brown eggs' as well as 'placid, pleasant and housewifely'.

Debbie thought that all three were hens, but it turned out that one was a cockerel. He was a fine-looking, assertive fellow – whom we named Mrs Doubtfire, on the basis that we had assumed him to be female – but we weren't sure we wanted a cock around the place. In fact we were fairly sure we didn't. For one thing, we didn't want chicks. For another, Mrs Doubtfire's crowing started at first light. And for another, I heard that in the presence of a cock, hens sometimes behave in an even more brainless manner than usual. This last snippet of information came from Nicola Lush, a former BBC press officer whom I'd known back in my *Mail on Sunday* days. She had long since left the Beeb and was now living idyllically in Somerset with a husband, and lots of children and chickens. She e-mailed me to say that her hens did a lot of squawking when they shared their run with a cockerel, and laid fewer eggs than they had before he arrived. 'I wonder whether it is for similar reasons that we don't allow men in our book club?' Nicola ventured.

Jane and I duly made the momentous decision to get rid of Mrs Doubtfire. But how? We had both made huge strides since leaving the city; I could now pick up a flapping hen without so much as a grimace, which didn't exactly make me David Attenborough or even Rolf Harris, but was a hell of a progression from a year earlier. And I was similarly cavalier about picking up and binning the dead shrews that Tess, even in her pregnant state, liked to deposit on the doorstep, preferably with their heads hanging off.

This was another feline characteristic that I didn't greatly care for. I have never worked out why people think it's cute when their cat brings its prey home, presumably so that they can applaud its killer instincts. My mate Dominic had a cat called Hector who used to drag half-dead rats and pigeons into the marital bedroom in the middle of the night, and both Dom and his wife Linda would describe these nocturnal visits affection-ately, as though they were talking about a kindly neighbour bringing round a rhubarb crumble. If a man made a habit of murdering other humans, and half-decapitating his victims before dragging them home to show the rest of the family, then sooner or later he'd wind up in Broadmoor with no chance of parole. Obviously it's different for cats. But I really don't see why we should congratulate them for it.

And yet, after picking up my first shrew with its innards on the outside, I stopped being the slightest bit squeamish about Tess's kills. But slaughtering a chicken, that was a different matter altogether. When it came to slaughtering chickens, I was still very much a townie. We discussed how I might dispatch Mrs Doubtfire. 'How about backing over him in the Volvo,' Jane suggested. She wasn't being wholly serious, but at the same time, she had no illusions that she had married Davy Crockett.

In the end we decided to call the nearest thing to Davy Crockett in Docklow: Malcolm. I knew Malcolm slightly from the King's Head, and he had been recommended to me for all manner of macho outdoors jobs. Malcolm said that he would come over straight away and see to Mrs Doubtfire. Would we like him back, oven-ready? 'Sure,' I said, in what I hoped was a macho, outdoorsy kind of way. If we were serious about keeping poultry, there was no point in getting sentimental about them.

Malcolm brought Mrs Doubtfire back a few days later, plucked, trussed and a shadow of his former self, as well as a lot quieter. 'Is he at all recognisable,' said Jane, peering anxiously into the plastic carrier bag. He wasn't. So we roasted him and had him for supper, just the two of us. We couldn't have fed him to the children, who thought that he had gone away to live happily on a farm.

Children can get seriously distressed about these things. Our friend Jane, a Stamford Heath mum, had once put her foot in it dreadfully with one of her son Jack's friends, a farmer's son, who had come round for tea. The little boy mentioned fairly cheerfully that his sheepdog Buster had been put down. 'What does "put down" mean?' asked Jack. Jane explained sensitively that when a dog gets very old it is given an injection which helps it to die without pain. She then became aware of the other boy looking at her, aghast, tears streaking his cheeks. He had heard his parents saying that Buster had to be put down by the vet, but when he asked what this meant they had told him that the vet would put Buster down in a really comfortable basket, then carry him off to live at the vet's house, where he could enjoy an even happier life than the one he had with them.

So when my own children come to read this book, the revelation that mummy and daddy ate Mrs Doubtfire might come as a traumatic shock. But if it's any consolation to them, he was as tough as old boots. I later found out that cockerels are best either braised or boiled up for stock, not roasted. He crowed at us even from the plate.

With only two Marans left following Mrs Doubtfire's sad demise, we had room for some more chickens. Although the bantams were entirely free-range, we had erected a large chicken run, in the orchard, for the bigger ones. So Jane went off to see a Mr Evans, who owned a farm at Knighton, on the Welsh border, and advertised his chickens in the *Hereford Times*. She phoned first, and ordered four Warrens, attractive pale brown birds and decent layers. It was arranged that she would pick them up the following week.

In the meantime, we consulted *The Big Book of Garden Hens* and other such volumes on how best to introduce new chickens to existing ones. Since 2001, I read somewhere recently, there has been a 400 per cent increase in sales of books about poultry-keeping. And most of them are books written very much with the bourgeois poultry-keeper in mind. The ones we read all but advised that, if you are introducing new birds to an existing brood, it is a good idea to throw a cocktail party at which they can get to know each other, perhaps with the existing birds serving mushroom vol-au-vents so that the new ones don't feel inferior. I exaggerate, of course. But not a lot. In *The Big Book of Garden Hens*, Ms Raymond advises that new birds being added to an existing flock 'must spend several days in purdah, cooped separately inside the run so the occupants can get used to each other little by little'. She also recommends making runs as attractive as possible, and keeping an old folding garden seat inside, 'so you can relax there too'.

Jane realised that we were perhaps fretting a bit too much about the welfare of the Warrens when she went to pick them up and consulted Mr Evans, too, on how to ease the new chickens into the society of the Marans. 'Oh, I should think they'll get along just fine,' he said gently, although Jane knew what he was thinking. 'They're just chickens, for fuck's sake!'

Mr Evans was right. Although chickens prefer to grub around with their own kind, the Marans and the Warrens got on without any bother. We also kept Bramble the rabbit in the chicken run, and he seemed to enjoy the company of the Warrens as well, as was manifest in his forlorn yet impressively persistent efforts to mate with them.

Unfortunately, the Warrens did not seem to be producing eggs. We checked in the henhouse every afternoon but all we kept finding were the two daily Maran eggs. Then one day I saw a Warren walking with a purposeful air into the rabbit hutch, and when I looked upstairs in the hutch I found no fewer than twenty-eight eggs.

No wonder Bramble was looking so pleased with himself; he clearly thought this fecundity had something to do with him. How old the oldest egg was, we had no idea. It had to be at least a week old and probably older. But we subjected them all to Delia Smith's freshness test, which holds that a completely fresh egg can be placed on its side at the bottom of a bowl of water and will not move. If it is less than completely fresh, it will tilt slightly upwards, and if it is stale, it will stand upright. All twenty-eight eggs conformed to Delia's measure of absolute freshness, yet – and if you find these things interesting, here's the really interesting thing – when we applied the same test to six supermarket eggs well within their use-by date, they all tilted slightly upwards!!! Which discovery is far more worthy of three exclamation marks than the entry in the hotel comments book by the people who'd had rumpy-pumpy in the Canadian hot tub, I think you'll agree.

In her paddock, which adjoined the chicken run, Zoe the Shetland pony watched the feathered comings and goings with interest. It was now April and she was supposed to be in the last few weeks of pregnancy, but a strange thing had happened: for a month or so she hadn't been getting any bigger. We began to wonder whether she had ever been pregnant in the first place, and phoned Margaret Shillitoe in Devon. She assured us that Zoe had been covered, as the expression goes, and by a very handsome chap, too. But that, she conceded, didn't mean she had ever been pregnant. She had looked pregnant, but maybe that was just her bulky winter coat, a mistake Jane had on one awful occasion made with an acquaintance in Crouch End, asking her when her baby was due. Mind you, that wasn't as big a faux pas as that committed by the mother of my friend Pam, who once stood on a street corner in Hartlepool talking to a neighbour she hardly knew, and absent-mindedly tried to remove a stray black hair from this other woman's cheek, only to find, when a little triangle of skin bulged out with it, that the hair was attached.

As for Zoe's phantom pregnancy, we thought back to the visit by the vet, Mike Devoy. He hadn't actually checked that she was pregnant, but why would he? We'd told him she was expecting and reasonably enough he had taken our word for it. But now that we were pretty sure she wasn't, it meant that Zoe would no longer be producing her own companion. On the bright side, it meant that I wouldn't have to spread out her placenta and check it for tears.

The children were disappointed, but Jane and I certainly weren't. Zoe, of unusually cheerful disposition for a Shetland pony yet still perfectly capable of trying to take the odd chunk out of a human thigh, was more than enough horseflesh to keep us busy. And there was nothing phantom about Tess the cat's pregnancy. We had been told by those who knew more about the feline world than we did, which was more or less anyone who'd ever seen an episode of *Top Cat*, that Tess would find somewhere secluded to have her kittens, and then slink off to give birth with the minimum of fuss.

In cat years, Tess was very much a teenage mum; she wouldn't even be a year old until June. The rascal who had taken advantage of her adolescent naivety we assumed to be a black-and-white tom, which we had seen prowling round the neighbourhood looking for trouble. We didn't know whether he belonged to anyone. And as soon as he had impregnated Tess, he disappeared off the scene. It's not only in The Far Side cartoons that animals display distinctly human characteristics, or is it our characteristics that are distinctly animal? Either way, if an irresponsible male gets an unworldly young female up the duff at prime time on BBC1, it might be *EastEnders*, or it might be *Wildlife on One*.

Whatever, we realised one Wednesday that we hadn't seen Tess for a few hours, and then she came padding into the kitchen, no longer pregnant. We looked high and low for the kittens, and eventually found them under the bed in an attic bedroom. We'd been told that a first litter, at such a young age, would be unlikely to comprise more than two kittens. So naturally there were five. Nothing at Docklow Grange seemed to happen in small measures. If Zoe had been pregnant, she probably would have had quins.

I still viewed cats with a certain amount of circumspection. Certainly their faeces hadn't grown on me, so to speak. But I could see that the kittens were adorable, and the sudden manifestation of Tess's maternal instincts represented a genuine miracle of nature. Teenage mum she may have been, but she no longer went out clubbing and drinking alcopops. I was truly impressed.

One day we found her carrying the kittens in her mouth from under the bed in the attic room and depositing them one by one under the wardrobe in Jacob's bedroom. This, we were told, was a common instinctive strategy on the part of a mother cat, shifting her offspring every so often to keep one step ahead of predators. Which I suppose made perfect sense in the wild, although if I had anything I wanted to keep safe, the bedroom of a 4-year-old boy, especially this particular 4-year-old boy, would be absolutely the last place I would hide it. On the other hand, maybe Tess was following the old dictum about keeping your friends close, but your enemies closer. At any rate, we told Jacob that he should feel truly special that Tess had chosen his room to house her kittens, and he seemed to take the compliment on board. It didn't stop him dragging them out to have a look at them from time to time, but at least he took reasonable care while doing so.

The children were keen for us to keep all the kittens, but that, I told them, would have to be over their father's dead body. In fact, I gave them the choice, and was rather hurt to see them equivocating. I told them they could choose one and the rest would have to go. It wasn't as though I was proposing to stuff four little balls of fur into a sack and take them all down to the River Lugg; Ali and Chris had said they would take two, my old university friends Doug and Rosie were having one, as were Jane and James, our mates from Stamford Heath. So all the children had to do was choose a kitten, and then give it a name. Needless to say, this was easier said than done, but eventually they picked a black-and-white cutie and called it Tiger Lily, Jacob's sugges-tion of Snot, which seemed absolutely splendid to me, having been narrowly rejected by three votes to two.

For a time, though, while the kittens were still relying on Tess for sustenance, we were a six-cat family. I can safely say that I had never expected to live under the same roof as six cats, although once they became too big to live under Jacob's wardrobe we moved them to the back hall, where at least they were safely con-tained. For a few weeks nobody got to visit the house without being taken into the back hall to admire the kittens, including our Really Distinguished Visitors.

Our Really Distinguished Visitors were Monique and Albert Heijn, our local billionaires. Not many people lived for long in north Herefordshire without becoming aware of the Heijns. He was Dutch, the scion of the Albert Heijn supermarket dynasty which, I was told by people in the know, was the Dutch equiva-lent of Sainsbury's. She was also Dutch, but had lived in

Herefordshire since 1967. She was his second wife; he was her third husband. When they married, she wanted to continue living in Herefordshire, where her children had been raised.

As the marital home the newlyweds chose Pudleston Court, a vast, castellated Victorian folly built in 1848 for Elias Chadwick, a Lancashire coal baron (and just as all pig farmers should be called Mr Tudge, so should all nineteenth-century Lancashire coal barons be called Elias Chadwick). But since old Chadwick's time, the house had been through many incarnations. During the Second World War it was a military hospital, and one of the patients was a chap called Alf Wight, whose pre-war career as a veterinary surgeon in Yorkshire later formed the basis for some rather successful books written under the pseudonym James Herriot, books which later still inspired the televison series *All Creatures Great and Small*, a popular Sunday evening drama which some years afterwards had me nervously contemplating the prospect of thrusting my arm up a pony's vagina. Small world.

After the war, Pudleston Court became a local authority borstal. Local authorities being what they are, someone in the education department talked to someone in the transport department and came up with the bright idea of using up a job lot of rubberised yellow paint, the stuff used for painting yellow lines on roads, to decorate the interior of Pudleston Court. When the Heijns bought the house, in 1993, they were determined to restore it pretty much as Elias Chadwick would have known it, and money being no object, did so. But they still had a devil of a job getting the rubberised yellow road paint off the cornicing, apparently. Still, at least nobody had parked there between the hours of 8 a.m. and 6 p.m. Monday to Saturday.

I don't know whether the Heijns intended to invoke the spirit of Elias Chadwick as well as recreate his living conditions, but they certainly behaved like old-fashioned Victorian benefactors, committing huge amounts of money to projects that cannot possibly have yielded any significant financial return on their investment.

One such is the Left Bank Village in Hereford, a splendid complex of shops and bars overlooking the River Wye. It is splendid not least because of its sheer improbability. For example, those who stroll into the Left Bank's excellent delicatessen without knowing anything about the Heijns must wonder why there is such a strong Dutch flavour to the place. Why on earth is the café there called De Koffie Pot and why does the deli sell every imaginable variation of gouda: with cumin; without cumin; with a little bit of cumin but not too much; mature; very mature; extra-mature; Victor Mature? Did William of Orange perhaps sail up the River Wye in the spring of 1581 and seize Hereford, leaving some of his men under the command of his loyal lieutenant Count van Nistelrooy to establish a stronghold, marry the local women and spawn generations of Dutch-jawed Herefordians who even 425-odd years later prefer jars of *rodekool mit appel* – also available in the deli – over red cabbage with apple? It sounds almost plausible.

When I was a student I landed a job for two or three summers driving American tourists round Scotland and showing them the sights. To our eternal discredit, my friend and fellow guide Angus MacLeod and I used to spin some ridiculous stories, usually involving Mary, Queen of Scots, which the Americans naturally took as gospel. I'm ashamed to say it pleases me to think that from New Jersey to North Dakota there must still be photograph albums containing pictures of crumbling Scottish castles captioned: 'This is where Mary, Queen of Scots, invented the game of Twister' or 'This is where Mary, Queen of Scots, who was only 3ft 8ins, escaped by hiding under her maid's hat.' Angus and I constantly used to try to outdo each other, although I could never quite match his convincing air of solemnity. He is now, incidentally, a highly respectable member of the clergy.

Had we been showing tourists round Hereford twenty years later we could have concocted a marvellous story to explain the Dutchness of the Left Bank Village. Not that the story of the Heijns needed the slightest bit of make-believe to render it any more fascinating. In 1887 Albert's grandfather, also Albert, had taken over his father's humble corner shop in the town of Oostzaan, and turned it into a food emporium. Its slogan was 'cheap enough for the man in the street and good enough for the millionaire', which perhaps sounds catchier in Dutch, although come to think of it, nothing sounds catchier in Dutch. Whatever, the emporium became a chain and the chain became a retailing empire.

Albert duly went into the family business and became chairman in 1962. But his was not just the everyday tale of a rich man born to run a corporate giant. I heard that he had been crippled by polio in 1944, which explained why the Left Bank catered for disabilities even to the extent of displaying notices in Braille. I also heard that he helped to invent the bar code, which is to the supermarket industry what penicillin is to medicine and therefore made him the Sir Alexander Fleming of the checkout or, if you prefer, Lord of the Aisles. Most intriguing of all, I heard that in 1987 his brother, also an executive in the company, had tragically been kidnapped and murdered, and that consequently the security around Pudleston Court would not disgrace a nuclear weapons compound. I wanted to know more.

Fortuitously, the Heijns' Dutch butler had used our cottages to accommodate his parents when they came over from the Netherlands to see him and his wife. One day while they were with us I asked him if he would ask the Heijns whether I could pay them a visit. He said he would put in a word. After a couple of weeks I had pretty much given up hope of hearing from him, when he phoned to say that Mrs Heijn had invited me for tea the following Thursday afternoon.

I had driven past Pudleston Court many times. The Antons lived that way, and with them we had also spent one or two cheerful evenings at Pudleston village hall, which was occasionally visited by a mobile cinema. The cinema, operated by an excellent organisation called Arts Alive, trundled through rural Herefordshire and Shropshire under the irresistible name of Flicks in the Sticks.

A short diversion from the Heijns is in order here, just to tell you about Flicks in the Sticks. One of our many concerns about leaving London was that we would no longer be able to go to the cinema on a whim, let alone on a W7 bus, as we sometimes did to the Muswell Hill Odeon.

Or if we did, the whim would involve a round trip of more than an hour to the Warner Village in Worcester. Yet as with so many of our concerns, this one was misplaced. We hadn't known about the joys of the Assembly Rooms in Ludlow, for example, where you could watch a film, listen to a lecture, drink a glass of wine and attend a yoga class, if not at the same time then sometimes on the same day. And we hadn't known about Flicks in the Sticks, which we could certainly go to on a whim, as long as the whim was once every two months.

We were enchanted by our first visit to Flicks in the Sticks. For us, cinema-going had long since become a predictable business, whereby we would purchase our tickets in advance and turn up twenty minutes early to queue for a wheelie-bin-sized bucket of popcorn, argue about which child was going to hold it, and then settle down in an overheated room to wait for the film to start, which was generally the point at which one child, often the one holding the popcorn, needed to go to the toilet. Even when it was just Jane and me on our own, cinema-going in London had become a prosaic experience.

Flicks in the Sticks at Pudleston village hall changed all that. We were back to the world of mid-feature reel-changes, and shadows on the screen if anyone stood up during the film, and occasional lip-sync problems: back, in other words, to the magic of the movies. The first film we went to see there was *About a Boy*, the adaptation of Nick Hornby's novel – which I do believe is the second mention that novel has received in these pages, constituting a reasonable claim for this book to get a mention in his next one, I'd have thought – starring Hugh Grant.

Jane and I bought two glasses of sauvignon blanc, another civilised dimension to Flicks in the Sticks, and took our seats. Then, just as the film was about to start, a woman in the row behind us whispered loudly to her companion, obviously in con- clusion to a conversation which regrettably we hadn't heard: 'It makes you wonder who else in the village is a nudist.'

It was the worst-possible curtain-raiser, in that we were torn between watching the film and wanting to know what marvellous piece of gossip had provoked that intriguing observation. It was especially frustrating for Jane, who had inherited the eavesdrop- ping gene from her mother. If there were a Nobel Prize for eavesdropping, Anne would be its most distinguished laureate. For ten days every summer we go with my parents-in-law to a characterful hotel in Cornwall, which has a rather formal dining room. It is a real old-fashioned, English seaside hotel, right down to the real, old-fashioned hors d'oeuvres trolley. It is just the kind of place where Agatha Christie's sleuths Hercule Poirot and Captain Hastings might have stayed, and then solved the mystery of who poisoned the elderly American woman, and why was her salamander brooch missing?

But Anne, believe me, would have left Hercule Poirot himself for dead in the information-gleaning department. At the dinner table she sits back in her chair with an inscrutable half-smile on her face, ostensibly listening to what Bob, Jane and I are talking about, but in fact concentrating raptly on an exchange going on at a table behind her between a man and wife.

Or seemingly a man and wife. Because she then leans forward and says, 'They're not married. He's divorced, lives in Kent, and she's never been married, although she had a six-year relationship with a jazz saxophonist who was ambidextrous.' Then she sits back and after a few moments leans forward again. 'And his ex-wife, Denise, has started going out with a builder, Harvey, who has two grown-up children, the elder of whom, Jonathan, is quite badly asthmatic. Jonathan's training to be a quantity surveyor, by the way.' It's engrossing stuff. But it has lured me well away from Pudleston village hall, and even further from the Heijns, whom, the following Thursday, I prepared to meet.

The vast iron gates to Pudleston Court, into which were woven an A, for Albert, and an M, for Monique, were firmly closed. On the intercom I spoke to a servant, who confirmed that the Heijns were expecting me. The gates swung open slowly, and I pointed my decidedly humble Volkswagen Polo up the majestic drive, passing a couple of ornamental lakes and a small herd of alpacas, as you do when you are calling on neighbours.

A housekeeper let me into a splendid entrance hall, where I

was greeted warmly by Monique Heijn. She was a handsome, charismatic woman, I estimated to be in her mid-fifties. She led me into an even-more splendid drawing room, with the kind of furnishings Elias Chadwick would have appreciated and absolutely no sign of double yellow lines round the cornicing. At first I was not aware of an elderly man sitting quietly in an armchair: Albert Heijn. I liked him immediately. He had a soft voice and a face that radiated kindness. It was hard to think of him as a multimillionaire anything, although if I'd had to guess, I might have guessed grocer. I stayed for about an hour and a half, drinking tea from a delicate china cup and trying very hard not to slurp. Mrs Heijn did most of the talking, about Pudleston Court, about Leominster, about Herefordshire, about her family. She also expressed some interest in seeing our house, which she had passed many times. I said we'd invite them round.

They came a few weeks later, bang on the appointed hour of 4 p.m., in a chauffeur-driven Bentley. Dr Heijn was in a wheelchair, and the chauffeur and I lifted him, and it, into the house. The chauffeur then left with instructions to return for them an hour and a half later, and we showed them around the ground floor, including the rather smelly back hall where the kittens were, although I had never pushed a wheelchair before and it later occurred to me, to my embarrassment, that once or twice I had left one of Holland's wealthiest and most venerable tycoons gazing at a wall.

As for afternoon tea, Jane made her pear and almond tart, a house speciality, although a nod of acknowledgement must be made to the excellent *River Café Cookbook*. The children briefly joined us and, of course, made no concessions to our visitors' grandeur. They were just another old couple. Perhaps, I reflected, there was a lesson there for us, although that did not stop me also reflecting, as I poured the tea, that we should have bought a new teapot for the occasion. It wasn't that I wanted to put on airs, but even so, this was almost certainly the first time the Heijns had encountered a slightly chipped white teapot from Ikea.

Again, Mrs Heijn did most of the talking, while Dr Heijn smiled and occasionally ventured an opinion in his quiet voice. They both seemed to derive great pleasure from watching Eleanor and her friend Sarah cavorting in the neighbouring field, and as she surveyed the scene Mrs Heijn offered the marvellously feudal tip that whenever I saw a farm hand in the field driving his tractor, at least after lunch, I should wave an ice-cold beer. This I later tried, and the Trueloves' tractor driver, Sam, seemed duly appreciative, although having cheerfully waved the beer I then watched it explode all over his blue cheesecloth shirt. I realised too late that Mrs Heijn had probably intended me to hold the bottle in one hand and wave with the other.

She left insisting that we were close neighbours – which in rural Herefordshire terms I suppose we were – and should do as close neighbours do, and drop in whenever we were passing. We never did. After all, the huge gates and security fence did not exactly encourage the drop-in, not that I blamed them for taking such precautions after the terrible fate of Dr Heijn's brother, Gerrit Jan.

At Docklow Grange we had far more banal reasons for securing our property, but reasons nonetheless. Our friends Dom and Linda had given us, as a housewarming present, a magnolia tree. I planted it outside the conservatory and lavished almost as much love on it as I did on my children, and without ever having to scold it for not using its knife and fork properly, either. In fact the greatest danger it faced was not a hard frost but being smothered with affection. I watered it assiduously during a unseasonally dry April, and checked on its progress every day. Then I came home one afternoon from a three-day overseas assignment for the *Independent*. I kissed Jane and Jacob, who were in the garden playing swingball, and strode over purposefully to admire the magnolia. It had gone! In fact, not only had it gone, but there was no sign that it had ever been there. I stood in stupefaction for a second or two, and then, a bit like Basil Fawlty looking for the elusive duck à l'orange, started manically scraping at the soil where the tree had so elegantly stood. There was no hole or anything. Clearly it had been pinched by someone with green fingers.

When I told my friend Geoff Ingham about this, he pointed out that in all the best mysteries, the guilty person is the one least likely to be the perpetrator. The finger of suspicion, said Geoff, therefore pointed directly at Jane. Which reminded me of the Edgar Allan Poe story, set in Paris as I recall, in which a man convinces his wife that she is mad by hiding all the signs that she ever existed. But what could have been Jane's motive? Jealousy? I imagined her reluctantly submitting to a polygraph test and eventually cracking. 'You loved that bloody magnolia more than you loved me, so, yes, I paid Harold from the garden centre to rub it out!'

But Jane, obviously, was as flummoxed as I was. And when you are flummoxed, your imagination takes flight. It could hardly have been an opportunistic theft, because hardly anyone would have had the opportunity. Could it have been someone staying in one of the cottages, angry that their duvet was too warm? Or Ted, the odd-jobman, exacting revenge for my dastardly trick of hiding a radio in the bushes to make him think that there were ghosts about? Or Sam, the tractor driver, getting his own back on me for giving him a booby-trapped beer? Or perhaps an enemy of my 'Tales of the Country' column? I didn't think there was anything in there to provoke too much ill will, apart from my unforgivable behaviour towards the septic tank, but you could never, ever tell. There was the twazzock episode, after all. Moreover, although we had been shown much kindness by people in and around Docklow, the television writer Simon Nye had based an entire comedy series – the brilliant *How Do You Want Me?* – on the resentment felt by some country folk towards newcomers from the city. We knew it was out there.

And yet, would such a person go to the trouble of not only stealing a magnolia tree but carefully filling the hole in afterwards? Surely not. It would have been helpful to engage some professional expertise in solving the mystery, but we could hardly call in the West Mercia constabulary. Herefordshire's crime figures were relatively low, yet not as low as my sister-in-law Jackie made out during one of her visits, when she was pursued for a while along a country lane by a police car with its siren blaring, and remarked to her daughter Rachel that someone, somewhere, must have kicked over a milk churn. The local police had more important things to do than investigate a case of magnolia-rustling. We never did find out what had happened. Or even get a package through the post containing a ransom demand and a twig.

It was ironic, I suppose, that the flowering of my interest in gardening was inspired by a magnolia I never saw in flower. I had never been much of a gardener, or indeed any kind of gardener at all. In Southport my mother had occasionally detailed me to push the lawnmower, but grass cuttings played havoc with my hay fever. She only had to say 'Please will you cut the grass' for my eyes to start puffing up. So that was one more job for my mum, along with washing, cleaning, cooking and driving to

Liverpool every day to pack bras in a rat-infested warehouse just off the supremely misnamed Paradise Street, which was the unglamorous reality of being in the 'job business'. If I never apologised to her then for being an obnoxious teenage layabout with some annoying personal habits, and I don't suppose I did, I can at least do so now.

Even once I had grown up, gardening never seemed like something that was ever likely to concern me. I admired a nice flowerbed as much as the next person, but couldn't get excited about potting up and pricking out, or even excited enough to find out what such terms meant. Besides, I'd never really had a garden to get excited about. In Crouch End it was just a fifteen-foot-square space to utilise in as many ways as we could, and the shed, the treehouse, the rabbit hutch, the sandpit and the small trampoline left precious little room for anything as non-utilitarian as flowers. But the garden at Docklow Grange was a different matter. A rather intimidating matter, in fact. We had Tom, the hard-working lad who had first alerted me to the distant spectacle of Lord Hereford's Knob, and who came once a week. And there was Ted, who cut the extensive, supposedly haunted lawns. But with nearly five acres to look after, we needed to become engaged ourselves.

We also needed some proper advice. Fortuitously, I had an old schoolfriend, from King George V days, who had become a highly successful landscape gardener. An invitation to him and his family to come to stay for the weekend seemed overdue.

My friend's name was Anthony Richards but at school he had been known to everyone, including some of the hipper teachers, as Mozzer. Until a few months before we moved to Docklow, I hadn't seen Mozzer for more than fifteen years; the last I'd heard of him had been in the mid-1980s when he'd been living in the West Indies.

However, another old schoolfriend, Chris Taylor, then told me that he'd heard Mozzer was now based, less exotically, in Liphook, Hampshire, where he was running a thriving company called Graduate Landscapes. Out of the blue I phoned him, wondering whether he would still be the Mozzer I had known.

Mozzer, to put it mildly, was a character. At the beginning of Woody Allen's wonderful film *Broadway Danny Rose*, a bunch of friends sit around a table at the Carnegie Deli in Manhattan swapping stories about Danny Rose, an accident-prone theatrical agent whose acts included a lethal hypnotist. 'If your wife never wakes up again,' Danny anxiously promised a comatose victim's distraught husband, 'I promise I'll take you to the restaurant of your choice.'

For me and my old schoolfriends, Pete, Mike, Chris and Johnny, Mozzer was our Danny Rose. He had been a lad of irresistible cheek and charm, who was always stonier-broke than the rest of us, always scrounging money for a bag of crisps. No matter that none of us had seen him for the best part of twenty years, he had left a legacy of stories that we would carry into our dotage. There was the one about him being invited to play at a ritzy squash club in Southport, and sitting in the changing room after the game, absent-mindedly picking his toenails and then chewing them. A member looked on in horror. 'That is so rude,' he said. 'Oh I'm sorry,' said Mozzer breezily. 'Would you like one?'

But my all-time favourite also concerned other members of his family. Mozzer's grandmother, who lived with them in a terraced house near the shrimping grounds on the Ribble estuary, was an extremely frail old lady. One day, suddenly, she died. It was sad, but not wholly unexpected, and not exactly a tragedy. Mozzer's older sister was due to play in a hockey tournament the following day and nobody saw any reason why she shouldn't go ahead and take part. However, she had left her hockey stick at school. She phoned the school and left a message asking her PE teacher, who conveniently lived in the next street, to bring her hockey stick round that evening.

Meanwhile, Mozzer was told the news when he got home from school that his granny had died. His mother explained that the undertaker had been called for and would be arriving soon to deal with granny, who was stretched out on the settee in the front room, where she had expired. Mozzer went to pay his last respects.

A few minutes later the bell rang, and Mozzer opened the door to a youngish man holding what appeared to be a hockey stick. 'Where is she then?' the man said cheerfully. 'Er, she's in there,' said Mozzer, vaguely wondering why the undertaker had come equipped to play hockey but, being Mozzer, not thinking to question the fact. He showed the man into the front room, then carefully closed the door behind him, to allow him to get on with his business. An ashen-faced PE teacher emerged a moment or two later, and had to be calmed down with a mug of strong, sugary tea. That, improbable but true, is a typical Mozzer story.

Happily, when at last we met again, I found him unchanged, if slightly less hirsute on top. Although he no longer had to scrounge the money to buy a bag of crisps, indeed far from it, he remained eminently capable, in polite company, of picking and chewing his toenails. And I mean that as a compliment. In fact, there is nobody I was at school with for whom I have more respect. His was a truly unprivileged, if not underprivileged background, and by dint of hard work and not inconsiderable charisma, he had built up a company with a staff of more than thirty and a multimillion pound turnover. Which was not in itself unusual, except that he was still exactly the same easy-going, engaging guy he always had been, which perhaps wasn't so usual. And best of all, he was very happy to come for the week-end with his friendly wife, Wendy, The Woman Who Married Mozzer, and three lovely daughters, and give me some free advice on what to do with the garden.

Of course, free advice was one thing, but ours was a garden that was never going to be cheap either to maintain or improve. It did need some attention. The Openshaws had gone for the charming, overgrown look, which certainly had its merits, but Mozzer was adamant that certain things needed doing urgently. We had a 100-foot long yew hedge, for instance, that wasn't all that far short of being as high as it was long. It needed to come down by at least ten feet. Yew, Mozzer told me, is the only conifer that regenerates from old wood. I wasn't at all sure what that meant or how I was supposed to react, so I just nodded solemnly and, feigning complete understanding of the yew situation, said 'right'.

After telling us which trees he would take down and what he would replant in their place, and where he would install a water feature, and for the second time that yew is the only conifer that regenerates from old wood, he added what I already knew, that we would be wise to find someone like him, only locally, and pay them to oversee some changes to the garden. After all, this was going to be our garden for at least the next ten years; it made sense to invest in it properly. We didn't have much money left after the work we'd had done in the house, but we might as well see how much it would cost. We arranged for a Bromyard-based garden designer called Julia Hancock to call round.

Julia turned out to be a highly appealing bundle of energy and enthusiasm with a fantastic line in malapropisms. Oddly, most of them were food-related. She told us that this planting scheme might not 'cut the custard', and that another planting scheme would probably involve having to get rid of some established bushes, in which case we would just have to 'bite the biscuit'.

It occurred to me that the English language should find room for biting the biscuit, perhaps as the very opposite of biting the bullet. 'I'm just going to have to bite the biscuit and get on with it,' we could say, on contemplating an entirely pleasant, indeed pleasurable prospect. Don't you think it would enhance the vocabulary? 'I've been offered a Centre Court ticket for finals day at Wimbledon. I'm just going to have to bite the biscuit and go.'

Julia's malapropisms also reminded me of an exchange Jane's dad had once overheard, at a colliery in South Yorkshire. Bob was standing in an office where a mining-equipment salesman was giving the colliery manager a seemingly interminable sales pitch.

'Reet,' said the salesman eventually, 'let me just put all that in a nutcase.'

The manager looked daggers at him. 'I'm t'bloody nutcase,' he snapped, 'standing 'ere listening to thee.'

With or without those slips of the tongue, Julia's visits were always a joy. Her enthusiasm for our garden and its potential was infectious, and it wasn't that she was looking forward to lining her own pockets; we'd given her a limited budget within which she knew she would have to operate. Nor was she in any hurry to take our money. She told us that we would have to be extremely patient, and having emptied the long border beneath the yew hedge of all vegetation, spend at least a year feeding the soil with compost and fertiliser until we were ready to bite the biscuit and get on with her planting scheme.

In the meantime, I applied myself to trying to understand the rudiments of gardening. May had arrived, and summer would soon follow. Our first full summer in the country. I wanted to engage with the garden, not simply stand back and let others do the work.

There was, at least, plenty of work to go round. And some of it was work that I couldn't very easily ask anyone else to do. Tackling the molehills, for example. Tackling them the way I had been advised to, anyway. We had dozens of molehills, much to the fascination of our Swedish neighbours, Ingemar and Kerstin, who told me that moles were unknown in Scandinavia and wanted to know more about them. Ingemar and Kerstin, a charming, retired couple from Gothenburg, were renting Limetree Cottage, one of the properties that had originally belonged to the grange but which the Openshaws had retained. Describing the characteristics of a mole to a pair of Swedes, it struck me, was one of the more surreal things I had had to do since moving to the country. And yet events were about to take an even more surreal turn.

One night, over a game of pool in the King's Head – the pool table having been reinstated by the new management, a family from Bromyard with no previous experience in the pub trade – Owen and Georgie had assured me that a good way of discouraging moles from exploding on to a lawn was to urinate on all the fresh molehills, or better still, to place a fresh dog turd on top of them. I was already aware of some of the useful ways in which one's urine can be deployed. Someone had told me years before that the best way to deal with a frozen car lock – in the absence of a can of antifreeze, anyway – is to wee on it. I could even testify to the efficacy of this. It had been a bitterly cold night, I'd been standing outside my cousin Stuart's house in a smart road in Highgate, north London, unable to get into my car, and had resourcefully taken the matter in hand. Naturally, I first made sure that there was nobody watching. Behaviour like that in Highgate has the police out in no time; it's armed robberies that they're slower to tackle.

Anyway, despite all that, the glint in Owen's eye made me wonder whether he was having me on. After all, people have been carted off in straitjackets for antics less peculiar than carefully positioning fresh dog turds on the tops of molehills. And although we had bonded that night when we got drunk and shared our respective family histories, I still felt pretty sure that Owen was capable of orchestrating a few good laughs at my expense. What greater laugh than the thought of me wandering round the garden at twilight, piddling on fresh molehills or even arranging an up-to-date collection of turds on top of them?

So I sought a second opinion, which I think is wise when someone tells you to wee on a molehill. I knew that our friends William and Claire, the same people who'd had their pony treated by a chiropractor, had a dreadful molehill problem. I phoned William and asked whether he had ever heard of what I assumed was known in horticultural circles as the pee and poo method? He had. He had even tried it. But the little varmints had kept coming back, so he had taken the more radical step – mole-lovers, avert your eyes – of attaching a hosepipe to the exhaust pipe of his diesel-powered car, feeding it into one of the latest molehills, and letting rip.

Before he'd tried this, however, he'd phoned his trusty local mechanic, Nigel, to ask whether diesel would yield the same potentially deadly carbon-monoxide fumes as ordinary petrol. It only occurred to him later, having not explained the reason for the enquiry, that Nigel probably wondered whether to refer him to the Samaritans.

I did not go down the exhaust-pipe route myself. I did try the weeing approach and it seemed to have some limited success. But it was not what anyone could call gardening. I wanted to be able to call myself a gardener, wanted to get some dirt under my fingernails, although – and this was possibly a hint that I would never be entirely at ease as a gardener – I also wanted to get the dirt out of my fingernails. Although not an especially fastidious chap, I had always had a bit of a thing about clean fingernails. Gardening, I found, even gardening with gloves on, spelt trouble for the fingernails.

When I shared this problem with the readers of my column, I received all kinds of helpful suggestions. One man recommended Grune Tante, a soap containing fine wood shavings, while another wrote to say that he always wore latex surgical gloves, thereby keeping his hands and nails spotlessly clean, and also enabling him to do the fiddly things that you can't necessarily do wearing big chunky gardening gloves. In the following week's column I aired this excellent suggestion, and wondered whether I might be able to find someone who could wear a nurse's uniform and snap the latex gloves on for me, before passing me a trowel, followed by some secateurs. The same man then wrote again to express his hurt, and effectively said that if he'd known I was going to take the piss then he wouldn't have bothered offering advice. I was mortified.

But there was another, worse kind of mortification to come.

9

Val Doonican: The Special Years

Over the second weekend in May, Jane took the kids up to her parents' house in Yorkshire. I stayed at home to work and look after the animals. On the Sunday morning, there was no sign of Tess, the cat, although that wasn't particularly unusual. Since we'd got rid of all the kittens except Tiger Lily, Tess had resumed her nights on the tiles. We didn't have to worry about her getting pregnant again, though; a few days earlier we'd had her spayed, just in case she bumped into that randy black-and-white tom again.

At midday I got a phone call from a man who lived hard by the A44. He'd found a dead cat lying on the road and thought it might be ours; could I come and identify the body? Sure enough, it was Tess, dutiful mother of five, not yet a year old, and now flattened by a car. So much for nine lives. She'd scarcely had time for one.

The children were predictably devastated by Tess's untimely death. Well, Eleanor and Joseph were; Jacob just wanted to prod the corpse.

We decided to bury her in the woods, close to a Victorian headstone which had crumbled over the years, although it was still possible to make out a year, 1884, and the age of the deceased, fourteen years and nine months. The Openshaws had told us that it marked the grave of a beloved family dog and there seemed no reason to doubt this, even though for Ted, the odd-jobman, it represented all the evidence he needed to confirm that the garden was haunted. 'How d'you know it's a dog, look?' he asked, and I had to concede that I couldn't prove it wasn't, although I told him emphatically that the Victorian occupants of Docklow Grange would not have buried a human being in unconsecrated ground.

Assuming this to be the historical burying ground for family pets, then, we dug Tess's grave. If you will accompany me on another tangential excursion here, can I just share with you something that I learnt once from a South African game warden about elephants' graveyards? I am aware that elephants and cats have very little in common, as you will know if you have ever tried to stroke an elephant while watching *Countdown*, but I can't imagine that I will get another opportunity to use this in print.

Apparently, elephants' graveyards are always in areas where the vegetation is soft, because as elephants get older their teeth get worn down, and they keep seeking food that is easier to eat, until finally they have hardly any teeth at all, can't eat, have a starvation-induced heart attack and die. That's why lots of elephant bones are found together. It used to be thought that there was something faintly mystical about elephants' graveyards, but it's a pretty humdrum explanation, really. Until someone invents dentures for elephants, and a big enough glass to put them in, and a big enough bedside table to put the glass on, nature will continue to take its course in this manner. At least in those areas where nature is allowed to prevail over gangs of nasty poachers.

Getting back to domestic pets, Tess's demise was not the first we had suffered. There had been Molly, our rabbit in Park Avenue South who was carried off by a fox. And Mary, the guinea pig who survived her mauling at the paws of the next-door neighbour's cat but was never quite the same again, and died fairly soon afterwards. Mary's misfortune had triggered our first encounter with a vet, and more specifically a vet's bills. Mary had spent two nights at the veterinary hospital in Hornsey for which the bill came to £115. She had cost £8. When Jane was handed the bill by the receptionist she was shocked. She asked whether Mary had made excessive use of the mini-bar or something. Later, we found out from our friend Ali, while she was training to be a florist, that the north London shop where she worked sent out several bouquets a week to people whose pets had died, conveying sympathy on the part of the vet. 'Our condolences on the sad loss of Scooby Doo' was one such heartfelt message. But I don't imagine for a second that the cost of Ali's lovely floral arrangement was ultimately borne by the vet.

Still, the expenditure was almost worth it for the entertainment. During that first visit with a traumatised Mary, Jane was sitting in the reception area when the receptionist called to the vet, 'Mr Hawkins, I've got Mrs O'Shaughnessy on the phone. You saw Bodie last week and now Doyle's not very well.' Jane looked round, assuming that everyone in the waiting room of the right sort of age to know that Bodie and Doyle were named after TV's *The Professionals*, and visualising macho Martin Shaw and smooth Lewis Collins, would be suppressing a giggle, as she was. Or at the very least wondering what kind of creatures Bodie and Doyle were. But nobody looked the slightest bit amused or even interested.

At the Ryelands Clinic in Leominster charges were mercifully below London levels, but there was a similar level of seriousness where pets' names were concerned. I suppose there comes a point where, if you work in a veterinary surgery or even spend much time in the waiting room, these things stop being funny.

All the same, I would like to see a standard procedure introduced so that whenever you take a pet in for treatment, whether in Andover or Auchtermuchty, you know whether to give your own name to the receptionist, or the animal's name. Assuming it to be the animal's name that was required, our friend James – whose wife, Jane, it was who unwittingly made her son's friend cry by explaining that the beloved old family collie had been sent to sleep for eternity – once took their cat Meaty in for an inoculation, and found himself walking self-consciously through to the treatment room having been loudly called as Mr Meaty.

At the Ryelands Clinic, conversely, it was the animal that was given the family name. One day, shortly after Tess died, Jane had come home with a runtish, bow-legged, black male kitten, one of a litter that another parent at school had been, quite understandably in my opinion, trying to dispense with. I was none too keen to have a second cat again, but, of course, the children were delighted, and with devastating originality called the new addition Sooty. In due course, Jane took Sooty to be castrated, poor little thing, and had to sit in the waiting room until the receptionist, deadpan as always, called 'Sooty Viner'. What a hoot. For

Jane's dad, who greatly enjoyed this story, the cat became, and remained, Sooty Viner.

With Sooty Viner's induction into the family, we had been at Docklow Grange for an entire life cycle, more or less, acquiring Tess as a kitten, seeing her raise her own kittens, then burying her and replacing her. That seemed symbolic, as did the impending first anniversary of our move to the country. We had decided to throw a party on 12 July, a year to the day since we left Park Avenue South for the last time as Crouch Enders. We were going to throw together all our friends from London with all our friends from Herefordshire, a prospect as intriguing as it was exciting. What, for example, would the chic Crouch End women make of Owen, with his bulldog tattoo and propensity for making a (thunderously authentic) farting noise by sticking a hairy hand in a hairy armpit when the person next to him sat down?

But before that we faced the biggest test yet of our skills in the hospitality business. A man called Martin Kinghorn, taking us slightly unawares, had responded to the celebration package idea we had advertised on the website. It was his wife's sixtieth birthday celebration, and there would be ten of them. He wanted all three cottages, with the four-course dinner in our house to take place on 5 July. That was the Saturday before the party, which was more than a little unfortunate. On the other hand, the income from that weekend would go some way towards paying for the live band, the disco, the catering, the children's entertainer, and everything else we had booked for the following weekend. In any event, we couldn't turn it down. We had always wanted to prove ourselves as hoteliers, and this was our chance.

Our first eleven months in the holiday cottage business had gone in fits and starts. They had been empty at times we'd anticipated them being full, and full when we might have expected them to be empty. During these former periods, Jane in particular, mainly because she was the one who paid the domestic bills, became thoroughly despondent. Far from the income covering the extra mortgage repayments, the cottages were costing us money. We had got them looking more or less as we wanted, but to do so we had spent far more on them than we had expected to, or than we had, for that matter.

There had also been the unfortunate business with the Stonehouses and then the Prices. And we had the perennial headache of how to market them. People kept saying that we had a great website, but every few days when Jane opened up her e-mails she would find 150 of them, 50 offering her a penis extension, 50 promising her a glimpse of hot teenage sex, 49 offering her Viagra, and one from somebody in Stevenage asking for a brochure. We sometimes wondered whether to hand all three cottages over to an agency such as English Country Cottages and leave it all to them. We'd certainly have fuller occupancy, but then we'd have to hand over a sizeable percentage of the rental fee.

On the positive side, we knew that businesses take time to grow, and we could at least take heart in the fact that most customers had left happy. Some we'd positively bonded with. One such customer was a man called Mark Lewisohn, who had stayed in Yewtree Cottage over Easter, with his wife, Anita.

This was a particularly fortuitous booking. For some years I had been mildly curious about the compiler of the magisterial *Radio Times Guide to TV Comedy*, whose name was Mark Lewisohn, wondering whether he could possibly be the same Mark Lewisohn widely considered to be one of the world's foremost experts on the Beatles. So when I found that a chap with this fairly unusual name had booked to stay with us, I wondered whether it might be the comedy bod or the Beatles bod or whether they were, perhaps, one and the same. And, good-day sunshine, so it was. Or rather, so they were.

In my book, a chap who knew all about TV comedy, all about the Beatles, *and* wrote us a cheque for £325, was a chap worth inviting round for a drink. I told him how much I had used his comedy guide, especially in my previous incarnation as a telly critic. I hoped I wasn't being too ingratiating, like Basil Fawlty with a prized guest, although it would not have been inappropriate to summon the spirit of Basil, first unleashed on an unsuspecting BBC2 audience, according to the entirely reliable *Radio Times Guide to TV Comedy*, on Friday, 19 September 1975.

Mark took my praise in his stride. He told me that he was looking forward to a few days of peace and quiet so that he could knuckle down to writing his latest book, a history of the Beatles in the year 1963. By a remarkable coincidence he had booked to stay at Docklow Grange before checking *The Complete Beatles Chronicle* (author: M. Lewisohn) in which he found that on Easter Monday 1963, exactly forty years earlier, John, Paul, George and Ringo had played the Riverside Dancing Club at the Bridge Hotel, Tenbury Wells, a lovely little town on the River Teme barely twenty minutes drive from our house, along – naturally – a long and winding road. Mark kindly gave me a copy of the notice in an April 1963 issue of the *Tenbury Wells Advertiser*: headlining on Easter Saturday at the Riverside Dancing Club were Erkie Grant and the Tonnets. On the Monday, the Beatles, supported by El Riot and the Rebels (3s. 6d. to members).

Mark duly took himself off to Tenbury to see what he could find. He was thrilled to find the Bridge Hotel not only still there but largely unchanged, to the extent that a man propping up the bar turned out to be Alec Cook, who'd been on the door the night the Beatles played. His wife, Jean, had booked them a few months earlier, for £100.

Since that booking, Mark told me, the band had had a number two hit with 'Please Please Me'. The record destined to be their first number one, 'From Me To You', had been released the Thursday before Easter. So the Bridge Hotel, Tenbury Wells, was somewhat more humble than the venues the Beatles could have been filling, but their manager, Brian Epstein, insisted on honouring all the dates already in the diary. Mark told me, with the authority of one who knew more about all this even than the people who were there at the time, that Beatlemania was still very much a localised phenomenon in April 1963. 'There were little pockets all over the country, and eventually they joined up. But Fleet Street didn't pick up on it until the October.'

He was also able to tell me that the night before they came to Tenbury Wells, John, Paul, George and Ringo had met the Rolling Stones – at the Crawdaddy in Richmond – for the first time. And the following night, they made their BBC television debut. So the Bridge Hotel, Tenbury, loomed large in an unusually eventful week even in the eventful evolution of the Beatles. This struck me as utterly fab, and yet somehow it was typical of the quiet little towns and rolling countryside which we had assumed to be such a cultural backwater.

Out and about in north London, I had never gone too long without spotting the winner of a Bafta or the Booker Prize or an Olivier award or even an Oscar. As one who also tried to be vaguely creative for a living, just to see these people was inspiring. I once followed the wonderful television writer Jack Rosenthal and his equally talented wife, Maureen Lipman, round Brocklehursts, a furniture shop in Muswell Hill, not quite daring to tell Rosenthal how much I admired his work, but hoping that if he sat down on a brown leather pouffe, and then I did, some of his brilliance might rub off.

It sounds silly, given that such encounters were so ephemeral as to scarcely be encounters, but I had been worried, in moving to the Welsh Marches, about stepping out of the society of my peers. And yet since moving to the Marches I had found that the number of distinguished writers, artists, musicians and sculptors, per capita, probably exceeded the numbers in north London. There seemed to be one down every lane. Just a few miles south of us was Broadfield Court, a vineyard with a charming café attached. The woman who ran it, an irrepressibly bubbly character called Alexandra James, turned out to have been an actress with the Royal Shakespeare Company. Her children's godfather was Sir Derek Jacobi, of *I Claudius* fame and rather a lot besides, who occasionally spent weekends at Broadfield Court to get away from the hurly-burly of the city, and was pressed into action waiting on tables in the café. Alex told us that sometimes when he saw customers struck by their waiter's resemblance to the stammering former Emperor Claudius, the great man took over their cappuccinos and asked 'w . . . w . . . whether they w . . . w . . . wanted t . . . t . . . to l . . . l . . . look at the s . . . s . . . sand-wich m . . . m . . . m . . . m . . . m . . . menu?' What a fine fellow.

There were creative forces at work in all directions. Or had been. One morning in May I read an obituary in the *Independent* of Jeremy Sandford. He had written *Cathy Come Home*, the massively influential documentary-drama directed by Ken Loach which, in 1966, bankrolled the homeless persons' charity Shelter practically overnight. And he had lived just a few fields away from us.

I'd already heard about Sandford from Monique Heijn, who, to put it mildly out of respect for the dead, was not a fan. He had formed a great affection for New Age travellers, in fact travellers of all sorts, and had encouraged many of them to live on his land. His kindness to travellers was commended in the obituaries but had apparently been less welcome in the lanes of Herefordshire.

All the same, I wished I had met him, and Shelagh Snell told me she wished she had met him, too. She recalled being told by someone, with considerable distaste, that Sandford gave parties at which people cavorted naked in the fields. That sounded pretty swell, Shelagh had reckoned, and wondered how to wangle an invitation. It reminded me, I told her, of a *Secret Lives* programme that I had once seen about Enid Blyton, which tried very hard to dish some dirt, but could find nothing more damning than the fact that Blyton liked to play tennis in the nude. My respect had instantly increased tenfold for the author of *Five Go to Billycock Hill*, as did Shelagh's for the author of *Cathy Come Home*. And respect is due to me, come to think of it, for getting *Cathy Come Home* and *Five Go to Billycock Hill* into the same paragraph. A literary first, surely.

Another first came a week or two after Sandford's death when, coincidentally, 3000 people described in the *Birmingham Post* as New Age travellers descended upon a village near Leominster for a three-day rave. Apparently, Leominster got a mention on Radio 1; that's the first I was talking about. And a woman with purple dreadlocks was sighted on Broad Street; yet another first. But it was no joking matter for all the people living nearby who complained about the bombardment of noise throughout the night – quite a bit of which, it had to be said, came from police helicopters. Nor was there much amusement among those farmers whose crops were trampled. According to the *Birmingham Post*, the 'revellers' (I've often thought it a shame that this nice word, like parochial, tends to be used pejoratively – revelling ought to be encouraged, not frowned upon) had been invited by a farmer who was about to have his farm repossessed because he had defaulted on his mortgage repayments. This was his way of getting his own back on society, which he felt thoroughly screwed by.

Sandford would probably have applauded. He had been a committed iconoclast. He had also, I was interested to discover, been a committed accordionist. While I was flicking through the pages of a local listings magazine to find someone who could provide live music for our party, I came across the following: 'Jeremy Sandford – accordion for your carnival, ceilidh, barn dance, French trad, circle dance, mystic, sprightly, weddings, birthdays, sacred, profane, solo or with fiddles, pipes, drums.' Nobody had thought to withdraw the listing, even though Sandford was now emphatically unavailable. Now that would have been one-upmanship, I thought. To have mentioned casually to some of our arty friends from London that the guy standing in the corner squeezing the bejesus out of his accordion was the author of one of the most influential pieces of televison ever made.

Instead, we booked a band called the Sultana Brothers, who as far as I knew had never so much as written an episode of *Hollyoaks*. But they were heartily recommended by our friends Avril and Ian. Ian was the guy who'd introduced us to that excellent local saying, 'get up the brook, Leonard'. He was a man of charm, wit, intelligence and joie de vivre, yet had lived his entire life, some forty-six years, in the small village of Richards Castle. Eleven months earlier I would have found that hard to comprehend. But if I had learnt anything since moving to the country, other than that 900 frogs having sex at the same time make a

noise like the purring of a giant cat, it was that you can live in the
sticks for ever and still have far more about you than someone
who has lived in London, New York, Rome and Los Angeles.
And having known a few people who had done just that, I was
able to make the comparison.

Besides, what was a working knowledge of the New York
subway system compared with an ability to impersonate the
warble fly? Ian could do that with uncanny accuracy, although
when he did, it was generally a good idea to protect anything you
didn't want covered in spit. The warble fly sounds like Freddie
'Parrot Face' Davies blowing a raspberry through a kazoo, and is
a noise which scares the living daylights out of cattle. To cattle,
even the smell of the abattoir is preferable to the sound of a
warble fly, which burrows into their hide and lays eggs there,
causing abscessed swellings and extreme pain. Even cows that
have not hosted a warble fly are genetically predisposed to act in
a terror-stricken way when they hear its approaching buzz, sticking their tails straight up in the air and thundering off in a panic.
So Ian could create quite a spectacle by doing his warble fly
impression while leaning on a five-bar gate looking into a field of
cattle. Not, he assured us, that he made much of a habit of it.
Not since his teens, anyway, when he had used it to impress girls.

My own efforts to impersonate a warble fly were poor enough
to do exactly the opposite, repel girls and attract cattle, curious to
find out why the chap leaning on the gate was issuing a noise like
a motorbike accelerating through a puddle of custard. But successful or not, it was yet another thing that I had never pictured
myself doing when I lived in the city.

Indeed, there were things that I couldn't imagine doing when
I lived London, that I now couldn't imagine not doing. Entering
pet competitions at village fetes, for example. By mid-June the

fete season was in full swing; it was not unusual to find three Herefordshire villages within a twenty-mile radius all having a fete on the same afternoon.

Some fetes, like some villages, were more appealing than others. The fete at Yarpole, between Leominster and Ludlow, was a classic of its kind, complete with Cutest Cat and Dandiest Dog competitions, a sack race, a coconut shy, a brass band playing a Beach Boys medley, capable women in flowery dresses offering strong tea and home-made flapjacks (not of the reclassified variety), and a bookstall full of enticing second-hand bargains, such as a 1979 edition of *1,000 Freezer Recipes* and a good-as-new copy of *Val Doonican: The Special Years*, both of which I bought, naturally.

There were also some morris dancers, of course. Who was it who said that everyone should try everything once, except incest and morris dancing? For years I had cheerfully subscribed to the notion that morris dancers must be irretrievably sad characters, the kind of people who wear socks under their sandals. In bed.

One of the funniest stories I had heard concerned some people we knew, the Higsons, who, like us, had moved out of London to Herefordshire. Like us, the Higsons were pathetically anxious that when their friends from the city came to visit, they did not think their new life unutterably boring. But when some friends from Shepherd's Bush arrived, late on the Saturday afternoon, they insisted on going out to buy some wine to go with that evening's dinner. Where could they buy wine? Steve Higson directed them to nearby Bromyard. But they returned empty-handed and faintly ashen forty-five minutes later. They had found nowhere selling decent wine in Bromyard, and one of the few shops open in the high street had been a haberdashery with a sideline, rather curiously, in life-size knitted effigies, notably

271

one of Margaret Thatcher. However, it was not true to say that the town had been devoid of life; outside the shop with the knitted Margaret Thatcher in the window, some morris dancers had been energetically giving their all. Apparently these friends of the Higsons' couldn't get back to Shepherd's Bush quickly enough.

Now, I hasten to add that Bromyard is a place of many charms, not to mention the distinction – and I was personally told this by the town crier – that it is the only place in the entire world called Bromyard. It also has Gilberts, a remarkable emporium – the word 'shop' really doesn't suffice – which always reminds me of the hardware store in *The Two Ronnies'* memorable 'Four Candles' sketch. I once stood behind a customer at Gilberts who bought a light bulb, some grass seed, a hammer, some tomatoes, an apron, a wok and a mole trap. The shop assistant didn't bat an eyelid, totted up the cost of everything on the list, and the customer had paid and gone before I had time to tap her on the shoulder and explain that she could save herself some money by weeing on her molehills.

But Gilberts did not sell fine wines, and I could see why, that particular Saturday afternoon, a couple from Shepherd's Bush might have thought Bromyard a trifle on the limited side. And also why the appearance of morris dancers might have reinforced their prejudices about rural England. On the other hand, just as I have stuck up for Bromyard, so I am going to stick up for morris dancing. The best part of a year in the country had taught me an appreciation of morris dancing. Not an appreciation of its finer points, obviously. I wasn't about to alert a morris dancer to the fact that he'd slightly mistimed his nurdle, or whatever it is that they do. But I had come to see in morris dancing a distillation of the best of England rather than the most idiotic: tradition, good cheer, mild eccentricity and National Health glasses.

So I was pleased to see them strutting, jiggling and waving their stuff at Yarpole fete, which, needless to say, was bathed in warm sunshine. Even the Almighty would think twice about defying those capable women in flowery dresses.

In his book *The English*, Jeremy Paxman quotes from a talk that John Betjeman gave to the BBC Home Service during the Second World War, in which he described a visit to a village in Kent, while the Battle of Britain was raging overhead, at which the local Women's Institute was staging a competition to find the best decorated table centre. 'For me,' said Betjeman,

> England stands for the Church of England, eccentric incumbents, oil-lit churches, Women's Institutes, modest village inns, arguments about cow-parsley on the altar, the noise of mowing machines on Saturday afternoons, local newspapers, local auctions, the poetry of Tennyson, Crabbe, Hardy and Matthew Arnold, local talent, local concerts, a visit to the cinema, branch-line trains, light railways, leaning on gates and looking across fields; for you, it may stand for something else, equally eccentric to me as I may appear to you, something to do with Wolverhampton or dear old Swindon or wherever you happen to live. But just as important.

The old boy would have enjoyed the Yarpole fete. Like the harvest auction months earlier at the King's Head, it was a parochial occasion in the best sense of that maligned word, with a large notice-board devoted to 'The Parish Plan: A Shared Vision', and another publicising a forthcoming talk on local glow-worm trails. Eleanor and her friend Sarah won the three-legged race, and even more excitingly, Tiger Lily came first in the

Cutest Cat competition. Joseph, who officially entered her, was given a rosette and £1 in prize money, and didn't stop beaming for three days. His delight was in no way diminished by the fact that the field was limited. Limited, in fact, to only one other contestant.

The field for the Dandiest Dog competition, by contrast, was positively Grand National-like. Eleanor entered Milo, and had to walk him round a parade ring, just like at Cruft's. Apart from once trying to roger a collie, Milo behaved with great decorum, but inexplicably didn't even make the top three. Meanwhile, the Prettiest Bitch prize went to Millie, a border terrier who belonged to our friends Jane and James. The £1 winnings was pocketed by James. 'Only £399 to go and she's paid for,' he muttered dyspeptically.

We realised, of course, that the appeal of village fetes would not last. The children would grow out of them, even if we didn't. But that summer we all got a kick out of chugging round the Herefordshire countryside in search of the next three-legged race. This was Betjeman's England, all right, complete with fierce pride and seething indignation over the outcome of the voting to determine Best Vegetable. At the Pembridge Show, alongside one of the specimens in class 77 – 'an old-fashioned cherry cake (recipe given)' – a judge had rather cattily written, 'What a shame this cake is overcooked, otherwise it would have won first prize.' I wondered how many years of polite acrimony between Mrs Turner, exhibitor, and Mrs Jones, judge, predated Mrs Turner's overcooked cherry cake.

Meanwhile, we prepared ourselves, mentally and physically, for the Eardisland Show. Children between eight and eleven, which included Eleanor and Joseph, were invited to enter up to five exhibits: a decorated wooden spoon, an animal made of vegetables, three decorated digestive biscuits, something new from something old, and a garden on a plate. Jacob, still not quite five, had just two challenges to ponder: to decorate a potato and to paint a fish. He thought hard about how he was going to tackle the fish-painting exercise, and only slowly did we realise that he had grasped the wrong, potentially fatal end of the stick, and was working out how to daub Teddy, our elderly goldfish. He was extremely disappointed to learn that it was a painting of a fish he needed to submit, not a painted fish. In any event, his decorated potato romped home and he was presented with a tiny trophy, which took pride of place on his bedside table.

Sometimes we took friends from London to these village festivities, past caring whether or not they thought us irredeemably sad for trying too hard to be country hicks. We were still having friends to stay most weekends, and had to think of something to do with them. Sometimes we just took picnics to our favourite spots, chief of which was a meadow stretching down to the River Arrow, just outside the beautiful black-and-white village of Pembridge.

One Sunday towards the end of June, that was where we took our Crouch End friends Liz and Jan, together with their three kids. An idyllic afternoon unfolded, with the children and the dog cavorting in the river, and the adults gorging themselves on a particularly indulgent picnic. The blissful languor of the afternoon seemed too precious to last, and it was. Suddenly, Jan started fiddling urgently in his shorts, which in itself was a strange turn of events, and then leapt to his feet and let out a bloodcurdling roar, as if he'd been stung on the balls by a bee, which in fact he had been. He hopped around in obvious agony, and sympathetic though we all were, I must confess that there was laughter. Jan laughed too, between yelps of pain, and took with admirable humour the predictable swelling gags.

All of which followed to the letter another of Viner's Laws, this one being Viner's Law of Idyllic Afternoons, which holds that as the communing with nature gathers pace, and the general feeling of contentment nears its zenith, someone will either be assailed by dreadful hay fever, step in a dog turd, or get stung.

We'd had a similar experience at the Docklow church fete the summer before, when that wasp stung my niece Hannah. And subsequently in our own back garden, too, one weekend when more friends from London, Steve and Mandy, were staying with us. A jolly barbecue was underway when a wasp somehow navigated its way into Jane's knickers and stung her on the bottom, although what bothered her most was not the pain, intense as it was, but that Mandy, whose own bottom was arguably somewhat more pert than hers, was the one who sympathetically dabbed malt vinegar on to the sting. Jane was aghast for days afterwards. It was obviously a girl thing. When we later told other friends about the incident, the men said, 'Oh no, not a wasp' or 'Oh no, not on your bum' while the women, without exception, said 'Oh no, not Mandy.' The whiff of malt vinegar lingered in the region of Jane's bottom, incidentally, long after the pain had gone. Even *in extremis*, you have to think these things through.

Apart from bees and wasps, the only things interfering with our enjoyment of summer weekends were the cottages. Happily, we had lots of bookings, but this also meant that we – or if I'm being honest, Jane – had to clean three cottages after they had been vacated, usually by ten on a Saturday morning, and have them ready by two in the afternoon for the new arrivals. Eventually we decided that the cottages were bringing in enough of an income for us to pay someone to help with this cleaning marathon, so we advertised in the *Hereford Times*.

We had ourselves responded to an advert in the *Hereford Times*, when we were looking for someone to do the jobs round the house that were beyond me; that is to say, most of them. We couldn't always wait for Jane's dad to come if we needed a shelf unit putting up properly, so we phoned a chap who advertised in the paper as Herman the Handy Husband. That made me feel rather like Brian the Rubbish Husband, but if it meant the difference between a shelf going up straight or at a jaunty angle, then it was worth swallowing my pride. And Herman turned out to be an excellent addition to our growing repertory company of manual labourers, not that Herman quite fitted the conventional image of a manual labourer; he was far more middle class than either Jane or me. He was, however, as per the advert, spectacularly handy. I had cause to phone him up at 7.30 one morning to be told by his wife that he was making fudge. Who makes fudge before 8 a.m.? Herman, I suppose. Later, indeed, he turned his fudge-making into a small commercial enterprise and we started adding his delicious 'Herm-made' Country Fudge to our cottage hampers.

Having so successfully answered an advert in the classified ads section of the *Hereford Times*, we now wondered whether we would be as lucky placing one. We were. Of the fifteen or so responses to our advert for someone to help clean holiday cottages, the first was from a woman called Mary, who lived the other side of Leominster, and who seemed so sound even on the phone that Jane felt tempted to give her the job there and then.

Mary was the answer to Jane's prayers, a woman of unflinching integrity, a rock-solid work ethic, and a keen if occasionally mischievous sense of humour. When Mary phoned her bank one day to enquire about the balance of her current account, she was asked to give her seven-letter password. She knew that it was a noun, and that it applied to the people she was dealing with at the bank. Mary was no lover of banks, and by thinking of a password that summed up how she felt about the functionaries at the other end of the phone, she felt sure she would never forget it. But she *had* forgotten it, and so ran through all the faintly insulting seven-letter words she could think of before being forced to tell the chap at the bank that she would have to call him back. She then phoned her daughter, who reminded her that the magic word was 'baboons'.

Mary was about fifty, an attractive woman in mid-menopause, as she often reminded us when we asked if we could make her a coffee. 'No thanks, I'm having enough hot flushes already today.' Mary had come from a background of genuine poverty, and like many women in Herefordshire of her age and background, had left school aged fifteen on a Friday, and started work at the Sun Valley factory in Hereford, plucking chickens, on the Monday. She had married her boyfriend Lenny, who came from a similar background, the following year. Almost thirty-five years, four children and several grandchildren later, they were still together and still devoted to one another. Moreover, they had seen all four children through the A-Levels that they had never had an opportunity to take, and one of them through Bristol University, then on to Reading to secure her PhD. Mary was herself study-ing part time at college, and took the job cleaning our cottages to pay for the course. She was perpetually cheerful, and funny, but with a strong sense of propriety. When a former employer, Sir somebody-or-other, had criticised her unfairly, she had appar-ently given him a stern lecture on manners. My admiration for her was boundless. I hope that doesn't sound patronising. If it does, she'll be the first to let me know.

10

Mr Hudson and Mrs Bridges

For the children, it was turning into another *Swallows and Amazons* summer. But they had never read *Swallows and Amazons*, and nor had I. When people asked me whether the kids were enjoying their new life in the country, I replied that, at best, theirs was a kind of *Swallows and Amazons* existence. As I understood it, that meant things like splashing around in rivers and looking for badgers. But I didn't know for sure. So when I saw Arthur Ransome's famous book for sale one day – in the tea-room at Worcester Shrub Hill station, improbably enough – I flicked through it with the intention of buying it. Jane and I had just finished reading the rather bloodthirsty *Harry Potter and the*

Order of the Phoenix to the kids at bedtime; *Swallows and Amazons* would be the perfect antidote.

The reason I didn't buy it, to my shame, is that my brief flick-through revealed one of the main characters to be called Titty. If I read a book to the children featuring a character called Titty then either they would keep giggling or I would. I did think of changing her name to Kitty, but that wouldn't work, because they often read over my shoulder. I also thought of lobbying the publisher to change Titty's name in the next edition, rather as the politically incorrect passages in the Famous Five books had been amended for these more sensitive, egalitarian times. ('"Dick, I'll make your bed," said Anne, shocked to see it made in such a hurried way' – *Five Get into Trouble*, 1949.) But that would have been ridiculous. So I just put it back.

Anyway, maybe reading a book about a blissfully bucolic summer would have been a mistake. It might have made us all feel as though we were missing something, because things are never as blissfully bucolic in real life as they are in fiction; I bet none of Arthur Ransome's characters ever got stung on the bum.

And I bet none of them ever found themselves urinating in front of an audience of bemused senior citizens. I'm aware that there has already been quite enough urinating in this book, not to mention other bodily functions (although frankly I'm surprised that I've managed to get this far without letting you in on my all-time favourite medical fact, the one fact I can remember from ante-natal classes, that if a man's bladder were powered by a muscle as strong as the uterus, he would be able to pee right across the Thames).

And I don't want to appear preoccupied with my wife's lower half, either. But it might as well be recorded that on our very first visit to Ludlow, almost a year earlier, we had all been merrily paddling in a shallow stretch of the River Teme, when Jane felt an overwhelming urge to pee. With no public toilets nearby, she found herself a secluded spot, protected by a screen of trees, crouched down and quickly did what she had to do. It was only in the act of straightening up that she glanced across to the opposite riverbank and saw what appeared to be a minibus party of elderly people, sitting on benches. They were eating their sandwiches and very much enjoying the show.

Our relationship with Ludlow, then, had inauspicious beginnings. When Jane, a few months later, caught the eye of an old man in a tearoom in Hereford, and he said 'Haven't I seen you somewhere before, my dear?', she decided not to ask him whether he had ever been on a nice minibus outing to Ludlow, with a picnic and unexpected cabaret by the River Teme.

Happily, we later came to associate Ludlow with more acceptable and, indeed, deliberate forms of exhibitionism, such as that insisted upon by the organisers of the town's annual medieval fayre. Normally I am not a fan of quaint olde English spellings, but fayre play to these people, they did a cracking job of evoking the Middle Ages. The fayre had taken place a few weeks before Christmas, in the castle grounds. It was superbly done, full of cowled monks and clanking knights, and with catapult-the-infidel rather than shoot-the-duck stalls, where Jacob was called 'young sir' and asked to hand over one groat.

I know that these themed fairs take place all over England all the time, but I don't suppose many of them are as atmospheric as the medieval fayre in Ludlow. I know that there are lots of them because I talked to the chap on the wool-dyeing stall, who was wearing a pair of pince-nez with, if you can picture this, a Plantagenet bridge. When I complimented him on his resourcefulness he said that he attended loads of fairs from

Anglo-Saxon to Victorian, and had appropriate eyewear for each one.

I have to take off my hat – in this case a rather handsome one in baggy green velvet – to people like this. Like the stalwart members of the Test Card Circle, assembling in Leominster every spring to discuss the Ceefax background music, they pursue their enthusiasms with extraordinary diligence, and give not a jot, or even a groat, for anyone who thinks them odd.

We had turned up to the fayre in mid-afternoon, not knowing that it shut up shoppe between 2 p.m. and 4 p.m., although that at least produced some marvellously anachronistic sights around town, such as Robin Hood buying a lottery ticket, and Thomas à Becket talking to a traffic warden. Even inside the castle grounds I had no doubt that there were anachronisms to horrify my old professor of medieval history, Prof. Leonard. I could imagine the old boy grimacing at the sight of a knight wearing a twelfth-century tabard over thirteenth-century armour alongside some fourteenth-century peasants dancing to fifteenth-century lute music. But it all seemed splendidly authentic to us.

The deal was that anyone with a stall had to wear period dress. I talked to a charming guy called Michael Leviseur, who ran a company called the Organic Smokehouse and was doing a roaring trade in smoked salmon, which hopefully compensated for the sackcloth robe he was forced to wear. It looked a trifle itchy.

We had met Michael before at the Ludlow Food Festival, a deliciously genteel affair, also held within the castle walls, which brought a flavour of olde England to the decidedly modern England carry-on of stallholders from Nuneaton trying to entice day-trippers from Walsall with their exciting new range of Ligurian stuffed baby artichokes. And unlike most food festivals, the Ludlow Food Festival was child-friendly. I can't claim to be an expert, but I'm told that when one takes one's offspring to some food festivals, the occasion is marred by them persistently asking when they can go for a Big Mac, and complaining that the cheese smells like poo. Our kids didn't do that, not because it hadn't occurred to them that the cheese smelled like poo, but because they found plenty to entertain them, not least the spectacle of people earnestly sampling olives stuffed with feta cheese as though their very lives depended on making the right choice between those and the olives marinated in walnut oil, garlic and cumin.

The sampling culture is not big in Britain, on the whole. When I was an impecunious student living in America, it was possible to stroll through a mall buying nothing but sampling everything. You didn't even have to feign intent to spend, as you do here, subtly brandishing your wallet as you ask if you can just try a sliver of the Stinking Bishop. In the States, with a broad smile, and a 'have a nice day', the shop assistant (probably wearing a lapel badge which read 'Arlene, Vice-President, Handing Over Crackers With Little Bits Of Cheese On') would usually convey the impression that watching you stuff yourself was the highlight of her week.

In Britain, by contrast, assistants in all but the most enlightened food shops are trained, or may even be genetically predisposed, to regard with the deepest suspicion anyone asking for a freebie. When they do hand something over, it's a neutron of cheese balanced on an atom of cracker. Yet at the Ludlow Food Festival, samples are practically forced on you. Which is not necessarily a good thing. On the day Jane and I went, I'd eaten garlic honey, some mature goat's cheese, some runner bean chutney, a Scotch egg, some free-range mayonnaise, some smoked organic salmon and a cardboard thimble of game sauce with port, all before 11 a.m., which quite ruined my plans for a lunchtime sortie to the exquisitely-named paella and faggot emporium.

The smoked salmon came from Michael, with whom we renewed our acquaintance at the medieval fayre. He was an interesting fellow. He had worked in either security or securities in London – over the lute ensemble energetically playing 'Greensleeves', I didn't quite catch which – but had given it all up to weave Harris tweed in the Hebrides. While up there he had learnt the rudiments of smoking fish, and had then set up his smokery in Clunbury, a few miles north-west of Ludlow. But he didn't only smoke fish, he also smoked cheese and butter, which had gone down a storm with a particularly distinguished visitor to his stall in Ludlow Farmers' Market. 'Smoked butter?' exclaimed the Queen. 'I've never heard of smoked butter!' She then continued on her royal walkabout, before twice returning to exclaim 'Smoked butter!' again.

Michael, not one to miss a marketing opportunity, slipped a small parcel of smoked butter to a lady-in-waiting, and a few days later phoned Buckingham Palace, managing to get through to some chap with a fabulously archaic title, the Chief Knob of the Royal Household, or something like that. 'I don't know whether the Queen was genuinely interested or whether she was just being polite,' said Michael. 'Oh no, you would have known if she wasn't interested,' said the Chief Knob, ordering more butter. There later came a further order from Balmoral, because the Duke of Edinburgh wanted some smoked butter for the family barbecue. I suggested to Michael that he could reasonably claim to supply the Queen 'by royal astonishment'.

Seven months later, as we prepared for our summer party, we

heard another nice story about the Queen. We were expecting about 120 people, and decided to hire someone to prepare some quiches and puddings and things, on top of the stuff we were going to do ourselves. A woman called Emma had been recommended to us, and she certainly had excellent credentials; every year she cooked for a shooting party at the home of Lord and Lady Fortescue-fforbes-Fotheringham, or some such people, at which the Queen and Prince Philip would occasionally make an appearance. But at the shooting party the previous year she had had to take her baby son, who was still being breast-fed. So having set out a couple of trestle tables groaning with game pies, home-made chutneys, cold meats and delicious salads, Emma then retired to the back seat of her Suburu, to feed the baby. Unfortunately, she couldn't get him to latch on. He was bawling and she was flustered, the more so when a sympathetic face appeared at the window and said, 'It can be awfully difficult, can't it?' Of all improbable moments to be engaged in conversation by one's sovereign, being in the back of one's Suburu while thrusting a breast at one's bawling baby must be right up there.

As well as Emma we also engaged Jean, a friend of the Johns, to prepare yet more food. And Legges of Bromyard were bringing a hog to roast. If anyone left the party complaining that there wasn't enough to eat, then it could only be that they had turned up to the wrong party. Apart from the weather, which in Herefordshire in mid-July can do just about anything, we felt we had all bases covered. We'd even found a clown, a bloke from Worcester called Steve Kaos, to entertain the kids. It was an expensive production, but a worthwhile one. After all, we were not only celebrating the anniversary of our move, it was also a belated housewarming. And a belated celebration of Jane's fortieth birthday, which had been somewhat eclipsed the previous August in the aftermath of the move. And for that matter an even more belated celebration of my own fortieth.

I had been forty when we moved to Herefordshire, and I was now forty-one. I hadn't had a body part pierced, after all. Nor had I started going clubbing or dyeing my hair or calling people 'dude', and I hadn't bought myself a pair of leather trousers or a powerful motorbike, those classic rites of passage into a chap's fifth decade. I had briefly toyed with the idea of buying myself a Yamaha GL900X with fluorescent orange mudguards, but wasn't sure whether I really needed an electric organ, especially one with fluorescent orange mudguards. No, my mid-life crisis, such as it was, had been entirely resolved by our move to the country. In fact, if anything had assumed the symbolic role of the leather trousers it was a pair of canvas gardening gloves.

Just as I had never pictured myself addressing a chicken as 'darling' while we still lived in the city, nor had I ever envisaged gazing with proprietorial pride upon a row of broad beans. But with the help of young Tom, and later of an experienced gardener called Alan, who came once a fortnight and was another recommendation of the Johns, I had created a vegetable garden at the back of Yewtree Cottage of which I was inordinately proud. Actually, to say that I had created it with their help is twisting the truth a little. They had created it with my help. Well, not my help, exactly. More my supervision. At any rate, I had said that it would be nice to have broad beans, and Tom or Alan had done the dirty work.

Alan was another treasure, as just about everyone had been who had helped us in the project of making a new life in the country. It would have been nice, if only for the purposes of recording the humorous consequences between these covers, to have employed a few incompetents: a colour-blind electrician, perhaps, or a roofer with vertigo.

We'd certainly had our share of them in London, notably a plumber who seemed moderately proficient before lunch, but after lunch turned into a walking disaster area, a metamorphosis possibly not unrelated to alcoholic intake. He only did a job for us once. He worked from 11 a.m. until noon, then took his lunch-break and returned at three, with noticeably shaking hands. In fixing a radiator to the wall in the loo, he then contrived to bang a nail into a water pipe which subsequently leaked into the utility room below and brought the entire ceiling crashing down. In the street a few days later, just after the insurance assessor had left, Jane spotted the painter-decorator who had recommended the plumber, and said, in what may actually have been a half-shriek, 'Have you any idea what bloody havoc that guy caused?' They had a brief conversation, featuring quite a few excited gesticulations, and then Jane stomped back to the house. Her parents were staying with us at the time, and had overheard this vigorous exchange. 'Did you just say "bloody"?' her mum asked, disapprovingly.

At Docklow Grange we had had no such bad luck. Our plumber, Mark, was a Koh-i-noor among diamond geezers, who, for all his despair at our strange configuration of oddly behaving pipes, seemed to regard it as a personal mission to smooth out all our plumbing difficulties. And although there was never a day when he was not Mr Busy from Busytown during a period with an unusually full diary, he had dropped everything on the couple of occasions we had had emergencies in the cottages. Twice we had been greeted with overflowing cisterns at the worst possible time, on a Saturday morning with guests having just left and new guests about to arrive, and twice Mark had shot round in a white van that didn't look like Batman's batmobile, but in a crisis shifted just as quickly, and was no less welcome.

Alan the gardener was another in Docklow Grange's short but happy tradition of reliable tradespeople. He was amazingly dedicated, turning up every other Tuesday rarely any later than 7.30 a.m., even though he lived a good twenty miles away. Alan was a man of few words, but shy rather than taciturn. When I took him a mug of coffee we sometimes conversed for a while about splitting snowdrops or whatever and then both stood there trying to think of something to say next. I was powerfully reminded of Ted and Ralph, as so sublimely played by Paul Whitehouse and Charlie Higson in *The Fast Show*, the difference being that I never so much as invited Alan to a Tina Turner concert, let alone fancied him.

Mind you, tickets to a Tina Turner concert were the least he deserved. He charged us £90 a day, which was why we couldn't afford him more than once a fortnight, yet one of Alan's days was worth several of most other people's. Indeed, I was shamed by his zeal for our vegetable garden into putting in some back-bending myself.

I also started reading books about growing vegetables. That's another sign of the ageing process. There was a time – several decades ago, obviously – when if I was browsing in a bookshop I would always sneak a look at a lavish book on nude photography, trying to convey the impression to anyone who might be watching me (and when you're looking at a book full of glossy nude photographs you're convinced that just about everyone is) that what I was interested in were the delicate nuances of light and shade, as represented by a recumbent female form which happened, by the by, to be starkers.

But one day, in Waterstones in Oxford as it happens, I realised that I was standing idly by the gardening section, and that it was books about vegetables that now turned me on. If *The Big Book of Garden Hens* had supplanted the *Rothmans Football Yearbook* on my bedside table, *The Big Book of Garden Hens* was now supplanted by *The Complete Book of Vegetables, Herbs and Fruit: The Definitive Sourcebook for Growing, Harvesting and Cooking*. It wasn't that my enthusiasm for the chickens had abated, any more than my enthusiasm for football had abated, or for the recumbent female form, for that matter. It was just that in those ten minutes between climbing under the duvet and turning off the bedside lamp, I had decided I wanted to learn things about globe artichokes rather than things about Rhode Island Reds or Plymouth Argyle. As for learning things about the recumbent female form, well, there was usually one next to me. I had learnt that it could go from 'night night' to full snore in less than thirty seconds.

The Complete Book of Vegetables, Herbs and Fruit: The Definitive Sourcebook for Growing, Harvesting and Cooking I should add, is not the easiest volume to wield when you are lying in bed. To do so with ease, it probably makes sense to first consult *The Complete Book of Biceps, Triceps and Pectorals: The Definitive Sourcebook for Increasing Upper Body Strength*. But I persevered, and discovered some wonderful things. Did you know that globe artichokes were introduced to France by Catherine de Medici, and to North America by French settlers in 1806? Me neither, although my favourite section was the section on herbs, which revealed that sorrel is also known as bread-and-cheese, sour leaves, Tom Thumbs, sour sauce and, best of all, a thousand fingers. And that cowslip is also known as Our Lady's bunch of keys, St Peter's keys, bunch of keys, keys of heaven and covekeys, although just as I thought I had hit upon a theme, I read on to discover that cowslip is also known as palsywort, cowflop, cowstripling, freckled face, golden drops, herb Peter, hot rod, long legs, nook maidens, titsy totsy, St Peter's herb, paigale, cowslop, cowslap, fair bells and fairy cups.

The trouble with these lists of alternative names for herbs, I thought, as I lay in bed waiting for sleep to overcome me, is that they begged far more questions than they answered. In fact, they didn't answer any questions at all. Who would open a book hoping to find an alternative name for sorrel? Hardly anyone. But who wouldn't wonder how sorrel possibly came to be called bread-and-cheese? Or whether there are any soup recipes calling for a thousand fingers to be mixed in at the last minute, in which case don't ask for it next time you stop for lunch in a leper colony. Or why the hell anyone would call cowslip 'titsy totsy', which sounded more like the name of a character in *Swallows and Amazons*. I wondered whether maybe all these names were made up, and made plans to write a herb book of my own, which would reveal that basil is also known as flopsy-mopsy, rat-up-a-drainpipe, beans-on-toast and Wayne Rooney. And with those intriguing if madcap thoughts clattering around in my head, I made my own contribution to the symphony of snoring alongside me.

Thanks to all Alan's work, and not a little of my own, the vegetable garden was looking wonderful by the start of July. I could hardly bring myself to harvest the potatoes, so splendid was their foliage. They were called Red Duke of Yorks, and again I had done my research, able to tell anyone who wanted to know, or who was perhaps immobilised in some way, that the Red Duke of York potato was of Dutch origin, had been introduced to the UK in 1942, and was the source of Marks & Spencer Heritage Crisps.

This information came from a booklet that I heartily recommend whether you grow vegetables or not: Alan Romans' *Guide To Seed Potato Varieties*. Like *A Complete Guide to British Moths* by Margaret Brooks, it enlightened me where previously I had never been aware I needed enlightening.

For one thing, I'd had no idea there were so many varieties of potato. There are royal potatoes – King Edward, British Queen, Princess, Ulster Prince, Caesar – and merely aristocratic potatoes – Duke of York, Lady Balfour, Lady Felicia, Ulster Chieftain. There are potatoes to travel in – Rocket, Concorde, Red Pontiac – and potatoes to travel to – Stirling, Ballydoon, Riviera. There are potatoes named after obscure American Congressmen – Russet Burbank, Pentland Dell, Edzell Blue – and potatoes named after Women's Institute branch secretaries – Maris Piper, Maris Peer, Maris Bard. There are potatoes that sound like eighteenth-century courtesans at Versailles – Belle de Fontenay, Amandine, Amour – and potatoes that sound like twenty-first-century hookers in Soho – Maxine, Mimi, Desirée. And, for that matter, potatoes that sound like services offered by Maxine, Mimi and Desirée – the Première, the Cabaret, the Majestic. Or, for clients with plenty of money and stamina, the Avalanche.

But I was happy with my Red Duke of Yorks, and looked forward to showing them off at the party, although arguably if I got to the point of escorting people round the vegetable garden, it wouldn't be much of a party.

Not that we were worried about people enjoying themselves. Jane and I were used to making parties. Given the weather, we felt pretty sure it would go well. In Crouch End we had always had a Christmas do for seventy or eighty people which we flattered ourselves was quite a fixture on the social calendar. The social calendar of those seventy or eighty people, anyway. So this one, while on a bigger scale, was not anything to worry about. Which was just as well, because the Kinghorns' celebration dinner was plenty to worry about.

We had e-mailed Martin Kinghorn with a suggested menu of mushroom risotto, roast guinea fowl in a cream and peppercorn sauce, local cheeses, and that old faithful from the *River Café Cookbook*, pear and almond tart. He e-mailed back to say the menu sounded splendid. He seemed like a nice chap, insofar as you can judge someone by the tone of an e-mail.

And so he was. He was rotund, northern and jolly, which in my book is very often an unbeatable combination. His wife Alicia was lovely as well; slim, northern and kind. Martin had found us on the internet and thought that Docklow Grange sounded like the ideal venue for Alicia's sixtieth. They were coming from Knutsford in Cheshire, but had friends coming from Cardiff, and others coming from Northampton, and we were located roughly in the middle of the triangle. So we were ideal for them, and they were ideal for us. A sixtieth birthday party seemed like an ideal baptism for our celebration package; they weren't likely to drink themselves into a stupor or play strip poker.

For Alicia the weekend was a surprise. She knew that she and Martin were going away somewhere, but not that they were meeting up with the four other couples who were their oldest friends. We cheerfully played a part in the deception, installing the Kinghorns in one-bedroom Manor Cottage and the others in Yewtree and Woodlands. The eight friends arrived on our doorstep at 7.30; I showed them into the drawing room and served them canapés and champagne. Then Martin and Alicia arrived at 7.45, and there was so much excitement – verging, I might even say, on rapture – that I thought for a moment that perhaps the evening would involve a few hands of strip poker. But they would have plenty to take off. Slightly alarmingly, they were all dressed to the nines; the men wore dark suits and the women their smartest frocks. I don't suppose we'd expected them to turn up in sweatshirts and jeans but even so, that they were so manifestly dressed for a special night out rather underlined the need for us to provide them with one.

We had bribed the children £5 each to stay quietly upstairs and put themselves to bed, although Jacob in particular was quite capable of forgetting the terms of the agreement and wandering down the stairs insisting that we wipe a huge bogey from under his nose, which the Kinghorns and their guests possibly would have found charming, although equally possibly it would have put them right off their roasted guinea fowl. We had a bit of family history with bogeys. When Joseph was three, walking through Haringey library with Jane, she stooped and with a swift motherly flourish, wiped a massive rogue bogey from his top lip. He was outraged. 'Hey,' he shouted, red-faced with fury. 'I was going to eat that!'

Fortunately, though, all three children kept to their side of the bargain, which left Jane and me to devote ourselves to keeping our guests happy. For Jane it was actually a treat to be confined to the kitchen while cooking for a dinner party. Excellent cook though she was, there had been occasions with friends round for dinner, when, while busy being gaily witty over pre-dinner drinks, she had forgotten to take something out of the oven, or even to put something in. This time she could dedicate herself entirely to the culinary arts, drizzling olive oil and scattering parsley with surgical precision. And she didn't have to worry about what to wear, although she couldn't be too slapdash; there was always the possibility that the Kinghorn party would insist on giving their compliments to the chef in person. We hoped.

We realised when we plated up the first course (plating up being the jargon that we professionals like to use) that mushroom risotto had been a mistake. There is simply nothing you can do with mushroom risotto that stops it looking like something a dog might have thrown up. Happily, that's not what it tasted like. Our guests tucked in merrily, and having started off the evening including me in their banter, and asking polite questions about the house, began more and more – in exact proportion with the amount of drink being taken, in fact – to disregard me. Which was exactly the way I wanted it. It was their house for the evening. I wanted them to be scarcely conscious of me. Besides, I needed to concentrate on carrying five loaded plates at the same time, as Emile, the camp head waiter at Roundtrees Restaurant in Southport, had taught me. He would have been proud of me, although he might have admonished me for not wiggling my bottom enough, or cocking my little finger.

At the same time, it felt decidedly odd to be a maître d' in one's own home. I couldn't help thinking about the folk who had lived in the Grange at the time that Mrs Goodfellow's mother had been the nanny, and how bizarre they would have thought the notion of making ends meet by inviting paying customers into the house and waiting on them. Using that excellent 1970s drama serial *Upstairs, Downstairs* as a reference point, it was as if Lord and Lady Bellamy had metamorphosed for the evening into Mr Hudson and Mrs Bridges, with the added, rather racy twist that Mr Hudson and Mrs Bridges would wake up in the same bed the following morning.

Still, if we managed to do more of these celebration dinners then we would have to get used to it. In any case, it was exhilaratingly odd rather than unpleasantly odd, with me updating Jane every time I went back into the kitchen on how much they were eating and what they were saying. I reported that the rest of the meal was going down as well as the mushroom risotto had, while looking very much less like dog's vomit. And after dinner Jane was indeed called through to take a bow, again like Mrs Bridges after a particularly triumphant meal at 165 Eaton Place. My only regret was that we couldn't leave the washing-up to Ruby the parlour maid.

After coffee, four of the five men went through to play snooker, and their cries of laughter gave me considerable pleasure, albeit mixed with the slight concern that they were not entirely, or even partly, sober. At one point I went in, on the pretext of offering port or brandy, but really to make sure that they weren't dancing a conga across the precious baize, or sword-fighting with the cues or something. Which, of course, they weren't. The snooker table had been a controversial acquisition – it had even been reported back to us that Mr Openshaw thought we had 'spoiled' his best room by installing it – but at last I could claim that it was a business asset as well as a personal indulgence.

The Kinghorns and their friends finally left just after 2 a.m., with Alicia repeatedly saying that her head felt like a helium balloon. 'It's going to keep floating off the pillow,' she brightly assured us, as Martin steered her down our front doorstep. After we had waved them into the night, and shut the door, there was a knock. We opened the door to find Alicia reminding us that her head felt like a helium balloon, and would keep floating off the pillow. We rather suspected that her head would feel less like a helium balloon the following morning, and more like a concrete ball, but plainly the evening, from their point of view, had been a great success.

As it had been for us. We felt as if we had come of age as professional hospitality-givers, and that we could now get more ambitious. Maybe I could start carrying six plates at once. Even more excitingly, maybe we could develop the fantasy of turning Docklow Grange into a venue for artistic weekend retreats. I resolved to e-mail Vanessa Redgrave, and reacquaint her with the idea I had suggested to her thirteen months earlier. What would be the worst outcome? That she would e-mail me back saying, 'Nice to hear from you. Unfortunately, I haven't got the foggiest idea who you are'?

The Kinghorns left the following afternoon, and Alicia still seemed high as a kite, or even a helium balloon, which was enormously gratifying. More gratifying still, Martin wrote us a cheque for £1195, the figure we had rather arbitrarily arrived at for our celebration package of dinner and accommodation for ten. We hoped he didn't consider it too steep. He seemed happy enough, and the price seemed about right to us. After all, we'd had to take into account the cost of bribing the children.

The children were giddy with excitement as the week wore on and the party got closer. Our fears that we might be rained on began to recede; there was a heatwave across the entire country, but especially intense in Herefordshire, Worcestershire and Shropshire, which was as good a sign as any that global weather patterns were going berserk.

On the Wednesday, Worcester was officially declared the hottest place in the country, at 28.7 degrees centigrade, and the fine weather was forecast to continue over the weekend. The following day a friendly chap called Vince from a company called Three Counties Marquees came round to erect a tent with a rather natty parquet dance floor. He told us proudly that we were the first customers for this particular marquee, and it

certainly looked impressively pristine. Unfortunately, not for
long. It took him hours to erect it but no sooner had he done so
than Vince strode into the house no longer looking friendly, in
fact looking faintly murderous. 'We've got a problem,' he said,
darkly. We followed him outside. 'Look,' he said. We looked.
And recoiled. Every one of the decorative ropes on the inside of
the marquee walls, what he told us was called Dutch lacing, had
been severed. We didn't need Miss Marple to lead us to the cul-
prit. The cuts were all at Jacob's shoulder height, and an hour
earlier Jacob had asked if he could borrow some scissors 'to cut
some shapes'. We put two and two together and arrived effortlessly at four, which coincidentally was his age.

Had I committed a crime of that magnitude when I was four,
I would have been spanked and sent to my bedroom. Such are
these enlightened times that Jacob's punishment was to be denied
any Pick 'n' Mix sweeties at the petrol station on that evening's
visit to see Stamford Heath School's end-of-term production, the
thrillingly titled *Zoom*. However, it had the desired effect. While
his sister and brother bagged up their chocolate mice and jelly
tots, Jacob could only watch. He was heartbroken, the more so as
Eleanor and Joseph were sternly instructed not to share their
sweets with him.

None of which repaired the Dutch lacing, however. We apologised to Vince as profusely as we could without licking his
boots clean, and said that, of course, we would pay for the
damage. In the event he charged us £100, for what, for Jacob, had
probably been twenty seconds' worth of satisfaction. Even Miss
Whiplash would have thought that equation a bit unfair.

Thankfully, there were no other disasters as Saturday
approached, and finally the day dawned, the first anniversary of
our move to Docklow Grange. There were twelve families from

Crouch End coming, as well as friends from school and university days, a few relatives, and lots of friends we had made since arriving in Herefordshire. It all felt highly symbolic, marrying our past with our present and indeed our future, not that there was much time to dwell on the symbolism. There was food to prepare, drinks to chill, decorations to put up, and more tents to erect, preferably without Jacob's help. Although we had kept the cottages free, and booked most of the B&Bs in the vicinity, there were still not enough beds for everybody. So several of our friends had declared they would camp, giving the place the look of a mini-Glastonbury. Most of them were experienced campers, pioneers in what was rapidly becoming a new middle-class enthusiasm. I read somewhere that since 2001, once the effects of the foot-and-mouth epidemic had begun to wear off, membership of the Camping and Caravanning Club had increased by 20 per cent, and that this huge increase was largely because canvas holidays had been embraced by the middle classes.

Our friends who arrived with tents mostly seemed to know exactly what they were doing, with the exception of one, Rob, who had borrowed a tent seemingly designed to accommodate a couple of battalions of soldiers, all wearing bearskins. Rob and his wife, Andrea, had four children with them so required a capacious structure, but this was just ridiculously huge in all directions, and took them about three hours to put up, which was almost three hours more than the amount of sleep they managed to get inside it, on account of it being hotter, as Rob evocatively and forcefully put it, than hell.

But I hope that if I were to ask them now, they would claim to have enjoyed the party immensely. Ditto my mother-in-law, Anne, whose trauma was that, shortly before the party began, as she was getting changed in our bedroom in what she thought was the utmost privacy, Steve Kaos the clown walked past the window on 20ft high stilts.

While the fifty-odd kids present were being entertained by Steve Kaos on what the Openshaws had known as the croquet lawn, almost certainly never intending it as a stage for fire-eating, Jane and I were being entertained by Owen, who was telling us about the time he found a chap he vaguely knew locked in full and energetic sexual congress with a sheep. 'Local businessman he was, look,' said Owen. 'Never married. He's dead now, poor bugger. Don't know about the sheep.'

As we laughed at Owen's stories, I thought how much more interesting my life had become since moving to Docklow. It wasn't that I derived particular fulfilment from tales of bestiality, in fact this was the first I had ever heard, but by the same token there had never been much likelihood in Crouch End of encountering someone who could describe exactly what it is like to stumble upon a man having sex with a sheep in a barn, right down, and I won't share too much detail with you, to the trousers carefully folded and placed on an adjacent bale of hay.

In a way, the party was a microcosm of our year in the country. Here I was laughing with Owen and introducing him to my friends from London, the same Owen who had been the personification of mistrust; whose disdain for us had been almost tangible. Maybe it still was, although if so, he at least concealed it well.

There were other ways, too, in which the party was a microcosm of our year. As a treat for Jane I had asked our friend Lou Dalgleish, the wife of my old school buddy Mike, to sing. Lou was a professional singer-songwriter and we loved her voice; in particular, Jane loved the way she performed the Elvis Costello song 'Indoor Fireworks'. But no sooner had Lou taken the microphone than there was a power cut. It wasn't like all the winter power cuts we'd suffered, in that we couldn't blame Powergen for this one. It was just that our own electricity system couldn't cope with the amplifiers and everything else required by the Sultana Brothers, our live band, and the circuit overloaded just as Lou was hitting the big notes. But even so, it seemed apt that a party to celebrate our first twelve months should experience the Docklow Grange phut! All we needed now was for the sky to darken with flies, like Japanese bombers advancing on Pearl Harbor. And maybe for Herman the Handy Husband to arrive, to get the power back on.

Not that we needed Herman, with my father-in-law Bob around. He flipped a few switches, and, after a couple of further electrical blips, Lou resumed. When she'd finished, she got a huge ovation, and I looked around at the smiling faces, and in particular at the faces that twelve months before had been entirely unknown to us. I looked at Jane and James: James who had had to walk through a veterinary surgery summoned as Mr Meaty; Jane, whose immensely kind and gentle demeanour hid a quick and at times risqué wit. We had celebrated her birthday at the Three Crowns, and after we had all perused the menu, someone guilelessly said, 'Jane, are you having tongue?'

'I hope so,' she replied, 'it *is* my birthday.'

I looked, too, at Shelagh, Jim, Nancy, John and John, the luncheon club stalwarts, of a different generation yet a like mind. And at Louise and Rupert Anton, so welcoming to us in those first few months. And at Avril and Ian: Avril one of the most generous-spirited women we had ever met; Ian with such an enviable warble fly impression. I was reminded of the night before we left Crouch End, of wondering who on earth our kindred spirits would be in Herefordshire. Well, here they were. And here we were; settled, contented, only periodically fretting about the exorbitant cost of our new lifestyle, and with so very much to look forward to, not least the exciting search for the right French Drain or nitrification tile or perforated plastic pipe to take the septic tank's effluent, as recommended by Mr Arthur J. Kirtley of Kimbolton.

Acknowledgements

Without the help, advice and encouragement of the following people, this book would not have been written – or at least, the experience of writing it would have been a sight less agreeable. My profound thanks to James Thompson, a keen *Independent* reader who kick-started the project by sending me an e-mail asking whether I was perchance thinking of writing a book. If I was, he said, then I should contact his wife, Suzanne Baboneau, at Simon & Schuster. So I did, and ended up in the patient and clever hands of Andrew Gordon, who has been a remarkably supportive editor. Edwina Barstow has done a great job of desk-editing, and my agent, Camilla Hornby, has been a consistent source of good advice, dispensed with tact and charm. My thanks also to Sam Ingleby, Nick Wallis, Fran Gibson and Fran Gibson's mum, who helped with research. And to my friend Chris Barry, who hardly helped at all, but did answer a question about nuclear physics.

I am grateful to Simon Kelner and Ian Birrell at the *Independent*, who have allowed me to plough my own furrow out here in Herefordshire, and to numerous other colleagues at the Indy – among them Lisa Markwell, Isabel Lloyd and Bernice Davison – who have looked after my country column in its various forms, and have hardly ever shouted at me about deadlines.

As for my wonderful children, the old gag applies, that without them this book would have been finished much sooner. But it would have been a thinner and duller volume; they have, wittingly and more often unwittingly, provided some marvellous material. Above all, I thank my wife, Jane, my soul mate in this enterprise and in so much else, and who, as Orville said of Keith Harris, feeds me most of my best lines.

Brian Viner, Herefordshire